GEORGINA CAMPBELL'S ireland

the Dublin guide

The best places to eat, drink and stay

Georgina Campbell Guides

Editor: Georgina Campbell

Epicure Press,
PO Box 6173
Dublin 13
Ireland

website: www.ireland-guide.com
email: info@ireland-guide.com

Cover Photographs courtesy of:
Dublin Tourism, Diep Le Shaker, La Stampa, Bord Bia.

Back Cover Photographs courtesy of:
Aya @ Brown Thomas, Bord Bia, BIM, Clarion Hotel IFSC, Dublin
Tourism, La Stampa, Merrion Hotel, Morrison Hotel, WM Nixon
(Ardgillan House, Skerries).

Design and artwork by The Design Station, Dublin
Cover concept: Chaos, Dublin
Image Scanning by The Design Station
Printed in Ireland by Colour Books Ltd.

First published 2005 by Georgina Campbell Guides Ltd.

ISBN: 1-903164-16-8

Introduction

Dublin is one of Europe's top short break destinations - and it is easy to see why. While the elegant Georgian architecture at its heart retains a timeless apeal, it is now balanced by youthful energy, seen in a skyline that has changed for ever, as once-neglected areas of the city now boast fine contemporary developments a-buzz with activity, especially in the old dockland areas and along the north quays. New hotels and restaurants open at a dizzying rate, which means greater choice for visitors, and accommodation standards overall are high -  all too often with prices to match, but this Guide will lead you to the hotels and guesthouses which offer value in all price ranges.

Recent changes that have profoundly affected the city include a complete ban on smoking in the workplace - which has proved a great success, making bars and restaurants pleasanter for both staff and customers - and the introduction of the Luas (tram) system, which is bringing new life to areas that were previously relatively inaccessible. On the Dublin dining scene, an increasingly cosmopolitan population has brought a growing number of authentic ethnic restaurants representing, for example, eastern European countries and some of the less familiar Asian cuisines. Other welcome changes include an increase in ingredients-led cooking, and a gradual move towards simpler cooking styles that allow quality ingredients to speak for themselves; contributing factors include the strength of the Irish branch of Euro-Toques (see page 6), enthusiasm (both consumer and professional) for the international Slow Food movement - and the growth of farmers' markets, which are now a popular weekly fixture in many areas.

But, ironically, Dublin's vibrant international dining scene means that Irish cuisine can be elusive - so we have made a point of highlighting establishments which usually feature Irish cooking, whether traditional or modern, on their menus. Simple traditional dishes, like Irish stew, may be easier to find in pubs than restaurants - and for many visitors the pub atmosphere is especially enjoyable too, so this is often a good choice.

This is an exciting time for Dublin, and we hope you will enjoy your experience of the city and its food - and, in tune with the national celebration of Irish food and drink, Féile Bia, let us say: "Blas agus sasamh go bhfaighe tu air" ("May you find it both tasty and satisfying")!

Georgina Campbell.

Georgina Campbell,

Editor.

How to Use the Guide

Finding your way around...

In **Dublin city**, postal districts are arranged in numerical order. Even numbers are south of the river Liffey and uneven numbers on the north, with the exception of Dublin 8 which straddles the river. Within each district, establishments are listed in alphabetical order and directions are given.

In **County Dublin** entries are divided into three sections, North, South and West. Within these sections, entries are broken down into named geographical areas and arranged alphabetically within them.

Map References

A map is given for the central city area (see inside front cover). A detailed map of the Temple Bar area is given at the beginning of the Dublin 2 section (page 26). For general information on location of entries in County Dublin, refer to the map inside the back cover. Directions are also given in each entry.

Key to Symbols

✓   indicates a particularly high standard of food and/or accommodation

♣   indicates an establishment where some traditional or modern Irish cooking may be expected

Ⓑ   indicates an establishment that is likely to be especially well suited to the business guest

féile bia   indicates an establishment that has signed the Féile Bia Charter (see page 12)

AWARDS referred to in the text relate to *Georgina Campbell's Ireland, The Guide*, see back flap for details of this guide to hospitality throughout Ireland.

Prices and Opening Hours

PLEASE NOTE THAT PRICES AND OPENING HOURS MAY HAVE CHANGED SINCE THE GUIDE WENT TO PRESS. TIMES & PRICES ARE GIVEN AS A GUIDELINE ONLY AND SHOULD BE CHECKED BEFORE TRAVELLING OR WHEN MAKING A RESERVATION.

Thanks and Acknowledgements

The publication of this guide would not have been possible without the support and encouragement of the sponsors, Bord Bia, also Dublin Tourism, Temple Bar Properties and many other individuals who have given invaluable assistance.

Contents

A Taste of Dublin

Today's visitors to Dublin find a thriving, fast-paced modern city - far from the traditional laid-back image of Ireland. But, although the Irish work hard to maintain their hard won prosperity and may have less time to chat these days, the good things in life - good food, drink and conversation - have not entirely disappeared, nor has the wish to share these good things with other people.

Price rises over the last few years have provoked much debate about value for money, an issue that has become a national preoccupation. Ireland certainly can't claim to be a low-cost destination but, at its best, the experience of Irish hospitality remains unique and, even in Dublin, there is good value to be found for discerning travellers (from home or abroad). And there is much to enjoy, both within the city and nearby: backed by the beautiful Dublin Mountains and flanked by many miles of coastline, the capital is blessed with a lovely setting, and many interesting places are easily accessible just beyond the bustle of the city, and perfect for day trips and short breaks (see Contents).

INFLUENCES & ETHNIC CUISINES

Much of the food served in Dublin is unashamedly international in tone, but there are also talented Irish chefs creating a more individual local style - typically they will be classically trained, and then bring back culinary influences from their travels and then give them an Irish twist. Over the last decade or so, the influence and strength of Euro-Toques (The European Community of Chefs) has been a real force for good in reawakening interest and pride in the value of locally produced, traditional foodstuffs and the leading chefs have put a creative, often innovative, spin on traditional Irish dishes. The aim is for a contemporary Irish style of cooking that is "entirely itself" reflecting the highly individual Irish approach to life and living - an aim supported by both Bord Bia and the Restaurants Association of Ireland.

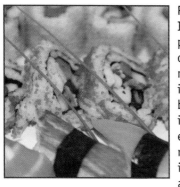

Prosperity has made Ireland an attractive place for people from all over the globe to settle; many have chosen to live in the capital, which has brought a rapid growth in the number and variety of ethnic shops and restaurants - and a growing emphasis on authenticity in **ethnic cuisines**. All the main food cultures are well represented and the best are included in the guide. While Italian, Chinese and Indian restaurants are most common, you'll also find a growing number of others including Spanish tapas, regional French, Thai, even Korean and Vietnamese.

TRENDS & VALUE

Some current trends include a welcome move towards simplicity in some of the better restaurants, with more emphasis on allowing the taste and flavour of ingredients to shine through, and a high value placed on seasonal and local food. Heeding customers' demand for better value, many restaurants have expanded the number of house wines and half bottles on their wine lists

and, in addition to an early dinner menu, there is often the option of a two-course menu at a keen price. Lunch remains the least costly meal - and lunch in one of Dublin's leading restaurants can offer a memorable experience, together with outstanding value for money. The **traditional Irish breakfast** is very much alive and well; known as "the full Irish", this is a substantial meal and taking it at a leisurely pace remains an essential part of a holiday or short break, both for visitors and Irish residents enjoying some time off. A Sunday curiosity to note is the extended lunch hour (often called brunch, although the menu may not necessarily reflect the name), which can run from noon to seven in the evening, or even later.

ARTISAN & SPECIALITY FOODS

The siren call "Ireland the food island" is more than a clever sales slogan. Although agriculture is less dominant than it once was, Ireland remains a food producing nation - and, in support of their mission to promote Irish food, Bord Bia (The Irish Food Board) has initiated programmes that have had a genuinely beneficial effect on the quality and diversity of Irish foods available to chefs and their customers including

the Féile Bia programme (a celebration of food), which is a partnership initiative between Bord Bia, The Restaurants Association of Ireland and The Hotels Federation of Ireland, supported by the farming community, and - a parallel initiative to support the development of small food producers - the Taste Council (acronym for traditional, artisan, speciality, trade expertise), is also coordinated by Bord Bia. Its main aim is to support the growing number of craft food producers to develop, distribute and market their products; membership of the council includes small food producers, organic growers, representatives of relevant organisations like Cáis (the Irish Farmhouse Cheesemakers Association), Euro-Toques (The European Community of Chefs), and retailers and distributors who specialise in traditional, artisan and speciality foods.

THE LOCAL FOOD MARKET REVOLUTION

Recent EU agricultural reforms are seen by many adaptable farmers as an opportunity to cut out the middle man and sell direct to the customer at food markets, where they also have the benefit of meeting fellow producers, getting feedback on their produce and ideas for improvement, and just interacting with consumers in a way that Irish farmers have not done for generations. The widespread revival of local food markets in Ireland is one of the most exciting recent developments in this country's re-emerging food culture - and there's a growing number to visit in Dublin city and environs.

FARMERS' MARKETS

DUBLIN CITY

DUBLIN 1:

- IFSC, Mayor Square; every Wednesday 10.30-4.00
- Wolf Tone Park Gourmet Food Market, 50 yards from Mary Street/Henry Street; Fridays 11-3
- Moore Street (not a farmers' market, but the oldest in Dublin and features fruit and vegetables and ethnic foods); daily

DUBLIN 2:

- Temple Bar Market, Meeting House Square; Saturday am
- Pearse Street Market, St Andrews Centre; Saturday 9.30-3.00

DUBLIN 6:

- Ranelagh (Multi-denominational School); Sundays, 10-4

DUBLIN 14:

- Marlay Park, Rathfarmham; Saturdays

DUBLIN 18:

- Leopardstown Farmers' Market, Leopardstown Racecourse (below the grandstand); every Friday 11-7.

COUNTY DUBLIN

- People's Park, Dun Laoghaire; every Saturday 11-4.
- Dun Laoghaire Ferry Terminal; Thursdays, 10.30-4
- Malahide Market, Church Road; every Saturday 11-5.
- Fingal Food Fayre, Fingal Arts Centre, Rush; last Sunday of each month, 12-5.

NB - Market times and locations may change, so check locally or log on to: www.bordbia.ie/consumers/farmersmarkets.htlm

OTHER USEFUL WEB ADDRESSES:
- www.farmersmarkets.ie
- www.templebar.ie
- www.dublinfoodcoop.com

SPECIALITY FOODS

Markets are a wonderful way of experiencing Irish food - a chance to buy food for a picnic, to taste traditional and innovative food products from traditional smoked wild salmon, trout, mackerel, smoked mussels, or smoked scallops, to fish patés, seafood soups and seaweeds (an ancient tradition in Ireland). Farmhouse cheeses are one of the glories of artisan producers and there about 70 farmhouse cheesemakers each producing cheeses that are unique to the family and farmland. Here you will also find distinctive Irish breads, biscuits and cakes - and a more surprising speciality is **handcrafted chocolates** filled with cream and Irish liqueurs; fine

examples are winners of Irish Food Writers' Guild Chocolate Lovers Awards: Gallwey's made in Co Waterford and Eve's made in Cork. Soft fruit and wild berries are often made into gorgeous preserves and chutneys. Traditional dry cures of bacon and ham are to be found alongside innovative smoked and cured meats, like the award-winning smoked Connemara lamb and smoked Irish beef, both innovative creations of young craft butcher James McGeough of Oughterard, Co. Galway, who has won top prizes at both The Irish Food Writers Guild Food Awards and The Craft Butchers Speciality Foods Competition.

Farmhouse cheese production has been *the* success story of Ireland's rejuvenating artisan food culture over the last 30 years and many of the earliest cheesemakers, who began back in the early '70s, are still in business today. The excellence of their products quickly attracted a loyal following - and encouraged others to follow their example. Today the range and diversity of cheeses made all over Ireland is truly astonishing;

there are literally dozens to choose from, with new ones coming on stream all the time - and there is a growing presence on restaurant menus in other European countries, especially in Britain, and also in specialist food shops in Britain and beyond. In Dublin, the acknowledged expert purveyors are

Sheridans Cheesemongers of South Anne Street, Dublin 2, and a visit to their shop is highly recommended.

Farmhouse cheeses are the pride of many a restaurant menu but they're also great for quick meals at home, or **picnics** - what could be more delicious than a simple ploughman's lunch of farmhouse cheese, with some good brown soda bread, a few stalks of crunch celery and some home-made chutney or a spoonful of Ballymaloe Country Relish? And they make versatile ingredients too - look out for Irish Farmhouse Cheese Recipes, a dinky pocket sized book of recipes for about 40 different varieties of farmhouse cheese, including Abbey Brie, Carrigaline, Drumlin, Gubbeen, Lavistown, St Gall and Wicklow Blue. Many of the recipes have been suggested by

the cheesemakers themselves, others have been donated by well-known chefs - and the book also includes a descriptive list of Irish farmhouse cheeses and tips for cooking and storing cheese. Supported by Bord Bia, it is widely available - and, at just one euro, is incredible value.

FOOD AT FARMLEIGH

The Bord Bia website (www.bordbia.ie) not only gives details of the regular farmers' markets, but also the special markets held at Christmas time, and in September during the Food At Farmleigh month. Farmleigh is an historic house in Phoenix Park which was quite recently acquired by the state; its main

function is to provide hospitality for state guests, but the house and grounds are open to the public at certain times and an annual Farmleigh Cultural Programme which runs during the summer months includes a series of food-related events (talks, demonstrations, seminars, Sunday food markets), for the whole of September. A particularly interesting event that has recently been developed by Farmleigh in collaboration with Bord Bia and the National Bakery School, at DIT is the **Artisan Bread Award**, which is open only to small owner-man-

aged bakeries producing bread by natural fermentation methods; after a blind tasting by an expert judging panel, the first Farmleigh Award for Artisan Bread went to a young Frenchman, Jean Baptiste Kapral, a baker at the bakery and café, La Maison des Gourmets in Castle Market, Dublin 2 (see entry). At Farmleigh itself, restaurateurs Eileen Dunne and Stefano Crescenzi (see entries for Dunne & Crescenzi) provide a combination of Italian and Irish food at **The Boat House Restaurant**, which overlooks an ornamental lake in the grounds, and light refreshments are available at **The Motorhouse Café**. Details of the house, its history, events and opening times are on the website (www.farmleigh.ie), or you can contact Farmleigh Reception, Tel: 01-815 5981.

FEILE BIA– CERTIFIED FARM TO FORK

Féile Bia is a year round programme that emphasises the importance of food sourcing in hotels, restaurants, pubs and workplaces throughout the country. Féile Bia was introduced in 2001 in response to growing consumer concerns on the origins of food offered when eating out.

Féile Bia is the consumer's reassurance that the fresh beef, lamb, pork, bacon, chicken and eggs being served are fully traceable from farm to fork and have been produced under a Quality Assurance Scheme.

When you see the Féile Bia logo displayed in a restaurant, hotel or pub you can be sure of the origin of the food being served. There are 1,300 members so far and the number is growing all the time. Those establishments recommended by the guide which have signed up to the charter are identified within the body of the guide by the use of the Féile Bia logo.

World cuisine has taken over Dublin recently, reflecting the diversity of an increasingly cosmopolitan population - and the capital's development as a cool modern city. There are some fine examples of cutting edge contemporary cooking to be found here, which can make for exciting dining, but it's all too easy for the **simple dishes and straightforward flavours of traditional Irish cooking** to be overlooked in the rush to be fashionable, so organisations like Bord Bia (the Irish Food Board) and the Restaurants Association of Ireland actively encourage Irish chefs to remember their roots and create modern dishes that are based on the best Irish produce, and reflect traditional themes. This is seen particularly through the Féile Bia campaign - recent

Dublin winners of the prestigious national Féile Bia Award include O'Connells of Ballsbridge and Avoca Café (Dublin 4 and Dublin 2, respectively - see entries); the 2005 Award was won by Lacken House in Kilkenny, which is close enough to Dublin to make an ideal short break (see page 140). These recipes illustrate far better than words how delicious modern Irish food can be - and they're easy to make at home.

Braised Beef in Guinness

Guinness is central to Dublin - and the scent of the mash wafting across the city on a calm evening is delicious, even to those who don't drink stout. It's great for enriching many traditional dishes, and beef  and Guinness is perhaps the all-time favourite combination. This updated classic was created by well known chef, John Howard, and is very special. **Serves 4:**

1kg/2 lb shoulder beef, cut into thin slices
2 tbsp olive oil
1 onion, chopped
2 leeks, 2 carrots, 2 celery sticks, chopped
2 cloves garlic, chopped
250ml/½ pt well reduced beef stock
125ml/¼ pt Guinness
Salt and black pepper
50g/2 oz butter
75g/3 oz streaky bacon, diced
100g/4 oz mushrooms, wild if available, sliced
50g/2 oz small onions, peeled
25g/1 oz flour

Heat the oil in a large pan, brown the meat well. Transfer the meat to a casserole, and sauté the onion, leeks, carrots and celery in the original pan. Add the vegetable to the meat, with the garlic. Pour in the stock and Guinness, season. Simmer gently for about 1½ hours, then remove the meat from the casserole and strain the liquid. Discard the vegetables. Place the meat back in the rinsed casserole, with the liquid. In a pan, sauté the bacon, mushrooms and onions in the butter. Add these to the casserole and reheat the lot. Blend the flour with remaining butter. Stir it into the sauce, stirring well, to thicken. Taste for seasoning. Serve in a deep dish with buttery mash.

Grilled Lamb in a Salad

This dish was created by the Co. Galway chef, Gerry Galvin, who has long championed the creative use of local produce. He would originally have used mountain lamb, which is one of Ireland's great speciality foods produced naturally in the wonderful hills of areas like Connemara, its lean meat flavoured by wild mountain herbs. (It is now available from renowned the Oughterard butcher McGeough's and selected outlets, as a smoked delicacy to be eaten in the same way as Parma ham.) But, of course, any good qality lamb can be used. **Serves 2**:

6 lamb steaks
2 tbsp olive oil
2 cloves garlic, crushed
2 tbsp chopped fresh herbs
Salt and black pepper
Mixed salad leaves

Place the lamb steaks in a shallow dish. Mix the oil, garlic, herbs and seasoning together. Spoon half this mixture over the lamb. Heat a griddle pan or grill until very hot. Cook the lamb steaks according to your preference. Mix the salad leaves with a dressing made with the remaining oil and herb mixture. Place on a the serving plates with the lamb steaks and serve with the cooking juices or a little lamb gravy.

Gortnamona Goats' Cheese Baskets

Goats' cheese starters feature on many a Dublin restaurant menu and this one, (from the Irish Farmhouse Cheese Recipes booklet), is easy to prepare and makes a refreshing beginning for a summer meal. Select large, ripe, evenly-sized tomatoes - best of all, use flavoursome home-grown tomatoes if you can. **Serves 4:**

190g/6½ oz Gortnamona, or other soft goats' cheese
8 good-sized tomatoes (or 4 beef tomatoes)
85g/3oz crème fraiche
30ml/2 tbsp chopped chives
5ml/1 tsp chopped basil
Mixed leaves to serve.

Wash and dry the tomatoes. Slice off the top of each tomato and scoop out the pulp; lightly salt the inside of each tomato and turn over to drain. Mix the cheese, crème fraîche, chives and basil in a bowl and fill the tomatoes with the mixture. Sprinkle with chopped chives and replace the caps over the cheese. Serve immediately on a bed of tossed leaves.

DUBLIN 1

Once the most fashionable part of Dublin - the great Georgian squares of Mountjoy and Parnell, built on rising ground with views across to the Dublin mountains, pre-date those in Dublin 2, while the Gresham Hotel, on O'Connell Street, was for many years <u>the</u> address to stay. Now, this area on the northern banks of the Liffey is again strongly in the ascendant. Aside from the controversial new landmark spire in O'Connell Street (known locally as 'The Spike'), the growth of the **International Financial Services Centre** over the last decade has put paid to many a southside joke (the traditional rivalry between the people of north and and south Dublin is legendary) and, in many ways, the tremendous vitality to be seen in the renewal of the north quays stems from the confidence engendered by this visionary project. Its continuing development is bringing many new enterprises to the area, with good food and drink increasingly respresented - by, for example, the **farmers' market** held at Mayor Square each Wednesday (10.30-4), and the choice of the IFSC as the location for one of Dublin's most respected independent wine shops, **Cabot & Co** (Custom House Plaza; 01 636 0616).

Although there have been a few good restaurants in this area for many years, it has never been a part of the city noted for any special interest in taking up the gastronomic challenge - except, of course, for the famous **Moore Street traders** (renowned for their Dublin banter while selling fruit and vegetables from stalls and prams) who have recently, somewhat unexpectedly, found themselves the centre of a rich ethnic mix as new arrivals from all over the world set up their stalls of exotica amongst the locals. Alongside the retail operations, we're also seeing the emergence of **authentic ethnic restaurants** (such as **Xhong Xing** and **China House**, for example, both on Moore Street); they're spartan, inexpensive, unlikely to take credit cards (unusual in Dublin) and it's anyone's guess how long any individual establishment may last, but the trend itslef looks as if it's here to stay. Then there's the gourmet shopping mall, the **Epicurean Food Hall**, on the corner of Lower Liffey Street and Middle Abbey Street, near the Ha'penny Bridge (see below). It encompasses a satisfyingly wide range of enterprises with quality as the common thread, some of which are listed below. Do have a browse and a bite to eat here - it's brilliant and developing all the time. And, happily, this vitality is reflected in the growing number of recommendations we can give in this edition for hotels and restaurants in Dublin 1 - and for the adjacent areas north of the river (see Dublin 7). This trend seems set to intensify in the next few years as redevelopment along both the north and south quays continues - bringing with it a host of new shops, restaurants and hotels, notably in the **chq** 'retail and dining destination' which it is rumoured that the Conran restaurant group has been eyeing - and a new swing pedestrian bridge will soon span the river from Mariners' Memorial at City Quay to Stack A, in the IFSC complex.

RESTAURANT

101 Talbot Restaurant

100-102 Talbot Street Dublin 1
Tel: 01 874 5011 Fax: 01 878 1053

féile bia Margaret Duffy and Pascal Bradley's ground breaking northside restaurant was here a decade ahead of the current gold rush to service the growing needs of the new "city" area in and around the maturing International Financial Services Centre. Its potential may be more obvious today but it is they who created the buzz here and, while the nearby Abbey and Gate Theatres and the constantly changing art exhibitions in the restaurant are partly responsible for drawing an interesting artistic/theatrical crowd, it is essentially their joyfully creative and healthy food that has earned the 101 such a fine reputation and it is heartening to see standards maintained in a busy city centre restaurant when so many around take the easier option. Mediterranean and Middle Eastern influences explain the uniquely enjoyable wholesomeness across the complete range of dishes offered on hand written menus, always including strong vegetarian options, such as celeriac rösti topped with spinach & blue cheese, with a sage cream sauce - and dietary requirements are willingly met. Interesting food, nice little details - friendly staff who welcome arriving guests promptly, the good complimentary breads offered at table, helpful advice with menu choices - and very reasonable prices ensure the continuing success of this popular restaurant. Just don't expect lavish decor - and try to ignore the drabness of Talbot Street, which seems to creep in a little up the lino-clad stairs. Children welcome before 8pm. **Seats 80.** Open Tue-Sat, 5-11. A la carte. Early D €21 (5-8). House Wine €17.95. Closed Sun & Mon, Christmas week. Amex, MasterCard, Visa, Laser. **Directions:** 5 minutes walk between Connolly Station and O'Connell Street. Straight down from the Spire.

RESTAURANT

Alilang Korean Restaurant

102 Parnell Street Dublin 1 Tel: 01 874 6766

A bright and simply decorated room with country pine furniture is home to this authentic Korean restaurant. serving tasty and exceptionally reasonably priced food. Aside from offering good quality for the price (endorsed by the local Asian community who frequent the restaurant), there's a unique feature at Allilang - each table has its own gas 'barbecue' ring set into it, allowing customers to finish their own dishes at table. In the oriental style, there are set menus which are a good choice for a first visit or, if you are in a group, the extensive main menus encourage wide-ranging orders and lots of sharing which would be more fun - starters like kimchi jun, for example (a potato pancake filled with the famous Korean relish, kimchi, and served with finely chopped leeks, garlic, sesame seeds & soy sauce), or the nine-variety Royal Appetiser which is a combination dish of thin pancakes, seasoned meat and vegetables and a dipping sauce. Then there are dishes to cook at your table - plenty to choose from, such as very lean and thinly sliced marinated beef, which you cook to taste and dip in sesame or chilli sauce, or wrap in lettuce leaves. All good fun, and you can choose between Asian beers, wine or green tea to wash it down - and the fresh sliced fruit offered to finish is a nice touch. **Seats 40.** Open 7 days.

RESTAURANT

Aya Deli @ IFSC

Mayor Street/Custom House Square IFSC Dublin 1 **Tel: 01 672 1852**

This younger sister of the highly successful Aya @ Brown Thomas (see entry) is run on similar lines, although with less seating and greater emphasis on food to go. Amex, MasterCard, Visa, Laser.

✓ Ⓑ ♣ RESTAURANT

Chapter One Restaurant

18/19 Parnell Square Dublin 1 **Tel: 01 873 2266**
Fax: 01 873 2330 Email: info@chapter.onerestaurant.com
Web: www.chapteronerestaurant.com

féile bia Chef-proprietor Ross Lewis and his partner, restaurant manager Martin Corbett, operate this superb restaurant in an elegantly furnished basement beneath the Dublin Writers' Museum and near The Gate Theatre - which you can visit after your main course and return later for dessert and coffee. The restaurant has great character, with understated modern decor providing a nice contrast to its underlying rusticity; arches create three main areas, of which one is an exceptionally welcoming reception/bar. Ross and Martin have built up a terrific kitchen and front of house teams who work together brilliantly to ensure that a visit to Chapter One is always a special occasion: this is a place where hospitality comes first and all the little niceties of a seriously good meal are observed from the moment you taste that complimentary amuse-bouche to the last petit four. Impeccably sourced ingredients have always been at the heart of this kitchen, where classic French cooking is lightly tempered with modern influences to produce meals of great creativity and technical excellence. Menus are strongly seasonal and invariably bring an agony of choice; on the evening à la carte, for instance, there are eight equally desirable starters - but also the irresistible option of the charcuterie trolley, which is brought to your table, offering half a dozen dishes ranging from West Cork ham with celeriac & mustard, or terrine of wild boar with apple & horseradish compôte to lamb tongue sauce gribiche, pig trotter boudin, with red wine & raisin jus, and a selection of West Cork salamis. Main courses will also bring out the indecisive in most guests: poultry and meat dishes (also game in season) may include several superb slow-cooked dishes - loin of lamb with slow-cooked shoulder, brioche dumpling & rosemary, perhaps - while four or five equally tempting fish dishes might include a fricassée of lobster (with summer vegetables, gnocchi, garlic and port, about €45). An exceptional selection of cheeses (invariably in perfect condition) is also offered and classic desserts - including a luscious apricot, coffee and amaretto trifle (with a glass of champagne, perhaps) that should be enough to bring that much-maligned treat back into fashion - round off the occasion in style. An excellent, informative wine list continues to develop and offers carefully selected house wines and wines by the glass, including a range of dessert wines. Chapter One was our Restaurant of the Year in 2001, reflecting the consistently memorable dining experience of that time - and (as we say every year) it just goes on getting better. *Chapter One also runs the café in the Writers' Museum, (10-5 pm Mon-Sat), and provides banqueting facilities for 60-80 people in the Gallery there. Small conferences. Air conditioning. Parking by arrangement with nearby carpark. Not suitable for children. **Seats 85** (private rooms,14 & 20). L Tue-Fri, 12.30-2.30, D Tue-Sat, 6-10.45. Set L €28.50. Pre-theatre menu €29.50, 6-5.45; D à la carte (Tasting Menu, for entire parties, €48.50). House wine €20. SC10%. Closed L Sat, all Sun & Mon, 2 weeks Christmas, 2 weeks August. Amex, Diners, MasterCard, Visa, Laser. **Directions:** Top of O'Connell Street, north side of Parnell Square, opposite Garden of Remembrance.

✓ Ⓑ HOTEL/RESTAURANT **Clarion Hotel Dublin IFSC**

Excise Walk IFSC Dublin 1 **Tel: 01 433 8888** Fax: 01 433 8801
Email: info@clarionhotelifsc.com Web: www.info@clarionhotelifsc.com

This dashing contemporary hotel opened on the river side of the International Financial Services Centre in March 2001 and was the Guide's Business Hotel of the Year in 2002. It is the first in the area to be built specifically for the mature 'city' district; now it is not only meeting the needs of business guests and the financial community admirably, but its high standards and central location have proved very popular with leisure guests as well, especially at weekends. Bright, airy and spacious, the style is refreshingly clean-lined yet comfortable, with lots of gentle neutrals and a somewhat eastern feel that is emphasised by the food philosophy of the hotel - a waft of lemongrass and ginger entices guests through to the Kudos Bar, where Asian wok cooking is served; the more formal restaurant, Sinergie, also features world cuisine, but with more European influences. Staff show a real desire to please, the standard of cooking and service are both consistently high. Uncluttered bedrooms have many facilities to appeal to the modern traveller, especially when on business: keycard, security eye and security chain are reassuring features and there are many other conveniences, including air conditioning, 2 phone lines (with voice mail and ISDN) also a pleasing element of self-containment, with tea/coffee-making, multi-channel TV, ironing facilities, power hairdryer mini-bar and safe. Generous semi-orthopaedic beds, good linen and bright bathrooms with power showers and bath, heated mirror, luxurious towels and top quality toiletries all add to the sense of thoughtful planning that attaches to every aspect of the hotel. There's even a 'Sleep Programme' to help you relax before bed! Leisure facilities, in the basement, are excellent and include an 18m pool and large, well-equipped gym. (Open to membership as well as residents' use). Rooms for meetings of anything between 8 and 100 people, theatre style have state-of-the art facilities. 24 hour room service. Lift. Children welcome (under 12s free in parents' room, cot available free of charge, baby sitting arranged). No pets. **Rooms 162** (17 suites, 81 executive, 81 no smoking). B&B €117.50 pps. Room rate €245, no SC. **Kudos Bar & Restaurant:** Mon-Fri,12-8.30; **Sinergie Restaurant:** L Mon-Fri 12.15-2.30, D daily, 6-9.45. Set L €18.95; Early D €28 (6-7); D €23.50-€35, also à la carte. House wines, from €18.50. Sinergie closed L Sat & Sun. Kudos no food Sat & Sun. 24-26 Dec. [*Comfort Inn, Talbot Street (Tel: 01-874 9202) is in the same group and offers budget accommodation near the IFSC.] Amex, Diners, MasterCard, Visa, Laser. **Directions:** Heading east, take the left lane on Custom House Quay. Hotel is in the 3rd block, after 2 sets of traffic lights.

RESTAURANT   # Condotti

38 Lr Ormond Quay Dublin 1 **Tel: 01 872 0003**

This stylish modern restaurant (previously Pasta di Milano) is part of the UK Pizza Express chain; ownership has not changed, but it is in new management. It is in an area that has so far eluded the tidy-up operation that comes with development but, once up the few steps from the pavement, you're in for a pleasant surprise as you enter a large and stylish restaurant with open stone walls and high wooden-beamed ceilings. The food style is as expected (youthful, Italian inspired dishes like bruschetta, Parma ham with rocket, pastas and a range of gourmet pizzas), generally well-executed and reasonably priced - the early dinner menu in particular offers very good value. However, judging by the Guide's visit when service was a weak point, some staff training remains to be done. Private room (24). Al fresco dining area for smokers. Open daily, 12 noon - midnight (Sun 11pm). 2/3 course early D, €12.50/15; also à la carte. Live jazz on Fri. Closed Christmas, Good Fri. Amex, MasterCard, Diners, Visa, Laser. **Directions:** On north quays, near Ha'penny Bridge (no parking but Temple Bar car park short walk across footbridge).

RESTAURANT   # D.One Restaurant

North Wall Quay IFSC Dublin 1 **Tel: 01 856 1622**

Proudly laying claim to be only restaurant in Dublin built right on the walls of the River Liffey, this contemporary glass cube takes full advantage of its location on the river side of the road. Although not large and often very busy (especially at lunchtime when hordes of hungry workers pour out of the nearby offices), it succeeds surprisingly well in achieving a sense of spaciousness through simple, minimalist furnishing which combines comfort with eye appeal. Clean-lined surroundings seem to underline the stated aim " to offer first class food with great service and, above all, to offer outstanding value for money" which is very welcome in a part of the city where good value is not often the first concept to come to mind. The owners - Cian Mooney and Chris Bailie - are also the chefs, their cooking style is contemporary, and specialities include D.One fish & chips and their variation on a modern Irish classic of roast breast of chicken stuffed with tomato & creamed cheese, wrapped in bacon, served with champ mash &

wholegrain mustard cream. Simplest choices are often the wisest here, and the early dinner menu offers especially good value. Perhaps reflecting demand from the heady world of high finance across the road, a brief wine list rather surprisingly includes four champagnes, with a top price of nearly €200. Children welcome. **Seats 80** (outdoor seating in summer, 20). Reservations suggested. Air conditioning. Toilets wheelchair accessible. L Mon-Sat, 12-3, Sun 12-5; D Mon-Sat, 5-10. A la carte. SC 12.5%. House wine €14.60. Closed D Sun, 1st week Jan. Visa, Laser. **Directions:** On the waterside at Customs House Quay, opposite Clarion Hotel. Street parking available 7pm-7am and weekends.

WINE BAR   # Enoteca delle Langhe

Blooms Lane Dublin 1 **Tel:** 01 888 0834 Email: info@wallace.ie

This shop-cum-wine bar is part of a new food court in Blooms Lane, where you will also find Wallaces Italian Food Shop, Café Cagliostro (great coffees) and a juice café. Food, while not exactly incidental, certainly plays second fiddle to the wines here, but they carry a good range of dried Italian meats, cheeses, paninis etc, and you can wander around at your ease checking out the wines displayed, or sit at a sturdy wooden table and have something by the glass (or choose any bottle, plus 10%), and a bite from their limited but interesting selection of quality food. You can have cold deli plates, for example, or plates of bruschetta (available in different sizes) with toppings like sundried tomato pesto, fresh tomato & sautéed courgettes, mortadella & black olive tapénade and perhaps a dessert of hazelnut biscuits with apricots & peaches in amaretto. It's all very relaxed and sociable, prices are reasonable - and it's a very pleasant way to shop for wine. **Directions:** Opposite the Millennium Bridge (new development).

Epicurean Food Hall

Lower Liffey Street Dublin 1

The Epicurean Food Hall brings together a wide range of gourmet foods, cooked and uncooked - and the wines to go with them. The hall is open during the day every day (opens later on Sunday, stays open for late shoppers on Thursday); there are lots of lovely little shops and cafes in the hall, these few are just a taster:

La Corte (01 873 4200): One of two north river outposts of Stefano Crescenzi and David Izzo's smart Bar Italia (see entry).

Miss Sushi (Tel 01 617 4820): Japanese food has taken great strides in Dublin in recent years and Miss Sushi, which was opened here in 2000 by a well-travelled Laois lady, Margaret Scully, features food (mostly free range and organic) prepared by a team of professional sushi chefs at The Japanese Food Company and delivered twice daily. There is, of course, much more to sushi than raw fish: it may have originated as a way to preserve fish in vinegared rice, but it has long since taken on a wider meaning and the vinegared rice is now often married with other ingredients. There's a lunch special, changed daily, individual pieces can be selected to taste, or there are Bento Boxes which are a good start. Soy sauce, wasabi, pickled ginger and rolling mats come with all sushi. Party platters are available (24 hours notice) and, although Miss Sushi is mainly a gourmet take-away, plated sushi can be eaten on the premises.

Itsabagel (Tel 01 874 0486): Domini and Peaches Kemps' classy bagel bar is very popular with discerning lunchers: choose from bagels, savoury breads with fillings, juices, muffins and cookies. Just delicious. Also at The Pavilion, Dun Laoghaire. **Directions:** On the corner of Liffey Street and Middle Abbey Street.

*Although not enclosed within a mall, or indeed a formal grouping of any kind, the nearby **Moore Street/Parnell Street area** - well known for its street markets and the recent arrival of specialist food shops catering for a newly cosmoplitan population - has become a hothouse of international flavours and is a place to wander for authentic, keenly priced food from different cultures.

RESTAURANT/CAFÉ

Expresso Bar Café I.F.S.C.

6 Custom House Square I.F.S.C. Dublin 1 **Tel: 01 672 1812**
Fax: 01 672 1813 Email: jcathcart@ireland.com

Sister of the Expresso Bar Café in Ballsbridge - Anne Marie Nohl and Jane Cathcart have applied the same winning formula to this stylish contemporary restaurant in Dublin's financial heartland. Breakfasts worth getting in early for kick off with freshly squeezed orange juice and lead on to a wonderful menu of temptations, from the best of traditional fries through the likes of pancakes with crispy bacon and syrup, or freshly baked pastries. Lunches are in a class of their own too, offering lots of lovely, colourful dishes - sweet mustard salmon with dill, new potatoes & fennel salad is a typical summer example, or stuffed chicken breast with roast veg, white wine & rosemary - all based on the best ingredients, impeccably sourced. Desserts are given daily on a board and there's a wide choice of coffees, minerals and a compact, well-selected wine list. Takeaway bagel menu also available. **Seats 85**. Reservations accepted. Open Mon-Fri, 8-10; Sat & Sun brunch, 10-5. Air-conditioning. Closed 25 Dec, bank hols. Amex, MasterCard, Visa, Laser. **Directions:** On corner, left of Custom Square, IFSC.

(B) HOTEL/RESTAURANT

The Gresham

23 Upper O'Connell Street Dublin 1 **Tel: 01 874 6881** Fax: 01 878 7175
Email: info@thegresham.com Web: www.gresham-hotels.com

féile bia This famous hotel has been at the centre of Dublin society since the early nineteenth century and is one of the city's best business hotels. A recent makeover has transformed the ground floor, including the lobby lounge, which is a favourite meeting place and renowned for its traditional afternoon tea, and also the Gresham and Toddy's Bars, both popular rendezvous for a pint. Business guests especially appreciate the newer air-conditioned bedrooms in the Lavery Wing and the hotel takes commendable pride in the quality of its staff. Dining options in the hotel offer a choice between the more traditional Aberdeen Restaurant, and a smaller contemporary restaurant "23" (see below), which is smart and welcoming, and gives guests a change of style. Conference/banqueting (350/280). Business centre; secretarial services; video conferencing. Fitness suite. Wheelchair access. Secure multi-storey parking. No pets. **Rooms 288** (4 suites, 2 junior suites, 96 executive, 60 no-smoking, 3 disabled). Lifts. B&B about €160pps, ss up to €100 (Room-only rate about €255).

Number 23: Friendly staff get visitors to this stylish contemporary restaurant off to a good start - and, with food, service and ambience to match this should be an enjoyable, perhaps even memorable, dining experience, in which excellent raw materials are handled with respect and cooked with finesse. The menu is lucid and informative, and cosmopolitan young staff certainly know their food and wine. The 2-course 'city' dinner menu offers especially good value. This is an ambitious project for an hotel and, on the whole, it works well. The wine list make up in interest anything it may lack in length, and is well priced. [Aberdeen Restaurant open for breakfast, lunch & dinner daily; "23": b'fst Tue-Fri, D Mon-Sat; 2-course D €23 +12.5%.] Hotel open all year. Amex, Diners, MasterCard, Visa, Laser. **Directions:** City centre, on north side of the River Liffey.

(B) RESTAURANT/BAR

The Harbourmaster

IFSC Dublin 1 **Tel: 01 670 1688** Fax: 01 670 1690

In a waterside setting at Dublin's thriving financial services centre, this old Dock Offices building has genuine character and makes a fine restaurant and bar. The bar is very busy at times, but there is also an impressive contemporary upstairs restaurant, The Greenhouse, in a modern extension which has been designed in sympathy with the original building. Most tables have an interesting (and increasingly attractive) view of the development outside but, as there are now several dining areas, it is wise to ensure you get to the right one on arrival. For fine weather, there's also a decked outdoor area overlooking the inner harbour and fountain, with extra seating. The Harbourmaster has that indefinable buzz that comes from being in the financial centre of a capital city and, while not necessarily a destination dining experience, the food is appropriately international and contemporary in style.

The Greenhouse Restaurant: L, Mon-Fri. Restaurant closed evenings and weekends (except for functions). Bar open Mon-Wed, noon-closing daily (Sun 12.30-11) Brasserie food all day, daily. Closed 25 Dec & Good Fri. Amex, Diners, MasterCard, Visa. **Directions:** In IFSC, near Connolly train station.

CAFÉ   # Insomnia

Unit 2 Lower Mayor Street Custom House Quay IFSC Dublin 1
Tel: 01 671 8651

This speciality coffee company has a small chain of outlets around Dublin (some under the brand Bendini & Shaw, whose complementary speciality is in sandwiches). All coffees made on the premises are based on top quality beans (Kenya, Java, Colombia and House Blend) and the range is wide. You name it, if it's quality coffee connected you can get it here: espresso-based drinks like cappuccino, caffe latte, caffe mocha and caffe americano and their cousins ('essence of coffee'), espresso, espresso con panna (with whipped cream), espresso macchiato (with foamed milk) , espresso ristretto (extra strong) and extras (espresso shot, flavoured syrup, whipped cream). Speciality teas, hot chocolates and chilled drinks like iced coffee are available too, and a selection of pastries (croissants, muffins, biscotti for dunking); Bendini & Shaw sandwiches also available. *Also at Charlotte Way, Dublin 1; Ballsbridge, Dublin 4; Main Street, Blackrock; Pavilion Shopping Centre, Swords. **Seats 45.** Open 7.30am-4pm daily. Closed 25-26 Dec. **Directions:** In IFSC.

Ⓑ HOTEL   ## Jurys Custom House Inn

Custom House Quay Dublin 1 **Tel: 01 607 5000** Fax: 01 829 0400

féile bia Right beside the International Financial Services Centre, overlooking the Liffey and close to train and bus stations, this hotel meets the requirements of business guests with better facilities than is usual in budget hotels. Large bedrooms have all the usual facilities, but also fax/modem lines and a higher standard of finish than earlier sister hotels; fabrics and fittings are good quality and neat bathrooms are thoughtfully designed, with generous shelf space. As well as a large bar, there is a full restaurant on site, plus conference facilities for up to 100 and a staffed business centre. No room service. Adjacent multi-storey car park has direct access to the hotel. **Rooms 239.** Room Rate from €108 (max 3 guests); breakfast €8-10. Closed 24-26 Dec. Amex, Diners, MasterCard, Visa. **Directions:** IFSC, overlooking River Liffey.

HOTEL   ## Jurys Inn Parnell Street

Parnell Street Dublin 1 **Tel: 01 878 4900** Web: www.jurysinns.com

féile bia A useful addition to the choice of city centre accommodation north of the Liffey, this new hotel is well placed for theatres and shopping, and brings the qualities of quality and value expected of Jurys Inns - no frills (and, specifically, no room service) but rooms are spacious and comfortably furnished, with double and single beds and, in many cases, a sofa bed too.

Rooms 253. Room rate from €108. Amex, Diners, MasterCard, Visa. **Directions:** At the new Moore Street Plaza.

CAFÉ   # Panem

Ha'penny Bridge House 21 Lower Ormond Quay Dublin 1
Tel: 01 872 8510 Fax: 01 872 8510

Ann Murphy's little bakery and café has been delighting discerning Dubliners - and providing a refuge from the thundering traffic along the quays outside - since 1996. Although tiny, it just oozes Italian chic - not surprisingly, perhaps, as Ann's Italian architect husband, Raffaele Cavallo, designed the interior - and it was way ahead of its time in seeing potential north of the Liffey. Italian and French food is prepared on the premises from 3 am each day: melt-in-the-mouth croissants with savoury and sweet fillings, chocolate-filled brioches, traditional and fruit breads, filled foccacia breads are just a few of the temptations on offer. No cost is spared in sourcing the finest ingredients (Panem bread is baked freshly each day using organic flour) and special dietary needs are considered too: soups, for example, are usually suitable for vegans and hand-made biscuits - almond & hazelnut perhaps - for coeliacs. They import their own 100% arabica torrisi coffee from Sicily and hot chocolate is a speciality, made with the best Belgian dark chocolate. Simply superb. Open Mon-Sat 9-5.30. Closed Sun & 24 Dec-8 Jan. **No Credit Cards. Directions:** North quays, opposite Millennium Bridge.

RESTAURANT   # Romano's

12 Capel Street Dublin 1 **Tel: 01 872 6868**

Widely recognised as one of the best value Italian restaurants in town, especially at lunch, generous-spirited Romano's gives great home cooking with a little extra oomph - and good value wines too. Lovely big homemade pastas, steaks, moreish espressos. Great place. Open 7 days. Wines from €18.50.

CAFÉ   # Soup Dragon

168 Capel Street Dublin 1 **Tel: 01 872 3277** Fax: 01 872 3277

This tiny place offers a stylish way to have a hot meal on a budget: a daily choice of soups and stews is available in three different sizes, with a medium portion and a selection of delicious home-made breads and a piece of fruit starting at about €6. Some change daily, while others stay on the menu for a week or a season. Choose from dahl (Indian lentil), potato & leek or carrot & coriander soup; or opt for something more substantial like beef chilli or a very fine Thai chicken curry from the blackboard menu. In keeping with their healthy philosophy, a range of wholesome and innovative breakfasts is offered, and also a range of freshly squeezed drinks (Red Dragon: strawberry, raspberry and cranberry or home-made lemon & lime lemonade) and smoothies, all made to order so they taste fresh and vibrant. Desserts include old favourites like rice pudding (served with cream) and a range of unusual home-made ice creams. Food to go is also available. **Seats 10**. Open Mon-Fri 8-5.30 & Sat 11-5. Closed Sun, bank hols, Christmas. **No Credit Cards. Directions:** Bridge at Capel Street.

✓ Ⓑ HOTEL/RESTAURANT   # The Morrison

Hotel Ormond Quay Dublin 1 **Tel: 01 887 2400** Fax: 01 874 4039
Email: sales@morrisonhotel.ie Web: www.morrisonhotel.ie

Located in the heart of the city close to the new Millennium Bridge over the River Liffey, this luxurious contemporary hotel is within walking distance of theatres, the main shopping areas and the financial district. Striking 'east meets west' interiors are by the internationally renowned designer, John Rocha: his simple, cool bedroom design - the essence of orderly thinking - contrasts pleasingly with the dramatic, even flamboyant, style of public areas, and in-room facilities are excellent. Public areas include a range of stylish bars and restaurants catering to the needs of different times - the Café Bar, for example, is ideal for morning coffee or light pre- and post-theatre meals, while The Morrison Bar is the place for cocktails and Lobo is a late night bar (open to 3 am on Friday and Saturday nights). Conference/banqueting (90/95). Children welcome (under 12 free in parents' room, cot available without charge, babysitting arranged). Pets permitted. **Rooms 90** (7 suites (inc 1 penthouse); 2 disabled). Lift. Room service (limited hours). B&B about €130 pps (weekend breaks about €280). Closed 24-27 Dec.

Halo: High drama comes into its own in the restaurant, which is on two levels, with angled mirrors giving a sense of unity and acres of curtains - notably a rich purple velvet - falling the full height. Head chef Jean-Michel Poulot presents stylish French and fusion menus at this fashionable restaurant; seafood dishes are a strength - a fillet of turbot with organic baby vegetables, lobster ravioli and shellfish sauce is a typically luxurious example - and imaginative vegetarian dishes make attractive mainstream choices. Original desserts (Morrison Surprise... The Spike) are spectacularly presented and a choice of dessert wines is offered by the glass. Service can be uneven, but value for money is generally good, especially at lunch time. **Seats 95**. Air conditioning. L& D daily, 12.30-2.30 & 6.30-10.15; Set L from €25, D from €35, also à la carte; house wine from €25; sc 12.5%. Amex, Diners, MasterCard, Visa, Laser. **Directions:** Located near the city centre beside the Millennium Bridge.

✓ RESTAURANT/BAR   # The Vaults

Harbourmaster Place IFSC Dublin 1 **Tel: 01 605 4700**
Fax: 01 605 4701 Email: info@the vaults.ie Web: www.thevaults.ie

These ten soaring vaulted chambers underneath Connolly Station were built in the mid-19th century to support the railway between Amiens Street and the Royal Canal and have since found many uses, including the storage of Jameson whiskey, in a tunnel running from Connolly to Westland Row! In 2002 this wonderful space entered a new and exciting era when Michael Martin - previously best known for his culinary expertise as head chef of the Clarence Hotel restaurant, The Tea Rooms - opened it as a multi-purpose venue. Despite the size - and a ceiling height of four metres - the atmosphere is surprisingly intimate: the Portland Stone floor is warm and welcoming and the vaults, which have been treated individually in styles ranging from sleek contemporary (brown leather booth seating) to neo-classical (salvaged lamps, aged sculptures) add up to a stylish and highly versatile space. Each has its own entrance, allowing a number of events to take place simultaneously and, in addition to high-resolution digital projectors allowing cinema quality audio-visual effects, surround sound and drop-down screens in three of the vaults, others have plasma screens - ideal for sports events (seats bookable in advance). Given Michael Martin's background, culinary expectations are high at The Vaults and Sardinian head chef Max Usai ensures that everything is made from scratch, including pasta, ice cream and breads; menus are simple - mainly grills, pizzas and pastas - but brilliantly executed and beautifully presented on plain white modern crockery. This place encapsulates the dramatic changes taking place north of the Liffey: simply stunning. **Seats 160** (private room 80). Reservations required. Food served 12-8 daily. Various menus - lunch, afternoon/evening, Saturday brunch and Sunday roast - à la carte. Vegetarian dishes on main menu. House wine €18. Late night bar. Closed 25 Dec, 1 Jan, Good Fri. Amex, MasterCard, Visa, Laser. **Directions:** Under Connolly station at IFSC.

Temple Bar Area

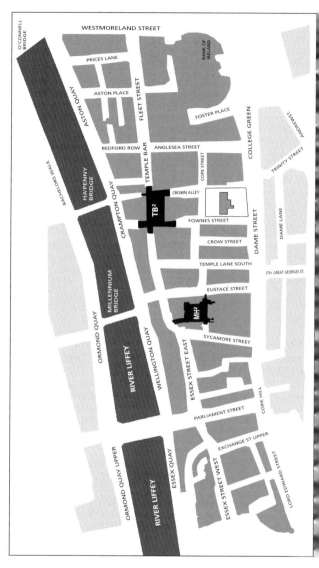

To be used in conjunction with City Centre Map on inside front cover.

- TB[2] - Temple Bar Square
- MH[2] - Meeting House Square

(Map courtesy of Temple Bar Properties)

Just south of the Liffey, this has been Dublin's most elegant and fashionable area for centuries: the great Georgian squares - Merrion and Fitzwilliam, St Stephen's Green, Dublin Castle, the old Irish parliament (now the Bank of Ireland), the Dáil (present parliament), Trinity College and the National Gallery are all within a few minutes walk of each other here and, of course, Grafton Street has always been the premier shopping area. Today, this part of the city offers a cross-section of just about everything that is best - or at any rate most typical - about Dublin's food and hospitality scene.

The most vibrant symbol of this diversity is **Temple Bar** which, only a decade or so ago, was derelict and designated for use as a giant bus terminal. Since then, it first became a victim of its own success as the rampant growth of night-life in the area quickly spiralled out of control and demanded re-direction, then the traders got together to clean up the act (and, specifically, to ban the stag and hen parties which were the most obvious problem). Now the underlying vitality of the area is resurfacing, allowing the emphasis to return to cultural events. Typical of these is *Diversions Temple Bar*, a free outdoor programme taking place during the summer in Meeting House Square and Temple Bar Square - for information on these and other events, call to Temple Bar Properties at 18, Eustace Street (Tel:01-677 2255).

Temple Bar is crammed with pubs and restaurants, many of which rely on passing trade for easy business; wise choices can be hard to make, so we've tried to reduce the risk by recommending a selection of the better places in all price brackets. But there's more to the area than restaurants and, from a food-lovers point of view, the most interesting cultural event is the **Temple Bar Food Market** on Meeting House Square. The brainchild of Toby Simmonds, of the Real Olive Co. (who is a stall-holder), the market first opened in May 1998 and now takes place every Saturday all year round, 9.30am-6 pm. The stall-holders who congregate here bring the best artisan-produced foods, many of them organic, from all over the country and beyond. Individual stalls vary from week to week, but you'll always find fish from Clare and west Cork, meat from Clare and Longford, cheese from Cavan, vegetables from north Dublin and Wicklow and fudge from Meath as well as locally made cakes, breads, chutneys - and all sorts of quality produce influenced by, or imported from, countries all over the world. Nearby the **Pearse Street Market** (St Andrew's Centre, Pearse Street, 9.30-3) is also on a Saturday. What the stallholders have in common is a commitment to fresh, natural produce - and many can be visited in their full-time workplaces as well: baker Sarah Webb's business **The Gallic Kitchen**, for example, is at her shop and café in Francis Street, and the legendary **Sheridans Cheesemongers** - who are so energetic in their pursuit of excellence and committed to enabling Ireland's developing food culture - are just up the road in South Anne Street, off Grafton Street.

Beyond Temple Bar and its satellites, the longer-established parts of this area provide a rich diversity of places for browsing gourmets to visit, offering everything from kitchenware to Asian ingredients - and plenty of chic café-bars and coffee shops to take a break from shopping. Or, if you prefer something down to earth and traditional, bar food is an option and there are plenty of fine **traditional pubs** to choose from, as many of the city's most famous ones are around here. Vegetarians will find good, casual eating places too, like **Juice,** on South Great Georges Street, **Café Fresh**, in **Powerscourt Townhouse**, which is well known for its delicious vegetarian and vegan food, and **Blazing Salads** in nearby Drury Street (just across from Asia Market), where you can get lovely vegetarian food to take away - salads, sandwiches - and they make their own superb bread on site.

To give an idea of the range for food shoppers, **La Maison des Gourmets** in Castle Market specialises in French fare, while **Asia Market** in Drury Street is the place for everything to do with eastern cooking and **Dunne & Crescenzi** in South Frederick Street are the experts on Italian artisan food. The **George's Street Arcade** is an increasingly interesting place for food lovers to browse - there are temptations a-plenty at the **Green Olive Food Co.** and **Claudio's Wine Shop** and, on the George's Street side, **Simon's Place** is a popular café for an inexpensive daytime bite.

On Nassau Street, '**Kilkenny**' sells lovely kitchen and tableware (and delicious foods that make great gifts, made on the premises) and, if kitchenware is your thing, other addresses to visit include **Sweeney O'Rourke** on Pearse Street (mainly trade, good for unusual items), the **Dublin Yeast Company** on College Street (specialist bakeware and cake decorating equipment), the kitchen shop at **Brown Thomas** on Grafton Street and **Kitchen Complements** on Chatham Street.

Anyone with an interest in food will want to linger a little in Chatham Street, where there are several fine shops specialising in the best of meat, poultry, fish and game - **Sawers, F.X. Buckley** - and, around the corner in Clarendon Street is **Magill's** (01 671 3830), one of the city's best-loved delis and purveyors of fine foods. Not far away, in Camden Street, you'll find a bit of the old Dublin in traditional (and kosher) butchers shops and **Listons**, a fine contemporary grocers shop with fine traditional values.

Up in the **Baggot Street area**, along from the Shelbourne Hotel, **Mulloys** is another fine butchers and, like Sawers, sells game in season. And there's wine to go with the food - **Mitchell's of Kildare Street** (and, more recently, Glasthule) is probably the oldest and definitely a must-visit, then there's the superb **Berry Bros & Rudd** in Harry Street, just beside the Westbury Hotel and, the newest kid on the block, **Corkscrew** on Chatham Street. And despite the name, there are good wines to be found at **The Celtic Whiskey Shop** on Dawson Street, as well as an exceptional range of whiskeys - a must-visit destination for gifts and treats to take back home.

As well as being something very close to a shopper's paradise, Dublin 2 is also where some of the city's finest accommodation is to be found - including, of course, the **Shelbourne Hotel**, on St Stephen's Green, which probably remains the greatest them all; at the time of going to press it has been acquired by an Irish consortium, and major investment is planned to bring it back to its former glory. It's the traditional place for an old-fashioned afternoon tea after the day's shopping is done - just what the doctor ordered.

RESTAURANT | **Acapulco Mexican Restaurant**

7 South Great Georges St. Dublin 2 Tel: **01 677 1085**

You'll find reliable Tex-Mex fare at this bright, cheap and notably cheerful place on the edge of Temple Bar. Recently refurbished in bright, warm tones of red, pinks and green, the decor matches the food which is authentic Mexican - nachos with salsa & guacamole, enchiladas, burrito, sizzling fajitas - and good coffee. **Seats 70.** Open 7 days: L 12-3pm, D 6-10.30pm (Fri 12-4pm & 6-11pm, Sat & Sun 2-10.30pm). Affordable wines, from about €17.95. 10% SC on parties of 6+. Amex, MasterCard, Visa, Laser. **Directions:** Bottom of South Gt George's St (Dame Street end).

✔ **Ⓑ** HOTEL   # Alexander Hotel

Merrion Square Dublin 2 **Tel: 01 607 3700** Fax: 01 661 5663
Email: alexanderres@ocallaghanhotels.ie Web: www.ocallaghanhotels.ie

féile bia Very well situated at the lower end of Merrion Square within a stone's throw of Dáil Éireann (Government Buildings), the National Art Gallery and History Museum as well as the city's premier shopping area, this large modern hotel is remarkable for classic design that blends into the surrounding Georgian area quite inconspicuously. In contrast to its subdued public face, the interior is strikingly contemporary and colourful, both in public areas and bedrooms, which are all to executive standard, spacious and unusual. Perhaps its best attribute, however, is the exceptionally friendly and helpful attitude of the hotel's staff, who immediately make guests feel at home and take a genuine interest in their comfort during their stay. Conference/banqueting (400/400). Business centre. Secretarial services. Video conferencing. Gym. Children welcome (Under 2s free in parents' room; cots available). No pets. **Rooms 102** (4 suites, 40 no-smoking, 2 for disabled). Lift. B&B about €105. Room-only rate about €295 (max. 2 guests). Open all year. Amex, Diners, MasterCard, Visa. **Directions:** Off Merrion Square.

RESTAURANT   # Ar Vicoletto Osteria Romana

5 Crow Street Temple Bar Dublin 2 **Tel: 01 670 8662**

Genuine little Italian restaurant, doing authentic, restorative food in a relaxing atmosphere and at very moderate prices - a set two-course lunch which includes a glass of wine and tea or coffee, is particularly good value. Very friendly helpful staff too - one of the pleasantest spots in Temple Bar. **Seats 35.** L &D daily. Children welcome. Air conditioning. Closed 24-25 Dec. Amex, MasterCard, Visa.

✔ ♣RESTAURANT   # Avoca Café

11-13 Suffolk St. Dublin 2 **Tel: 01 672 6019** Fax: 01 672 6021
Email: info@avoca.ie Web: www.avoca.ie

féile bia City sister to the famous craftshop and café who have their flagship store in Kilmacanogue, County Wicklow, this large centrally located shop is a favourite daytime dining venue for discerning Dubliners. The restaurant (which is up rather a lot of stairs, where queues of devotees wait patiently at lunchtime) has low-key style and an emphasis on creative, healthy cooking that is common to all the Avoca establishments recommended in the Guide. (Avoca Cafés received the Happy Heart Eat Out Award in 2000 and the Féile Bia Award for 2003). The importance of using only the very best ingredients has always been recognised at Avoca: their food is based on the best available produce, as much of it as possible local and artisan, and they were among the first to sign up to the Féile Bia Charter. Avoca's chic little menus speak volumes - together with careful cooking, meticulously sourced ingredients like Woodstock tuna, Hederman mussels, Gubbeen bacon and Hicks sausages lift dishes such as smoked fish platter, organic bacon panini and bangers & mash out of the ordinary. All this sits happily alongside the home baking for which Avoca is famous - much of which (along with other specialist produce) can be bought downstairs. Meals daily 10-5 (Sunday 11-5); à la carte. Bookings accepted but not required. Amex, Diners, MasterCard, Visa, Laser. **Directions:** Turn left into Suffolk St. from the bottom of Grafton St.

RESTAURANT   # Aya @ Brown Thomas

49/52 Clarendon Street Dublin 2 **Tel: 01 677 1544** Fax: 01 677 1546
Email: mail@aya.ie Web: www.aya.ie

This dashing contemporary Japanese restaurant was Dublin's first conveyor sushi bar, restaurant and food hall - it's owned by the Hoashi family, who established Dublin's first authentic Japanese restaurant, Ayumi-Ya, in 1983 - and was a runaway success from the day it opened, in 1999. The sushi conveyor belt has 35 stools and six 6-seater booths for communal diners, as well as à la carte seating for thirty. Wall-to-wall style remains the order of the day - and the menu includes a wide range of sushi, all authentically Japanese, and also some hot food, including Asian and Japanese tapas, as well as tempura and teriyaki dishes and additions with broader Asian flavours to tempt a wider range of customers. Aya Deli, nearby on South William Street, sells Japanese food, including sushi, and also has an ice cream counter selling Tipperary Organic Ice Cream. Children welcome before 8pm. **Seats 60.** Air conditioning. Open daily: L 12-4. D 5.30-11 (Sun to 10). Set L from €10; Set D from €21 (6-7pm), €25 (7-close). Also à la carte. House wine from €21. SC 12% (at night). Closed 25-26 Dec. Also at: **Aya Deli @IFSC** (Custom House Square, IFSC, Dublin 1). Tel: 01 672 1852. Run on similar lines, although with less seating and greater emphasis on food to go. Amex, MasterCard, Visa, Laser. **Directions:** Directly behind Brown Thomas off Wicklow Street.

RESTAURANT/CAFÉ
Ba Mizu / Mimo
Powerscourt Townhouse Centre South William Street Dublin 2
Mimo: Tel 01 679 4160 Bá Mizu: Tel 01 674 6712

These two attractive sister establishments are within a whisper of each other in the lovely Powerscourt shopping centre: Mimo, in the central focal area, is more of a café-cum-champagne bar while the Bá Mizu is a fully-fledged restaurant with full bar and a small alfresco eating area on South William Street - between them, you will find just about anything you could wish for in the way of interesting, freshly-prepared food and drink throughout the day and evening. Bá Mizu offers an extensive drinks menu, including a comprehensive choice of liqueurs and cocktails (both bars have a cool aquarium built in - something of a trade mark now, as there's also one in the ceiling of the newer Ba Mizu in Howth, Co Dublin), and the restaurant - which is in an atmospheric vaulted area and stylishly furnished with comfy leather chairs - offers a wide range of food from tasty bar bites to full meals, with seafood a particular strength: pan seared fillet of organic salmon with a lemon crème fraîche, wilted spinach, fired prawn & a gazpacho dressing (€12.20)attracted particular praise on a recent visit. That said, there's plenty else to choose from, including great steaks - all round an in place to go for a well-priced informal meal in a cool, trendy bar.Excellent bar bites too. A shortish wine list is on the dear side, and includes several champagnes. Children are welcome during the daytime. **Mimo:** Open 7 days, in shopping hours (closed bank hols); **Bá Mizu:** Open Mon-Wed, Thu 12 noon-1.30am; Thu-Sat 12 noon-2.30am. Closed 25 Dec, 1 Jan. Diners, MasterCard, Visa, Laser. **Directions:** In an 18th century listed building 2 minutes west of Grafton Street.

CAFÉ/RESTAURANT
The Bad Ass Café
9-11 Crown Alley Temple Bar Dublin 2
Tel: 01 671 2596 Fax: 01 671 2596
Email: bad_ass_@hotmail .com Web: www.badasscafe.com

The Bad Ass Café has been charming youngsters (and a good few oldsters) with its particular brand of wackiness and good, lively food since 1983, when most people running Temple Bar restaurants were still at school. Kids love the food (the Bad Ass burger is still one of the favourites, and can be very good), the warehouse atmosphere, the loopy menu and the cash shuttles (from an old shop) that whizz around the ceiling. Over twenty years after opening, the young still find it cool, the fun atmosphere makes it a great place for a family outing - and it gives value for money. Children welcome. **Seats 92.** Open daily

11.30-11.30. Lunch special €7.30 (11.30-4.30); Bad Ass Special €15.85, any time. A la carte also available. House wine from €17.50. Air conditioning. SC 10%. Closed 25-26 Dec, Good Fri. Amex, MasterCard, Visa, Laser. **Directions:** Behind the Central Bank on the way to the Ha'penny Bridge.

ATMOSPHERIC PUB   # The Bailey

2-3 Duke Street Dublin 2 **Tel: 01 670 4939**

Although it's now more of a busy lunchtime spot and after-work watering hole for local business people and shoppers, this famous Victorian pub has a special place in the history of Dublin life - literary, social, political - and attracts many a pilgrim seeking the ghosts of great personalities who have frequented this spot down through the years. Closed 25 Dec & Good Friday.

✓ RESTAURANT   # Bang Café

11 Merrion Row Dublin 2 **Tel: 01 676 0898**
Fax: 01 676 0899 Web: www.bangrestaurant.com

féile bia Stylishly minimalist, with natural tones of dark wood and pale beige leather complementing simple white linen and glassware, this smart restaurant is well-located just yards from the Shelbourne Hotel. It is on two levels with a bar in the basement; upstairs, unstressed chefs can be seen at work in one of the open kitchens: an air of calm, relaxed and friendly professionalism prevails. Head chef Lorcan Cribben's menus offer innovative, modern food: a starter of perfectly cooked foie gras served atop a crisp onion bahji with Sauternes jus is typical and well-balanced main course options include a signature dish of bangers & mash (made with Hicks sausages) now also on the menu at the new **Clarendon Café Bar** (see entry); also great fish dishes - using fresh fish from Bantry, in West Cork. Tempting desserts include several fruity finales (Scandinavian iced berries are a speciality) as well as the ever-popular dark chocolate treats, or there's an Irish farmhouse cheese selection. Attention to detail is the keynote throughout and this, seen in carefully sourced food and skilful cooking combined with generous servings and professional service under the management of Kelvin Rynhart, ensures an enjoyable dining experience and value for money (especially at lunch time). **Seats 90.** Private room, 35. Air conditioning. L &D Mon-Sat 12.30-3, 6-10.30 (Thu-Sat to 11). Set L €35, Set D €45. Also à la carte. House wine €20. 12.5% sc on parties of 6+. Closed Sun, bank hols, 1 week Christmas/New Year. Amex, MasterCard, Visa, Laser. **Directions:** Just past Shelbourne Hotel, off St Stephen's Green.

✓ RESTAURANT/WINE BAR   # Bleu Bistro Moderne

Dawson St Dublin 2 **Tel: 01 676 7015**
Fax: 01 676 7027 Web: www.onepico.com

féile bia A younger sister to Eamonn O'Reilly's excellent flagship restaurant **One Pico** (see entry), this modern bistro (now known generally as simply 'Bleu' or even 'Blue') opened to some acclaim in 2003 and, at its best, can be impressive. Smartly laid tables are rather close together (paper napkins at lunch time - linen at night) and hard surfaces make for a good bit of noise, but Head Chef Paul McDonald's food is based on carefully sourced quality ingredients, skilfully cooked and pleasingly presented on plain white plates: signature dishes include salmon fish cakes with cucumber pickle & saffron aïoli and loin of lamb stuffed with boudin noir, with fondant potato and mushroom & Madeira onion tart. Portions are on the small side, which may make value on the plate seem less than it looks on the menu (vegetables, salads etc charged as extras). The long opening hours can be an advantage - there's a very nice little afternoon menu offered between 3 and 6pm which, with an appealing list of wines by the glass, could make an enjoyable late lunch or early supper. *At the time of going to press a new branch, **Bleu Café Bar,** is due to open in Dundrum. Good wine list, with a dozen or so wines by the glass (from €5.50). **Seats 50** (outdoor seating 10/12). Reservations advised. Air conditioning. Open all day, 12-11 (Sun to 9). L 12-3 (Sun to 4), Set 2/3 course L €19.95/24.95. D 6-11 (Sun 5- 9). Early D €25 (6-7.30), otherwise à la carte. House wine from €20. Closed bank hols. Amex, Diners, MasterCard, Visa, Laser. **Directions:** At top of Dawson St. off St. Stephen's Green.

✔ Ⓑ HOTEL/RESTAURANT   # Brooks Hotel

59-62 Drury Street Dublin 2 **Tel: 01 670 4000** Fax: 01 670 4455
Email: reservations@brookshotel.ie Web: wwwbrookshoteldublin.com

féile bia A city sister for the Sinnott family's hotels in Galway (see entry for Connemara Coast), this boutique hotel is very well located, just a couple of minutes walk from Grafton Street. It has always been an attractive and discreet hotel, but recent developments have transformed it into one of Dublin's most desirable addresses, especially for business guests. The style is a pleasing combination of traditional with new minimalist touches, using a variety of woods, marble, wonderful fabrics and modern paintings - and, while a grand piano adds gravitas, there's a welcome emphasis on comfort (especially in the residents' lounge). All bedrooms have exceptionally good amenities, including well-designed bathrooms with power showers as well as full baths (some also have tile screen TV), air conditioning and many other features. State-of-the-art facilities for meetings and small conferences, include a 45-seater screening room. Fitness suite. Children welcome (under 2 free in parents' room; cots available without charge, baby sitting arranged). No pets. **Rooms 98** (1 suite, 2 junior suites, 7 executive, 90 no-smoking, some for disabled). Lift. B&B €125pps, ss €65. *Special breaks offered - details on application. Open all year.

Francescas Restaraunt: This ground floor restaurant has a young contemporary café style look, and a welcoming ambience with wooden floors, leather seating and an open plan kitchen where head chef Patrick McLarnon and his team can be seen at work from all angles, thanks to well positioned mirrors. Tables are elegantly appointed with classic linen cloths and napkins - and waiting staff, smartly attired in black, look after customers with warmth and professionalism. Patrick sources ingredients with great care (wild salmon, organic chicken, dry aged steak, peat smoked lamb. wild boar sausage), his cooking is imaginative - and there's a strong emphasis on fish and seafood: pan-fried Dublin Bay prawns, perhaps, with smoked bacon, white wine butter sauce and colcannon perhaps. [*Informal meals also available 10am-9.30 daily.] **Seats 70.** Reservations advised. Children welcome. Air conditioning. Toilets wheelchair accessible. D daily, 6-9.30, L Sun12-6. Early D €19.95 (6-7); also à la carte. Closed to non-residents at Christmas. Amex, MasterCard, Visa. **Directions:** Near St Stephen's Green, between Grafton and Great St. Georges Streets; opposite Drury Street car park.

HOTEL   # Brownes Hotel

22 St Stephen's Green Dublin 2 **Tel: 01 638 3939** Fax: 01 638 3900
Email: info@brownesdublin.com Web: www. brownesdublin.com

féile bia Stylish conversion of this fine period house on the stretch of St Stephen's Green between Grafton Street and the Shelbourne Hotel makes an impressive and exceptionally well-located small hotel. The house has something of the atmosphere of a private home about it, and the spacious bedrooms have well-finished bathrooms. Brownes Restaurant is attached to the hotel - along well-appointed split-level room, with well-spaced tables, comfortable chairs and fresh flowers, and big mirrors add interest and create a spacious feeling. The cooking is perhaps a little inconsistent, judging by the Guide's most recent visit, although menus remain interesting. *Recently taken over by Stein Group; major refurbishment is planned at the time of going to press. **Rooms 12** (2 suites). Lift. B&B about €200 pps. L Sun-Fri & D daily. Closed Christmas/New Year. Amex, Diners, MasterCard, Visa, Laser. **Directions:** Stephens Green North, between Kildare & Dawson Streets.

Ⓑ HOTEL   **Buswells Hotel**

25 Molesworth Street Dublin 2 **Tel: 01 614 6500** Fax: 01 676 2090
Email: buswells@quinn-hotels.com Web: www.quinn-hotels.com

féile bia Home from home to Ireland's politicians, this 18th century townhouse close to the Dáil (parliament) has been an hotel since 1921 and is held in great affection by Dubliners. Since major refurbishment several years ago, it now offers a fine range of services for conferences, meetings and private dining. Accommodation is comfortable in the traditional style with good amenities for business guests and it's just a few yards from the city's prime shopping and cultural area, making it an ideal base for private visits - and the lobby and characterful bar make handy meeting places. Conference/banqueting (90/50). Business centre; video conferencing. Children welcome (Under 3s free in parents' room; cots available without charge, baby sitting arranged). No pets. **Rooms 68** (2 suites, 4 shower only, 32 no-smoking, 1 for disabled). Lift. B&B €120pps, ss €50. 24 hr room service.

Trumans: This elegant, well-appointed restaurant has a separate entrance from Kildare Street, or access from the hotel. Quite extensive menus feature popular modern dishes such as a starter of crab caked with sweet chilli sauce, or prawn & saffron risotto with parmesan & chive oil, and have the little touches that endear guests to an establishment, such as a tasty little amuse-bouche presented before the meal 'compliments of the chef'. Wisely, given the likely clientèle, simpler dishes are always an option - notably rack of lamb, steaks presented various ways, or traditional fish & chips with tartare sauce - and vegetarian dishes are creative. Finish with a classic dessert like chocolate ganache with raspberry coulis - or Irish cheeses, perhaps. Children welcome. **Seats 44** (private room, 50). Reservations advised. L 12-2.30, D 5.30-10. Set L, €9.95; early D, €22 (5.30-7); Set D €35; also à la carte. House wine €18.50. SC discretionary. Closed 24-26 Dec. Amex, Diners, MasterCard, Visa, Laser. **Directions:** Close to Dail Eireann, 5 minutes walk from Grafton Street.

CAFÉ   **Butlers Chocolate Café**

24 Wicklow Street Dublin 2 **Tel: 01-671 0599** Fax: 01 671 0480
Email: chocolate@butlers.ie Web: www.butlerschocolates.com

Butlers Chocolate Cafés combine coffee-drinking with complimentary chocolates - an over-simplification, as the range of drinks at this stylish little café also includes hot chocolate as well as lattes, cappuccinos and mochas and chocolate cakes and croissants are also available. But all drinks do come with a complimentary handmade chocolate on the side - and boxed or personally selected loose chocolates, caramels, fudges and fondants are also available for sale. Open 7 days: Mon-Fri 8am-7pm, Sat 9am-7pm, Sun 11am-6pm. Closed 25-26 Dec, Easter Sun & Mon.

Also at: 31 Grafton Street (Tel: 01 671 0599); 9 Chatham Street (Tel: 01 672 6333); 18 Nassau Street (Tel: 01 671 0772), 31 Henry Street (Tel 01 874 7419); all of the above have similar opening times to the Wicklow Street branch, except Nassau St, Grafton St & Henry St open at 7.30 am on weekdays, but a branch at Dublin Airport is open every day from 5am-10pm. (Tel: 01 814 1486). Amex, Diners, MasterCard, Visa, Laser. **Directions:** 5 city centre locations & Dublin Airport.

RESTAURANT **Café Bar Deli**

13 South Gt George's Street Dublin 2
Tel: 01 677 1646 Fax: 01 677 6044
Email: dublin@cafébardeli.ie Web: www.cafebardeli.ie

Despite its obvious contemporary appeal - paper place mat menus set the tone by kicking off with Tasters, the first of which is home-made breads with three dips and marinated olives - the friendly ghosts of the old Bewleys Café are still alive and well in Jay Bourke and Eoin Foyle's inspired reincarnation of one of Dublin's oldest and best-loved comfort zones. Even the name is a play on what was the essence of a café in the old-fashioned sense - steaming pots of tea and milky coffee, with scones or a traditional fry; today it suggests a very different character. Tables may be old café style, with simple bentwood chairs, the original fireplace and a traditional brass railing remain but a smartly striped awning over the the large street window signals the real nature of the place from the outset. Imaginative salads are packed with colourful, flavoursome treats in the modern idiom - rocket, parmesan, anchovies, baby spinach, goat's cheese, hazelnuts, chickpeas, couscous, tapenade are the vocabulary of this menu - with pizza and pasta menus continuing in the same tone. The ten or so pizzas offered include a Café Bar Deli special, changed daily, as do the pastas - and there are also family sized bowls available (serves two for about €22). A sensibly limited wine list combines quality and style (sparkling and dessert wines included) with value; service is friendly and efficient and prices remarkably moderate - an attractive formula for an informal outing, and treating a family won't break the bank.

Branches at: Ranelagh, Dublin 6 (Tel 01 496 1886); Cork (Bodega); and Sligo (Garavogue). Children welcome. **Seats 150**. Open 7 days: Mon-Sat, 12.30-11; Sun 2-10. Air conditioning. A la carte. House wine €20 (litre). No reservations. Closed 25-27 Dec, 1 Jan, Good Fri. Amex, Diners, MasterCard, Visa, Laser.
Directions: Next door to the Globe Bar.

✓CAFÉ/PUB **Café en Seine**

40 Dawson Street Dublin 2 **Tel: 01 677 4567** Fax: 01 677 4488
Email: caféenseine@capitalbars.com Web: www.capitalbars.com

The first of the continental style café-bars to open in Dublin, in 1993, Café en Seine is still ahead of the fashion - the interior is stunning, in an opulent art deco style reminiscent of turn-of-the-century Paris. Not so much a bar as a series of bars (your mobile phone could be your most useful accessory if you arrange to meet somebody here), the soaring interior is truly awe-inspiring with a 3-storey atrium culminating in beautiful glass-panelled ceilings, forty foot trees, enormous art nouveau glass lanterns, and statues and a 19th century French hotel lift among its many amazing features. No expense has been spared in ensuring the quality of design, materials and craftsmanship necessary to create this beautiful Aladdin's cave of a bar. Lush ferns create a deliciously decadent atmosphere and the judicious mixture of old and new which make it a true original - and its many 'bars within bars' create intimate spaces that are a far cry from the impersonality of the superpub. Food is a major part of its appeal too: evening menus are equally informal, and menus offering simple bar food are left on tables - there's a sociable combination platter serving four people and hot dishes like steak sandwiches, scampi and quiches with salads are popular; everything is spotlessly clean and, while simple, the food is really tasty. There's also a snack bar offering desserts and takeaway sandwiches & baguettes with coffee, and an informal range of contemporary dishes is available over lunchtime every day, light bites all day and a popular Jazz Brunch every Sunday. Little wonder that so many people of all ages see it as the coolest place in town. Small al fresco covered section at front seats about 30. Lunch daily, 12-3; (Sun brunch 1-4). D daily: Sun-Wed, 5-9; Thu-Sat, 5-10. Wheelchair access. Bar open 10.30am-2.30am daily. Carvery lunch 12-3. Snack menu 4-10. Closed 25-26 Dec & Good Fri. Amex, MasterCard, Visa, Laser. **Directions:** Upper Dawson Street, on right walking towards St Stephen's Green (St Stephen's Green car park is very close).

🅱 HOTEL   # Camden Court Hotel

Camden Street Dublin 2 **Tel: 01 475 9666** Fax: 01 475 9677
Email: sales@camdencourthotel.com Web: www.camdencourthotel.com

Complimentary secure parking and a leisure centre with swimming pool are perhaps the two main attractions of this conveniently located modern hotel. All bedrooms have neat bathrooms, practical fitted furniture and the usual facilities (plus satellite TV which can show your room bill, speeding check-out). Friendly staff, business and leisure facilities and fairly reasonable rates for the location make this a city centre base to consider. Conference/banqueting (115/100). Leisure centre (swimming pool, gym, sauna, steam). Children welcome (Under 2s free in parents' room; cots available without charge). No pets. **Rooms 246** (1 suite, 13 no-smoking, 13 for disabled). Lift. 24 hr room service. B&B €92.50 pps, ss €57.50; no SC. Closed 23-28 Dec. Diners, MasterCard, Visa. **Directions:** City centre, 10 minutes walk from St.Stephen's Green.

🅱 HOTEL   # Central Hotel

1-5 Exchequer Street Dublin 2 **Tel: 01 679 7302** Fax: 01 679 7303
Email: reservations@centralhotel.ie Web: www.centralhotel.ie

Very conveniently located on the corner of South Great George's Street, this hotel is over a hundred years old and is a handy place to stay on business or for short breaks. Extensive renovations have recently been completed, it's relatively reasonably priced for the city centre and special offers are often available, including weekends. Conference/banqueting (200). Children welcome (Under 12s free in parents' room; cots available). Lift. No pets. **Rooms 70** (2 suites, 2 junior suite, 44 shower only, 14 no smoking). Lift. B&B from about €95 pps, ss €35. Closed 24-28 Dec. Amex, Diners, MasterCard, Visa, Laser. **Directions:** City centre, between Trinity College & Dublin Castle.

RESTAURANT   # Chatham Brasserie

Chatham Street Dublin 2 **Tel: 01 679 0055**

féile bia Just off Grafton Street, the large glass frontage and dainty tables and chairs outside Chatham Brasserie are welcoming - this is a handy place to take a break from shopping. Indoors, the chunky wooden tables with a single flower on each, bentwood chairs and a soothing combination of browns and creams give the room a slightly French elegance, underlined by effective lighting and a display of modern paintings. Menus offer something for everyone - there's a Kids Menu as well as a wide range of popular fare like pasta, pizzas, burgers etc; starters include one or two retro dishes like good old-fashioned shrimp cocktail with Marie Rose sauce, and main courses such as Cape Malay chicken curry (with poppadom, raita, chutney & rice, €15.95), and grilled organic Irish salmon fillet (with chive mash & caper butter, €17.50) are well thought out complete dishes, with delicious vegetables and salads. Dishes suitable for vegetarians and coeliacs are highlighted, also those unsuitable for anyone with nut allergies; some bottled beers are offered in addition to a short but interesting wine list. This is wholesome, satisfying fare, served by friendly (mainly French) staff - not a place for a romantic night out, perhaps, but ideal for refuelling after shopping. Open daily from 11 am - Sun-Tue to 11pm, Wed-Sat to midnight. Amex, MasterCard, Visa, Laser. **Directions:** Off Grafton Street.

RESTAURANT

Chili Club

1 Anne's Lane South Annes Street Dublin 2
Tel: 01 677 3721 Fax: 01 635 1928 Web: www.adlib.ie

This cosy restaurant, in a laneway just off Grafton Street, has great charm; it was Dublin's first authentic Thai restaurant and is still as popular as ever a decade later. Owned and managed by Patricia Kenna, who personally supervises a friendly and efficient staff, it is small and intimate, with beautiful crockery and genuine Thai art and furniture. Supot Boonchouy, who has been head chef since 1996, prepares a fine range of genuine Thai dishes which are not 'tamed' too much to suit Irish tastes. Set lunch and early evening menus offer especially good value. Children welcome. **Seats 40** (private room, 16) L Mon-Sat 12.30-2.30, D daily 6-11. Set L €15. Early D from €15 (6-7pm), Set D €30. A la carte D also available. House wine €19. SC discretionary. Closed L Sun, 25-31 Dec. Amex, Diners, MasterCard, Visa, Laser. **Directions:** Off Grafton Street.

✓ Ⓑ HOTEL/RESTAURANT

The Clarence Hotel

6-8 Wellington Quay Dublin 2 **Tel: 01 407 0800** Fax: 01 407 0820
Email: reservations@theclarence.ie Web: www.theclarence.ie

Dating back to 1852, this hotel has long had a special place in the hearts of Irish people - especially the clergy and the many who regarded it as a home from home when 'up from the country' for business or shopping in Dublin - largely because of its convenience to Heuston Station. Since the early '90s, however, it has achieved cult status through its owners - Bono and The Edge of U2 - who have completely refurbished the hotel, creating the coolest of jewels in the crown of Temple Bar. No expense was spared to get the details right, reflecting the hotel's original arts and crafts style whenever possible. Accommodation offers a luxurious combination of contemporary comfort and period style, with excellent amenities. Public areas include the clublike, oak-panelled Octagon Bar, which is a popular Temple Bar meeting place, and The Study, a quieter room with an open fire. Parking is available in several multi-storey carparks within walking distance; valet parking available for guests. Conference/banqueting (60); video conferencing on request. Beauty treatments, Therapy @ The Clarence (also available to non-residents). Children welcome (Under 12s free in parents' room, cots available without charge). No pets. **Rooms 49** (5 suites, incl 1 penthouse; 44 executive, 6 no smoking, 3 for disabled). Lift. Turndown service. Room rate from €300; no SC.

The Tea Room: The restaurant, which has its own entrance on Essex Street, is a high-ceilinged room furnished in the light oak which is a feature throughout the hotel. Pristine white linen, designer cutlery and glasses, high windows softened by the filtered damson tones of pavement awnings, all combine to create an impressive dining room. Solicitous staff move quietly, quickly offering aperitifs and menus. Now in his fifth year, head chef Antony Ely presents fashionably international seasonal menus that offer plenty of choice, including vegetarian options, but are not overlong or overpriced. Seasonal à la carte dinner menus offer around nine or ten starters and main courses in a modern European/Irish style that is bright and sassy, with strong but not overworked presentation. A wonderful Tasting Menu is also offered, at €65 per person (available for whole tables only): beautifully balanced and superbly cooked, the menu sampled on a recent visit included a number of dishes which allowed this skilful and creative chef to demonstrate tremendous finesse in, for example, a luxurious starter portion of pan fried foie gras, which was partnered with potato pancake, roast sweet onion and Guinness jus - a fascinating creation bringing together the traditions of classic French cuisine and local Irish ingredients. It is well worth treating yourself to the Tasting Menu when in a restaurant of this calibre - it allows the chef full freedom to be creative, and is excellent value for a memorable experience. Table d'hôte lunch menus offer especially good value too, and there's an "all-day" lunch in The Octagon bar offering a light à la carte and a different main course dish every day of the week. Very good wine list (well priced for the quality). **Seats 80**. Toilets wheelchair accessible. L Sun-Fri 12.30-2.30, D daily 6.30-10.30 (Sun to 9.30). Set L €30 (Sun €34); Set D €65. A la carte L & D available. House wine from €24.50. No SC. Octagon Bar Menu,11-5 daily. Closed L Sat; from L 24 Dec-27 Dec. Amex, Diners, MasterCard, Visa. **Directions:** Overlooking the River Liffey at Wellington Quay, southside.

CAFÉ/BAR

Clarendon Café Bar

Clarendon Street Dublin 2 **Tel: 01 679 2909** Fax: 01 670 6900

The Stokes brothers' stylish new contemporary café-bar just off Grafton Street is a sister to Bang Café and, although informal, the restaurant experience is seen immediately in details like really comfortable seating (chairs and banquettes), and quality tableware. It's a much bigger operation, over several storeys, but the same commitment to interesting food is promised on menus that offer tempting dishes like risotto of wild asparagus with squid (starter or main, €6/95/13.50), and house specialities of cod & chips (unfortunately not with home cut chips), and bangers & mash (an upmarket version, which come with a wholegrain mustard & shallot sauce); and, as well as a full range of 'proper' dishes, you can also have sandwiches or toasted sandwiches, made up to order. A couple of really good points about the menu - which is not over-extensive - include describing the cooking instructions given for steak, which is served with classic béarnaise & fries: 'rare; very red, cool centre' etc; this must make life a lot easier in the kitchen. And another highly commendable feature is the list of suppliers given at the end of the menu - full marks for this. The wine list is short, but makes up in interest anything it may lack in length - and an exceptional choice is offered by the glass. Open 10-11. Food served: Mon-Sat, 12-8; Sun 12-6. No reservations. Air conditioning. Toilets wheelchair accessible. A la carte. Wines from €15.50. Closed 25 Dec, Good Fri. Amex, MasterCard, Visa, Laser. **Directions:** From St Stephen's Green, walking down Grafton Street - 1st street on left, 100yards.

🅑 HOTEL

Clarion Stephen's Hall Hotel & Suites

14-17 Lower Leeson Street Dublin 2
Tel: 01 638 1111 Fax: 01 638 1122
Email: stephens@premgroup.com Web: www.stephens-hall.com

Conveniently located just off St Stephen's Green, this 'all-suite' hotel consists of units (bedroom, bathroom, living room, kitchenette) each with modem point, fax machines and CD players. **Rooms 33** (all suites, 9 no-smoking). Wheelchair access. Lift. Room rate from about €165. Free underground parking. Open all year.

Romanza (Tel 01-662 4800): George Sabongi took over this attractive semi-basement adjacent to the hotel in 2001 and with him came the piano bar concept for which he is well-known in Dublin. An enclosed coffee terrace at the back creates a pleasantly summery 'outdoor' atmosphere and, as the restaurant is accessible directly from the hotel and nearby offices, it's a popular lunchtime venue - and very convenient to the National Concert Hall in the evening too. Moderately priced menus include informal Italian fare like quality pizzas and pastas, but there's also a range of antipasti and substantial main courses like charcoal grilled rib eye of beef and barbecue leg of lamb, and Egyptian influence showing in a vegetarian dish such as koushery, which is based on black lentils. You can also just have a drink at the bar (10am-midnight); there's quite an extensive cocktail list and a short bar food menu,10.30-5.30. Live music at weekends. B'fst daily. L Mon-Fri, 12.30-3; D Mon-Sat 5-12. A la carte. House wine about €16. 10% s.c. on parties of 6+. Closed L Sat, all Sun. Amex, Diners, MasterCard, Visa, Laser. **Directions:** Just off St.Stephen's Green, on Lower Leeson Street.

✓ Ⓑ HOTEL   # Conrad Hotel Dublin

Earlsfort Terrace Dublin 2 **Tel: 01 602 8900** Fax: 01 676 5424
Email: dublininfo@conradhotels.com Web: www.conradhotels.com

Just a stroll away from the beautiful St Stephen's Green and right in the heart of the city centre, this fine hotel celebrated its fifteenth anniversary in 2005; service by committed staff is excellent and facilities are constantly upgraded. Many of the bedrooms enjoy views of the piazza below and across the city, and all have recently been refurbished in a contemporary style, offering luxuriously comfortable accommodation with everything required for visiting business guests. A state of the art fitness centre is reserved exclusively for the use of hotel guests. Public areas include a raised lounge, two restaurants, the Alexandra and Plurabelle Brasserie (breakfast, lunch and dinner served here), and Alfie Byrne's Pub, which is home to locals and visitors alike and opens on to a sheltered terrace. Conference/banqueting(300/270). Executive boardroom (12). Business centre; secretarial services; video conferencing. Underground carpark (100). Children welcome (under 12s free in parents' room, cots available without charge, baby sitting arranged). **Rooms 192** (9 suites, 7 junior suites, 165 no-smoking, 1 for disabled). Lift. 24 hr room service. Turndown service. Room rate from about €180, SC incl. Open all year. Amex, Diners, MasterCard, Visa, Laser. **Directions:** On the south-eastern corner of St Stehen's Green, opposite the National Concert Hall.

RESTAURANT   # Cookes Restaurant

14 South William Street Dublin 2 **Tel: 01 679 0536**

After a brief closure the old Cooke's Café re-opened, and got back to doing what Johnny Cooke and his team have always done best - smart modern café cooking. The Cookes' style is still hard to beat - the food has a classical French discipline in there somewhere, with sunny Italian overtones and, perhaps, a little bit of Irish in places. Great breads (but not complimentary, and neither are the olives that have become de rigeur to begin this kind of meal), superb salads and fish cooking, and outstanding pasta dishes remain the strengths of this kitchen - good dessert and coffee too. Old fans should not be disappointed - a revamped first floor dining room marks a return of the real Cookes style - the cooking is still great and prices are fairly reasonable. **Seats 60** (outdoor seating available). L daily, D Wed-Sat MasterCard, Visa. **Directions:** On corner of Castle Market and South William Street.

RESTAURANT   # Cornucopia

19 Wicklow Street Dublin 2 **Tel: 01-677 7583**
Fax: 01 6719449 Email: cornucopia@eircom.net

You don't have to be vegetarian to enjoy this long-established wholefood restaurant, which is well located for a wholesome re-charge if you're shopping around the Grafton Street area, but it might be a good idea to be with someone who is, on a first visit. It was originally a wholefood store with a few tables at the back and, although it has now been a dedicated restaurant for some time, a waft of that unmistakable aroma remains. It may give out mixed messages in various ways - the smart red and gold frontage and pavement screen seem inviting in a mainstream way, but the atmosphere is actually quite student / alternative so don't expect a trendy modern restaurant. It is very informal especially during the day (when window seats are well placed for people watching), and regulars like it for its simple wholesomeness, redolent of good home cooking. Vegetarian breakfasts are a speciality (lots of freshly squeezed juices to choose from) and all ingredients are organic, as far as possible. Yeast-free, dairy-free, gluten-free and wheat-free diets catered for and no processed or GM foods are used. Organic wines too. **Seats 40.** Mon-Sat 8.30am-8pm (Thu to 9pm), Sun 12-7. All à la carte (menus change daily); organic house wine about €16 (large glass about €3.95). Closed 25-27 Dec, 1 Jan, Easter Sun. MasterCard, Visa, Laser. **Directions:** Off Grafton St. turn at Brown Thomas.

RESTAURANT
Da Pino

38-40 Parliament Street Dublin 2 **Tel: 01 671 9308**
Fax: 01 677 3409 Email: m.jimenez@tinet.ie

Just across the road from Dublin Castle, this busy youthful Italian/Spanish restaurant is always full - and no wonder, as they serve cheerful, informal, well cooked food that does not make too many concessions to trendiness and is sold at very reasonable prices. Paella is a speciality and the pizzas, which are especially good, are prepared in full view of customers. Children welcome. **Seats 75.** Open 12-11.30 daily. 2-course L (Mon-Fri), €7.40; special D €18 (all evening), also à la carte. Wine from €15.90. Closed Christmas & Good Fri. Amex, Diners, MasterCard, Visa, Laser. **Directions:** Opposite Dublin Castle.

RESTAURANT
Darwin's

16 Aungier Street Dublin 2 **Tel: 01 475 7511** Fax: 01 475 9881
Email: darwinsrestaurant@eircom.net Web: www.darwinsrestaurant.ie

Proprietor Michael Smith's own butchers shop supplies certified organic meats to this new restaurant in an area known for its butchers but not, until now, so much as a dining destination. But, together with a strong team of head chef Brendan O'Sullivan (Irish, recently retuned from Australia) and restaurant manager, Rachel Clancy, Darwin's hit the ground running when it opened in the winter of 2004/5 and looks set to open up a whole new area for Dublin's discerning diners. Flavoursome cooking that pleases the eye as much as the taste buds combines sophistication with generosity, making the most of well-sourced ingredients, including excellent vegetables and delicious fish. Finish with a choice of gorgeous puds or mature farmhouse cheeses (attractively presented plated with fresh fruit and oatcakes) and a wack of irresistible Illy coffee. Good wine list - and fair pricing too. This place should do well. **Seats 48.** D Mon-Sat, 5.30 to 'late'; L Thu & Fri, 12-3. Early D about €25; also à la carte. Closed Sun. **Directions:** Opposite Carmelite Church.

---

❶ ⑧ HOTEL
The Davenport Hotel

Merrion Square Dublin 2 **Tel: 01 607 3900** Fax: 01 661 5663
Email: davenportres@ocallaghanhotels.ie Web: www.ocallaghenhotels.ie

féile bia On Merrion Square, close to the National Gallery, the Dáil (Parliament Buildings) and Trinity College, this striking hotel is fronted by the impressive 1863 facade of the Alfred Jones designed Merrion Hall, which was restored as part of the hotel building project in the early '90s. Inside, the architectural theme is continued in the naming of rooms - Lanyon's Restaurant, for example honours the designer of Queen's University Belfast and the Gandon Suite is named after the designer of some of Dublin's finest buildings, including the Custom House. The hotel, which is equally suited to leisure and business guests, has been imaginatively designed to combine interest and comfort, with warm, vibrant colour schemes and a pleasing mixture of old and new in both public areas and accommodation. Bedrooms are furnished to a high standard with every comfort for the leisure and business guest. Conference/banqueting

DUBLIN 2

(380/400). Business centre. Gym. Children welcome (Under 2s free in parents'
room; cots available, baby sitting arranged). No pets. **Rooms 115** (2 suites, 10
junior suites). Lift. 24 hr room service. B&B about € 97.50pps. Open all year.
Amex, Diners, MasterCard, Visa. **Directions:** just off Merrion Square.

♣ ATMOSPHERIC PUB   **Davy Byrnes**

21 Duke Street Dublin 2 **Tel: 01 677 5217**
Fax: 01 671 7619 Web: www.davybyrnes.com

Just off Grafton Street, Davy Byrnes is one of Dublin's most famous pubs -
references in Joyce's Ulysses mean it is very much on the tourist circuit.
Despite all this fame it remains a genuine, well-run place and equally popular
with Dubliners, who find it a handy meeting place and also enjoy the bar food.
The style is quite traditional, providing 'a good feed' at reasonable prices (most
meals, with hearty vegetables, are under €15). Oysters with brown bread &
butter, Irish stew, beef & Guinness pie and deep-fried plaice with tartare sauce
are typical and there's always a list of daily specials like sautéed lambs live
with bacon & mushroom sauce, pheasant in season - and, in deference to the
Joycean connections, there's also a Bloomsday Special (gorgonzola and
burgundy). And the literary history of Davy Byrnes has recently moved into a
new phase, with the introduction of their Irish Writing Award, with a prize fund
of €20,000 - details on application. Not suitable for children under 7. Outside
eating area. Bar food served daily, 12.30-9 (winter to 5). Closed 25-26 Dec &
Good Fri. MasterCard, Visa, Laser. **Directions:** 100 yards from Grafton Street.

WINE BAR/RESTAURANT   **Dax Wine Bar**

23 Upper Pembroke Street Dublin 2 **Tel: 01 676 3287**
Email: olivier@dax.ie Web: www.dax.ie

Olivier Meisonave - who will be warmly remembered by many from his previous
role as restaurant manager at Thornton's - named this new venture after his
home town in Les Landes, and this appealing wine bar-cum-restaurant is the
fruition of a longheld ambition. Flagged floors, light-toned walls and
upholstery set off simple contemporary darkwood furniture in the bar and
restaurant areas, and there is an open plan lounge area with comfortable
seating for those who prefer a casual bite - it all adds up to a tone of relaxed
contemporary elegance. Head chef Pól ó Héannraich's menus change weekly
and offer a carefully judged selection of dishes that can make up a standard 3
course meal, or stand alone as a light plate to enjoy with wine - a growing
trend in Dublin at the moment, and a welcome one. Charcuterie and tapas style
plates, for example which serve as starter or stand-alone dishes, and also
substantial main courses (in the cuisine grand-mère style, perhaps - perfect for
a chilly day), good puds and an exceptional range of European cheeses
French, Italian, Spanish and, of course, Irish - on a trolley that is also available
to anyone who drops in for a glass of wine between lunch and dinner. An
extensive and carefully selected European wine list includes a large selection
by the glass. Children welcome (but not really suitable for very young children).
No wheelchair access but help available (6 steps) and no steps inside. **Seats
65**. D Tue-Sat, 6.30-10.30, L Tue-Fri; also open during the day as a wine bar.
Closed Sun. MasterCard, Visa, Laser.

RESTAURANT   **Diep Le Shaker**

55 Pembroke Lane Dublin 2 **Tel: 01 661 1829** Fax: 01 661 5909
Email: info@diep.net Web: www.diep.net

This fashionable two-storey restaurant is elegantly appointed with comfortable
high-back chairs, good linen and fine glasses, while sunny yellow walls and
long skylight along one side of the upper floor create a bright, summery

atmosphere and the ambience is always lively. Head chef Taweesak Trakoolwattana, who has experience in five star hotels in Thailand, joined the restaurant in 2002 and the cooking can be very good; the Chinese dishes previously listed have all but disappeared as a team of Thai chefs has developed the newer Royal Thai Cuisine to replace them: signature dishes include Hoi shell Neung, a subtle dish of steamed scallops with fresh ginger and light soy sauce, and Goong Phad Numprig Pao (stir fried king prawns with oyster mushrooms, ginger, peppers and scallions. Service is invariably charming and solicitous. Not suitable for children after 9 pm. Air conditioning. Toilets wheelchair accessible. Jazz Tue & Wed night. **Seats 120**. Reservations required. L Mon-Fri 12.30-2.15, D Mon-Sat 6.15-11. Set L €31.50; D à la carte. House wine from €19.90. SC 10%. Closed L Sat, all Sun, bank hols, 25 Dec. Amex, MasterCard, Visa, Laser. **Directions:** First lane on left off Pembroke Street.

ⒷRESTAURANT   # Dobbins Wine Bistro

15 Stephens Lane Dublin 2 **Tel: 01 661 3321** Fax: 01 661 3331
Email: dobbinswinebistro@eircom.net

féile bia This 'Nissen hut' hidden away near Merrion Square is something of a Dublin institution, having been run since 1978 by the late John O'Byrne and manager Patrick Walsh. A visit to this unique oasis is always a treat and, along with great hospitality and food which is consistently delicious in a style that shows an awareness of current trends without slavishly following them, they're renowned for their wines, which have always been at the centre of their philosophy: the exclusive 'Front Page Wines' on the regular list are available for off-sales, by the bottle or case - which greatly pleases the many wine buffs who frequent the restaurant, as they are sold at half the list price. They also hold a wine fair every December, buying bin ends and selling them a vineyard prices; needless to say it's very popular with customers - and sorts out the Christmas shopping very pleasantly too. Leisurely lunches have been known to run on a bit too long, hence the warning on the menu: "Bar closes at 5.30pm and re-opens at 7.30 for dinner service." The only down side to this conviviality is that tables for two can seem a little forlorn, so it's best to make up a party. Dobbins was selected for the Guide's Wine Award in 2003. Children welcome. Air conditioning. **Seats 120** (private room, 40). L Mon-Fri 12.30-2.30, D Tue-Sat 7.30-10.30. Set L €24.50, D à la carte. House wine from €20. SC discretionary. Closed L Sat, all Sun, D Mon, bank hols, Christmas week. *At the time of going to press, Dobbins is to close for major renovations, expected to take several months. Amex, Diners, MasterCard, Visa, Laser. **Directions:** Between Lower & Upper Mount Street.

ATMOSPHERIC PUB   # Doheny & Nesbitt

5 Lower Baggot Street Dublin 2 **Tel: 01 676 2945** Fax: 01 676 0655

Only a stone's throw from Toner's (see entry), Doheny & Nesbitt is another great Dublin institution, but there the similarity ends. Just around the corner from the Dáil (Irish Parliament), this Victorian pub has traditionally attracted a wide spectrum of Dublin society - politicians, economists, lawyers, business names, political and financial journalists - all with a view to get across, or some new scandal to divulge, so a visit here can often be unexpectedly rewarding. Like the Horseshoe Bar at the nearby Shelbourne Hotel which has a similar reputation and shares the clientèle, half the fun of drinking at Nesbitt's is the anticipation of 'someone' arriving or 'something' happening, both more likely than not. Although it has been greatly extended and is now in essence a superpub, it has at its heart the original, very professionally run bar with an attractive Victorian ambience and a traditional emphasis on drinking and conversation. Closed 25 Dec & Good Fri.

RESTAURANT # The Dome Restaurant

St Stephens Green Shopping Centre St Stephens Green Dublin 2
Tel: 01 478 1287

féile bia At the top of the shopping centre, this bright and airy daytime restaurant has a lot going for it before you take a bite: beautiful views over St Stephen's Green, a friendly atmosphere, fresh flowers - and even live background music. A self-service section has a full chalk board description above, and a salad bar opposite. Everything on display is very appetising and friendly chefs are at hand, behind the counter, to assist your choices. The food style is basically French and Mediterranean, also a full breakfast which is served from 8.30am, and afternoon meals every day. Main courses like duck with orange sauce, chicken with cream and salmon with cream sauce, or prawns with dill should tempt the most determined sandwich muncher - and there are lovely desserts supplied by the Mardi Cake Shop, next door. Children are made very welcome too, with high chairs, changing facilities and bottle warming available. And they even have jazz guitarists playing, from 3.30-5.30 Mon-Sat. Great value for money too. **Seats 200**. Air conditioning. Open Mon-Sat, 8-6 (Sun 12-6). A la carte. Wines (1/4 bottles) from about €4.60. SC discretionary. Closed 25-26 Dec, 1 Jan, Easter Sun. **No Credit Cards. Directions:** Very top floor of St Stephens Green Shopping Centre.

RESTAURANT/DELI # Dunne & Crescenzi

14 South Frederick Street Dublin 2 **Tel: 01 677 3815** Fax: 01 677 3815

This much-loved Italian restaurant and deli very near the Nassau Street entrance to Trinity College delights Dubliners with its unpretentiousness and the simple good food it offers at reasonable prices. It's the perfect place to shop for genuine Italian ingredients - risotto rice, pasta, oils, vinegars, olives, cooked meats, cheeses, wines and much more - and a great example of how less can be more. Menus offer sandwiches or panini, antipasti and desserts: How good to sit down with a glass of wine (bottles on sale can be opened for a small corkage charge) and, perhaps, a plate of antipasti - with wafer-thin Parma ham, perhaps, several salamis, peppers preserved in olive oil, olives and a slice of toasted ciabatta drizzled with extra virgin olive oil... There are even some little tables on the pavement, if you're lucky enough to get them on a sunny day. Indoors or out, expect to queue: this place has a loyal following. A short Italian wine list **Seats 30**. Air conditioning. Open 9-7 Mon & Tue, to 10 pm Wed-Sat. Closed Sun. A la carte; wine from about €11. ***Now also at** Sandymount, Dublin 4 (Tel 01-667 3252) and, at the time of going to press, a more formal new Italian restaurant, **Nonna Valentina**, is due to open in Portobello, Dublin 8; it will specialise in north Italian cuisine. Amex, MasterCard, Visa, Laser. **Directions:** Off Nassau Street, between Kilkenny and Blarney stores.

✓ RESTAURANT # Eden

Meeting House Square Temple Bar Dublin 2
Tel: 01 670 5372 Fax: 01 670 3330
Email: bookings@edenrestaurant.ie Web: www.edenrestaurant.ie

This spacious two-storey restaurant was designed by Tom de Paor and has its own outdoor terrace on the square; modern, with lots of greenery and hanging baskets, there's an open kitchen which adds to the buzz and provides entertainment if service is slow. A well-established house style has become very popular - seasonal menus are quite extensive and make use of organic produce where possible, in updated classics which suit the restaurant well. Head chef Michael Durkan's menus are clear and to the point: a starter of smokies (smoked haddock with spring onion, crème fraîche and melted cheddar cheese) is simple, as stated, and amazingly good, and chargrilled sirloin of organic beef with red onion, chips and a classic béarnaise sauce is a revelation, the roasted red onion sweet and wonderful, simply halved and cooked perfectly. Vegetables are a particular strength - they always cook a vegetable of the day and use a great variety in season: a Moroccan mixture of celeriac, carrot, sweet potato and spices is typical, and even the humble cabbage gets the treatment - shredded and stir-fried in oil and utter, with ginger and garlic added. A three-course pre-theatre menu, offers four choices on each course and is great value at about €22. A well-balanced and fairly priced wine list offers several wines by the glass. Great food and atmosphere, efficient service and good value too - long may Eden continue to do what it does best. Children welcome. **Seats 110** (private room, 14; outdoor seating, 48). Air conditioning. L daily,12.30-3 (Sat & Sun brunch from 12). D daily 6-10 (Sat & Sun to 10.30). Set menus offered, also à la carte. House wine €22. SC discretionary. Closed bank hols, 25-29 Dec. Amex, Diners, MasterCard, Visa, Laser. **Directions:** Next to the Irish Film Theatre, opposite Diceman's Corner.

RESTAURANT   **Elephant & Castle**

18 Temple Bar Dublin 2 Tel: 01 679 3121 Fax: 01 679 1399

This buzzy Temple Bar restaurant was one of the first new-wave places in the area and, although not quite what is was in the early days, its specialities remain the same: big, generous and wholesome salads (their special Caesar salad is renowned), pasta dishes, home-made burgers and great big baskets of chicken wings. Not a place to drop in for a quick bite - waiting staff are usually foreign students and, although willing and friendly, it can take longer than anticipated to finish a meal; however, the lively atmosphere is perhaps the strongest attraction here, so the time passes agreeably. Children welcome. Air conditioning. **Seats 85**. Open Mon-Fri, 8am-11.30pm; Sat, 10.30am-11.30pm, Sun from 12. Toilets wheelchair accessible. Closed Christmas & Good Fri. Amex, Diners, MasterCard, Visa. **Directions:** Behind Central Bank, Dame Street.

✓ Ⓑ ♣ RESTAURANT/WINE BAR   **Ely Winebar & Café**

22 Ely Place Dublin 2 **Tel: 01 676 8986**
Fax: 01 661 7288 Email: elywinebar@eircom.net

féile bia Just around the corner from The Shelbourne and a stone's throw from the Merrion Hotel, Erik and Michelle Robson's unusual wine bar and café occupies the ground floor and basement of an imaginatively renovated Georgian townhouse - polished wooden floors, brick arches and contemporary furnishings are completely at home here, a successful and refreshing blend of old and new. Ely's remarkable wine list is the main attraction, offering a vast number of carefully selected wines, with about fifty by the glass thus providing the opportunity to taste wines which would otherwise be unaffordable to most people. Although not the first restaurant to try this, it is done with great dedication and style at Ely - and the exceptional wine list is backed up by other specialities including a list of premium beers and, on the food side, organic produce, notably meats from the family farm in Co. Clare, are a special feature - and not just premium cuts, but also products like black pudding and home-made sausages which make all the difference to simple dishes like sausages and mash or beefburgers. Although food was originally presented more or less as an accompaniment to the exceptional wines, quite extensive lunch and evening menus are now offered - including, many visitors will be glad to hear, Kilkee oysters with brown bread and traditional Irish stew made with Burren lamb as well as many contemporary dishes. Mature Irish and continental cheeses make the ideal accompaniment to a glass of wine and they also serve great coffee, and a fine selection of hand-made Irish chocolates. A recent refurbishment has created lots more room and greater comfort for adventurous sippers, and a wine list that is bigger and better than ever - Ely was selected for our Wine Award of the Year for 2005 (in the Ireland Guide). **Seats 120.** Open Mon-Sat 12 noon-12.30 am. L 12-3, D 6-10.45 (Bar open to midnight). Wines from €22 (W)/24.50 (R). SC 12.5% on groups of 6+. Closed Sun, Christmas week, bank hol Mons. Amex, Diners, MasterCard, Visa, Laser. **Directions:** Junction of Baggot Street/Merrion Street off St Stephens Green.

Ⓑ RESTAURANT   **Fadó Restaurant**

Mansion House Dawson Street Dublin 2 **Tel: 01 676 7200**
Fax: 01 676 7530 Email: info@fado.ie Web: www.fado.ie

The Mansion House has been the official residence of the Lord Mayor of Dublin since 1715 - the only mayoral residence in Ireland, it is older than any mayoral residence in Britain. The room previously known as The Supper Room has been imaginatively renovated as a restaurant - the room itself is of sufficient interest to be worth a look even if you haven't time to eat - and the contemporary food served somehow seems very appropriate to this sparkling restoration. Since opening in 2000, Myles Tuthill's team have worked hard to achieve a well-earned reputation for hospitality and attention to detail, in both food and service. Well-balanced menus, which include a quick set lunch, as well as quite extensive à la carte menus, perhaps lean a little towards seafood - specialities include salmon fish cakes - but meat and poultry are well-represented and vegetarian options are imaginative too: a main course of butternut squash ravioli with a cream sauce, pinenuts and sage is a typically tempting example from a lunch menu. Desserts tend to be classic and there's always a cheese plate (supplied by Sheridans cheesemongers). The wine list includes some serious bottles, and a fair choice of half bottles and wines by the glass. *At the time of going to press a change of management is anticipated. Hopefully the essential character of this lovely restaurant will remain unchanged. Open Mon-Sat, 12-10. L 12-5, Set L €18; D 6-10, €37. A la carte also available. House wines from €18.95. Closed Sun, bank hol Mons, 25 Dec, Good Fri. Amex, MasterCard, Diners, Visa, Laser. **Directions:** City centre, beside the Lord Mayor's residence, the Mansion House.

RESTAURANT   **Fitzers Restaurant**

51 Dawson Street Dublin 2 **Tel: 01-677 1155**
Fax: 01-670 6575 Email: fitzcat@indigo.ie

féile bia Reliable Cal-Ital influenced cooking in a dashing contemporary setting with a heated al fresco dining area on the pavement. Open daily 11.30am-11pm. Closed Dec 25/26, Jan 1, Good Friday. Amex, Diners, MasterCard, Visa. **Also at:** *Temple Bar Square, Tel: 01-679 0440 (12-11 daily, cl 25 Dec & Good Fri) *National Gallery, Merrion Square Tel: 01-663 3500 Mon-Sat 9.30-5, Sun 12-4.30, closed Gallery Opening days). **Directions:** Halfway up Dawson Street, on the right heading towards St Stephen's Green.

Ⓑ HOTEL   **The Fitzwilliam Hotel**

St Stephens Green Dublin 2 **Tel: 01 478 7000** Fax: 01 478 7878
Email: enq@fitzwilliamhotel.com Web: www.fitzwilliamhotel.com

This stylish contemporary hotel enjoys a superb location at the top of Grafton Street. Behind its deceptively low-key frontage lies an impressively sleek interior created by Sir Terence Conran's design group CD Partnership: public areas combine elegant minimalism with luxury fabrics and finishes, notably leather upholstery and a fine pewter counter in the bar, which is a chic place to meet in the Grafton Street area. In addition to the hotels' premier restaurant, Thornton's (see separate entry), breakfast, lunch and dinner are served daily in their informal restaurant Citron, on the mezzanine level. Bedrooms, while quite compact for a luxury hotel, are finished to a high standard, and care has been lavished on the bathrooms too, down to details such as high quality toiletries. Informal meals served at the fashionable 'The Inn on the Green' bar. Conference/banqueting (80/60). Secretarial services. Children welcome; (under12s free in parents' room; cots available free of charge). 24 hour room service. **Rooms 128** (2 suites, 128 executive, 90 no-smoking, 4 for disabled). Lift. B&B about €160pps No service charge. Open all year. Amex, Diners, MasterCard, Visa, Laser. **Directions:** On the north-western corner of St Stephen's Green.

RESTAURANT | **Franks**

The Malting Tower Grand Canal Quay Dublin 2

féile bia There are no special lunch or dinner menus at John Hayes and Elizabeth Mee's new restaurant - and anyone who remembers the excitement of the fresh flavours and gutsy, simple food they brought with them when they opened Elephant & Castle way back when, will recognise the style - albeit a grown up version - here at Franks. Despite its unlikely location under a railway arch and its pared down simplicity it's a smart little place - and well suited to the sassy bistro menu that these old hands have devised. Starters kick off ordinarily enough with soup of the day - then come rock oysters (at a very reasonable €7.50 for six, €15 the dozen) and a little French chic kicks in with other unusual choices like potted shrimps with poilane toast. Salads to die for might include a classic combination of endive, roquefort & pear, with roasted walnuts (available, like most of the salads, in small or large portions), then there are great main courses (including lots of good red meat, in classic steak tartare, for instance, and home made beef burgers). And the sandwiches... suffice it to say they include croque m'sieu and croque m'dame; ah heaven indeed. There's even an egg menu - what a place to go for brunch. An interesting and informative wine list provides a great read and includes a good choice of out-of-the-ordinary house wines and half bottles. **Seats 75.** Reservations accepted. Air conditioning. Toilets wheelchair accessible. Open 11.30 am-11 pm daily. Children welcome. Closed 24-26 Dec, Good Fri. **Directions:** First right after Kitty O'Shea's - just across canal bridge.

RESTAURANT | **Good World Chinese Restaurant**
---

18 South Great Georges Street Dublin 2
Tel: 01 6775373 Fax: 01 6775373

One of a cluster of interesting ethnic restaurants around Wicklow Street and South Great George's Street, this was one of the first and is popular with the local Chinese community, who appreciate the high standard of their Dim Sums - a selection of which can be had after 6pm at about €5 per item. A more interesting and authentic Chinese menu is available as well as the standard one, offering unusual dishes such as 'Fish Slices Congee' - a sort of rice porridge not often seen even in London - other variations are beef, chicken, salted eggs and pickle. Another satisfying concoction consists of assorted meats (chicken, pork etc) and also seafood including squid, prawns and scallops) with tofu, mushrooms and Chinese leaf - delicious and a real bargain at about €14. The restaurant prides itself on an especially full range of Chinese dishes, suitable for both Chinese and European customers, and service is both friendly and efficient. **Seats 95.** Open 12.30pm-midnight daily. Closed 25-26 Dec. Amex, Diners, MasterCard, Visa, Laser. **Directions:** Corner of Sth Gt George's Street & Wicklow Street.

RESTAURANT

Gotham Café

8 South Anne Street Dublin 2 **Tel: 01 679 5266** Fax: 01 679 5280

A lively, youthful café-restaurant just off Grafton Street, the Gotham does quality informal food at reasonable prices and is specially noted for its gourmet pizzas - try the Central Park, for example, a Greek style vegetarian pizza with black olives, red onion & fresh tomato on a bed of spinach with feta & mozzarella cheeses and fresh hummus, which is just one of a choice of sixteen tempting toppings. Other specialities include Caesar salad, baby calzoni (two miniatures - one with chèvre, prosciutto, basil & garlic; the other with baby potato, spinach, caramelised red onion, mozzarella & fresh pesto) and Asian chicken noodle salad (satay chicken fillets on a salad of egg noodles tossed in a light basil & crème fraîche dressing). There's a good choice of pastas too - and it's a great place for brunch on Sundays and bank holidays; consistent quality at fair prices. [*A sister outlet, **The Independent Pizza Company**, is at 28 Lr Drumcondra Road, Dublin 9]. Children welcome. Air conditioning. **Seats 65** (outdoor seating, 12). Open daily: Mon-Sat 12 -12 (L 12-5, D 5-12); Sun brunch, 12-4 & D 4-12. A la carte. House wine €15.95. SC discretionary (10% on parties of 6+). Closed 2 days Christmas & Good Fri. Amex, MasterCard, Visa, Laser. **Directions:** Just Off Grafton Street.

Ⓑ HOTEL

The Grafton Capital

Stephens Street Lower Dublin 2 **Tel: 01 6481100** Fax: 01 6481122
Email: info@graftoncapital-hotel.com Web: www.capital-hotels.com

In a prime city centre location just a couple of minutes walk from Grafton Street, this attractive hotel offers well furnished rooms and good amenities at prices which are not unreasonable for the area. Rooms are also available for small conferences, meetings and interviews. The popular 'Break for the Border' nightclub next door is in common ownership with the hotel. Small conferences (22). Business centre. Wheelchair access. Parking by arrangement with nearby carpark. Children welcome (Under 12s free in parents' room; cots available; baby sitting arranged). No Pets. **Rooms 75** (3 junior suites, 19 no-smoking, 4 for disabled). Lift. B&B about €96pps, ss €40. Short breaks offered. Closed 24-26 Dec. Amex, Diners, MasterCard, Visa, Laser. **Directions:** Near St. Stephen's Green (opposite Drury Street carpark).

Ⓑ GUESTHOUSE

Harrington Hall

69/70 Harcourt Street Dublin 2 **Tel: 01 475 3497** Fax: 01 475 4544
Email: harringtonhall@eircom.net Web: www.harringtonhall.com

Conveniently located close to St Stephen's Green and within comfortable walking distance of the city's premier shopping areas, Trinity College and the National Concert Hall, this fine family-run guesthouse was once the home of a former Lord Mayor of Dublin and has been sympathetically and elegantly refurbished. Echoes of Georgian splendour remain in the ornamental ceilings and fireplaces of the well-proportioned rooms, which include a peaceful drawing room. Bedrooms, which are both comfortable and practical, have sound-proofed windows and ceiling fans, and neat en-suit bathrooms. All round this is a welcoming alternative to a city-centre hotel, offering good value and with the huge advantage of free parking behind the building; luggage can be stored for guests arriving before check-in time (2pm). Snack menu available (with wine list). Small conferences (12). Children welcome (under 3s free in parents' room, cot available without charge). Staff are friendly and helpful. Parking (8). **Rooms 28** (2 junior suites, 3 shower only, 6 executive, all no smoking). Lift. 24 hour room service. B&B about €86.50, ss €20. Open all year. Amex, Diners, MasterCard, Visa, Laser. **Directions:** Off southwest corner of St Stephens Green (one-way system approaches from Adelaide Road).

B HOTEL   # Hilton Dublin

Charlemont Place Dublin 2 **Tel: 01 402 9988** Fax: 01 402 9966
Email: reservations_dublin@hilton.com Web: www.dublin.hilton.com

féile bia Overlooking the Grand Canal, this modern hotel, is beside a Luas station, and caters well for the business guest; at the time of going to press a major refurbishment programme is in progress. A buffet-style breakfast is served in the well-appointed **Waterfront Restaurant**, where accomplished cooking is offered in the evening. Conference/banqueting (350/270). Underground carpark. Children welcome (Under 12s free in parents' room; cots available). No pets. Lift. **Rooms 189** (78 no-smoking, 8 for disabled). Room rate from about €110 (max. 2 guests). Weekend specials from €176. Open all year. Amex, MasterCard, Visa. **Directions:** Off Fitzwilliam Square.

B HOTEL   # Holiday Inn

99-107 Pearse Street Dublin 2 **Tel: 01 670 3666**
Fax: 670 3636 Email: info@holidayinndublin.ie
www.holidayinn.dublincitycentre.ie

With all the advantages of a city centre location, plus good business / conference facilities - and secure parking - this new hotel is not only a convenient base for leisure visitors, but has quickly become a favourite for business and corporate guests too. Residents' gym. Businss centre. Conferences (400). **Rooms 101**. B&B from €45pps. Open all year. Amex, Diners, MasterCard, Visa.

RESTAURANT   # Hô Sen

6 Cope Street Dublin 2 **Tel: 01 671 8181** Web: www.hosen.ie

The chefs at Ireland's first authentic Vietnamese restaurant are trained in Vietnam and take pride in bringing their cuisine to this pleasingly simple restaurant in Temple Bar - and in introducing this lighter, clear-flavoured Asian cooking style at prices which are incredibly reasonable by Dublin standards - so word spread like wild fire and, from the outset, this has been a busy place. Vietnamese cooking is said to be among the healthiest in the world and, although the familiar Asian styles feature - spring rolls, satays, stir fries and pancake dishes, for example - fresh herb flavours of mint, coriander and lemongrass are the dominant flavours, and there is a light touch to both the flavours and the cooking. And the cooking here is as exciting as the welcome is warm - this place is a little gem. **Seats 30**. Open 7 days. Wines from about €16. **Directions:** In Temple Bar, behind the Central Bank.

RESTAURANT/WINE BAR   # Il Primo Ristorante

16 Montague Street Dublin 2 **Tel: 01 478 3373**
Email: alto.primo@iolfree.ie

Dieter Bergman's cheery little two storey restaurant and wine bar between Harcourt Street and Camden Street was way ahead of current fashions when it opened in 1991. Separate air conditioned dining rooms are simply furnished, but the essentials are right: warm hospitality and good, imaginative, freshly cooked modern Italian food that includes gourmet pizzas (with smoked salmon & spinach, for example), excellent pastas and lovely salads (try the insalata misto, with mixed leaves, cheese, olives & French beans). Unusual speciality dishes include Ravioli Il Primo - open ravioli filled with chicken breast, parma ham and wild mushrooms, in a cream sauce - and lasagne with crabmeat and leek. The wines are Dieter's special passion: the list is impressive (mainly Italian and French, with a little nod to the rest of the world), and Dieter also organises regular wine tastings and dinners. Fresh flavours and buzz sum up Il Primo best - a visit here is always fun. Separate dining/function rooms available (30). Children welcome. **Seats 80**. Air conditioning. L Mon-Sat, 12.30-3, D daily 6-11 (Sun to 10); à la carte. House wines €25 (per litre). SC10%. Closed L Sun. Amex, Diners, MasterCard, Visa, Laser. **Directions:** 5 mins from Stephens Green between Harcourt Street & Wexford Street.

RESTAURANT **Imperial Chinese Restaurant**

12A Wicklow Street Dublin 2 **Tel: 01 677 2580**
Fax: 01 677 9851 Email: imperial@hotmail.com

Mrs Cheung's long-established city centre restaurant has enjoyed enduring popularity with Dubliners and has also a clear vote of confidence from the local Chinese community, who flock here for the Dim Sum at lunchtime - a good selection of these delectable Cantonese specialities is available between 12.30 and 5.30 daily. Fried Seafood Noodles is a good dish with lots of succulent prawns, scallops and squid with Pak Choi; crispy aromatic duck is another speciality from a wide-ranging selection of Chinese dishes. Children welcome. **Seats 180**. Private room available. Open daily 12.30-11.30 (L12.30-2.10 Mon-Sat). Set L about €12, Set D about €30. Also à la carte. House wine about €17. SC 10%. Closed 25-26 Dec. Amex, MasterCard, Visa, Laser. **Directions:** On Wicklow Street near Brown Thomas.

ATMOSPHERIC PUB **The International Bar**

23 Wicklow Street Dublin 2 **Tel: 01 677 9250**

Just a minute's walk from Grafton Street, this unspoilt Victorian bar makes a great meeting place - not a food spot, but good for chat and music. Closed 25 Dec. & Good Friday. **Directions:** Corner of Wicklow Street & St Andrew Street.

B ♣ RESTAURANT **Jacobs Ladder**

4 Nassau Street Dublin 2 **Tel: 01 670 3865** Fax: 01 670 3868
Email: dining@jacobsladder.ie Web: www.jacobsladder.ie

féile bia Adrian and Bernie Roche's smart contemporary restaurant is up a couple of flights of stairs and has a fine view, overlooking the playing fields of Trinity College. The decor is on the minimalist side with a wooden floor (which can be noisy) and paintings for sale by new Irish artists; good-sized tables with classic white linen and comfortable high-back chairs bode well for the meal ahead. Aidan is one of Dublin's most talented younger chefs; the cooking style is modern Irish and, while there is a leaning towards fish, his wide ranging seasonal menus always include some less usual meat dishes: roast loin of rabbit, perhaps, with its kidney and livers - and imaginative vegetarian dishes - which, along with 'healthy eating' dishes, are considerately highlighted. Several menus are offered including a compact à la carte selection at lunch, and a short 3-course set dinner which is very good value. An 8-course tasting menu, for complete parties, is also offered. Service can sometimes be a little slow but food is cooked to order. It's worth allowing time to finish off with a classic dessert (warm chocolate pudding with pistachio oil & white chocolate ice, perhaps) or Irish farmhouse cheeses, which come from Sheridans cheesemongers, and are served with tomato chutney & oat biscuits. The wine selection is limited for a restaurant of this calibre, but includes a fair number of half bottles and a fine wine list. Children welcome. **Seats 80** (private room, 50). L Tue-Sat 12.30-2.30; D Tue-Sat, 6-10; Set D from €21 (6-7); Menu Surprise €70, L à la carte. House wine from €21. No SC. Closed Sun & Mon,1 week Aug, 2 weeks from 24 Dec, all bank hols, 17 Mar, Good Fri. Amex, Diners, MasterCard, Visa, Laser. **Directions:** City centre overlooking Trinity College.

RESTAURANT   **Jaipur**

41-46 South Great Georges Street Dublin 2 **Tel: 01 677 0999**
Fax: 01 677 0979 Email: info@jaipur.ie Web: www.jaipur.ie

féile bia This custom-built restaurant is named after the "Jewel of Rajasthan" and offers a contemporary image of ethnic dining. It's a cool and spacious place, with a large modern spiral staircase leading up to an area that can be used for private parties; warm colours send the right messages and it is a pleasing space. Head chef Armit Wadhwan is keen to make the most of Irish ingredients, notably organic lamb (Khato Ghosth - Wicklow lamb braised in yoghurt with carrom seeds & mustard oil, finished with asafoetida and dried mango powder - is a signature dish), while importing fresh and dried spices directly. Menus offer an attractive combination of traditional and more creative dishes - try Jaipur Jugalbandi, an assortment of five appetisers, to set the tone. Jaipur was the first ethnic restaurant in Ireland to devise a wine list especially suited to spicy foods. Service is attentive and discreet. **Seats 110.** D daily, 5.30-11.30. Set D from €20. A la carte. House wine from €15. Closed 25-26 Dec. ***Also at:** 21 Castle Street Dalkey, Co. Dublin, Tel: 01 285 0552; 5 St. James' Terrace, Malahide, Co. Dublin, Tel: 01 845 5455. Amex, MasterCard, Visa, Laser. **Directions:** At the corner of Sth Great Georges Street and Lower Stephens Street.

ATMOSPHERIC PUB   **John Mulligan**

8 Poolbeg Street Dublin 2 **Tel: 01 677 5582**

One of Dublin's oldest and best-loved pubs, Mulligan's 'wine & spirit merchant' is mercifully un-renovated and likely to stay that way - dark, with no decor (as such) and no music, it's just the way so many pubs used to be. The only difference is that it's now so fashionable that it gets very crowded (and noisy) after 6pm - better to drop in during the day and see what it's really like.

PUB   **Kehoe's**

9 South Anne Street Dublin 2 Tel: 01 677 8312

One of Dublin's best, unspoilt traditional pubs, Kehoe's changed hands recently and added another floor upstairs, but without damaging the character of th original bar. Very busy in the evening - try it for a quieter daytime pint instead. Closes 25 Dec and Good Friday.

♣RESTAURANT/CAFÉ   **Kilkenny Restaurant & Café**

5-6 Nassau Street Dublin 2 **Tel: 01 677 7075**
Fax: 01 670 7735 Email: info@kilkennyshop.com

féile bia Situated on the first floor of the shop now known simply as Kilkenny, with a clear view into the grounds of Trinity College, the Kilkenny Restaurant is one of the pleasantest places in Dublin to have a bite to eat - and the food matches the view. It looks good and the experience lives up to anticipation: ingredients are fresh and additive-free (as are all the products on sale in the shop's Food Hall) and food has a home-cooked flavour. Salads, quiches, casseroles, home-baked breads and cakes are the specialities of the Kilkenny Restaurant and they are very good. They also do an excellent breakfast: high quality ingredients, good cooking and appetising presentation make this a rewarding place to start the day. For quicker all-day bites, Kilkenny Café, offers Italian panini and cappuccino and the same principles of quality apply. A range of Kilkenny preserves and dressings - all made and labelled on the premises - is available in the shop. Children welcome. **Seats 190.** Open 8.30-5 (Thu to 7), Sat 9-5, Sun 11-3. Breakfast to 11.15, lunch 11.30-3. A la carte. Licensed. Air conditioning. Closed 25-26 Dec, 1 Jan, Easter Sun. Amex, Diners, MasterCard, Visa. **Directions:** Opposite TCD playing fields.

GUESTHOUSE

Kilronan House

70 Adelaide Road Dublin 2 **Tel: 01 475 5266** Fax: 01 478 2841
Email: info@dublinn.com Web: www.dublinn.com

The Luas tram passes just beside Rose and Terry Masterson's attractive white Georgian house, and it is within comfortable walking distance of Stephen's Green and the National Concert Hall. The foyer, which leads off to a large sitting room and dining room, is impressive, with a great mirror, chandeliers and mahogany furniture echoing the Georgian origins of the house, and a winding stairway that leads to bedrooms which all have direct dial phones, TV and tea/coffee making, and most have full bathrooms. Breakfast is a special feature, with Baileys porridge among house specials which also include other favourites like scrambled eggs with smoked salmon and warm pancakes with maple syrup. A conveniently located and reasonably priced alternative to hotel accommodation in the area. **Rooms 15** (2 shower only). B&B €45-85pps (mid-week about €60), no ss. MasterCard, Visa. **Directions:** At the Harcourt Street end of Adelaide Road.

✓ Ⓑ ♣ RESTAURANT

L'Ecrivain

109a Lower Baggot Street Dublin 2 **Tel: 01 661 1919** Fax: 01 661 0617
Email: mary@lecrivain.com Web: www.lecrivain.com

féile bia On two levels - spacious and very dashing - Derry and Sallyanne Clarke's acclaimed city centre restaurant is light and airy, with lots of pale wood and smoky mirrors - and lovely formal table settings which promise seriously good food. Derry's cooking style - classic French with contemporary flair and a strong leaning towards modern Irish cooking - remains consistent, although new ideas are constantly incorporated and the list of specialities keeps growing. Special treats to try include a wonderful signature starter of baked rock oysters with York cabbage & crispy cured bacon, with a Guinness sabayon - perhaps followed by a main course of roast rump of lamb and smoked fillet with pomme fondant, mint jelly and celeriac purée. Thoughtful little touches abound - a fine complimentary amuse-bouche before your first course, for example - and there are some major ones too, like the policy to add the price of your wine only after the 10% service charge has been added to your bill: a gesture like this endears this restaurant to customers who happily dig deep into their pockets for the pleasure of eating here. Wonderful puddings are presented with panache and might include a hot soufflé or a classic vanilla crème brulée with lemon curd ice cream. Attention to detail - garnishes designed individually to enhance each dish, careful selection of plates, delicious home-made breads and splendid farmhouse cheeses - is excellent. Lunch, as usual in top rank restaurants, offers best value. A fine wine list is augmented by a tempting selection of coffees and digestifs. **Seats 104** (private room, 18. outdoor seating, 20) L Mon-Fri 12.30-2, D Mon-Sat 7-10.30, Set L €30. Set D €65 (Vegetarian Menu about €50). Tasting Menu €95. House wine €28.50. 10% SC (on food only). Closed L Sat, all Sun, Christmas week, bank hols. Amex, MasterCard, Visa, Laser. **Directions:** 10 minutes walk east of St Stephens Green, opposite Bank of Ireland HQ.

RESTAURANT

L'Gueuleton

1 Fade Street Dublin 2 **Tel: 01 675 3708**

This no-frills French restaurant took Dublin by storm when it opened in the autumn of 2004, and expansion plans developed forthwith. The format: simple premises and no-nonsense French bistro decor, with tightly packed tables and a few seats at the bar (with views into the kitchen), and a menu that makes no distinction between courses and offers a combination of less usual dishes (organic parsley soup with frogs legs) and the classic (blanquette of lamb). Add to this great cooking, a short, all French wine list (by Simon Tyrrell), pretty efiicient service and terrific value for money - and you have the kind of format that Dubliners have been praying for. Vive la France. **Seats 35**. Open Mon-Sat, L 12.30-3, D 6-10. Closed Sun. A la carte. House wines €18. No reservations MasterCard, Visa, Laser. **Directions:** At Hogans pub.

RESTAURANT   # La Cave Wine Bar & Restaurant

28 South Anne Street Dublin 2 **Tel: 01 679 4409** Fax: 01 620 5255
Email: lacave@iol.ie Web: www.lacavewinebar.com

féile bia Wine bars were not a noticeable feature of Dublin's hospitality scene until recently, but Margaret and Akim Beskri have run this characterful place just off Grafton Street since 1989 and it's well-known for its cosmopolitan atmosphere, late night opening and lots of chat. An excellent wine list of over 350 bins (predominantly French) includes 15 bubblies, an exceptional choice of half bottles and 30 by the glass. With its traditional bistro atmosphere, classic French cooking ("food for the gourmet at reasonable prices"), it makes a handy place to take a break from shopping, for an evening out, or for a party. Classic menus with the occasional contemporary twist make a refreshing change from the ubiquitous eclectic fare that has taken over the restaurant scene in recent years: paté de campagne, crab & gruyère tartlet with leeks, Wicklow lamb cutlets with a thyme jus, warm salad of kidneys and chocolate mousse au Grand Marnier all indicate the style. Many of the dishes are ideal for a one plate light meal - perfect for a shopping break. A private room upstairs (with bar) is ideal for parties and small functions. No children after 6pm. **Seats 25** (private room, 32). Air conditioning. Open Mon-Sat 12.30-11, Sun 5.30-11. Set L €29.50. Early D €15. Also à la carte. House wine from €16. SC discretionary. Closed L Sun, 25-26 Dec, Good Fri. Amex, Diners, MasterCard, Visa, Laser. **Directions:** Just off Grafton Street.

RESTAURANT   # La Corte

Top Floor Powerscourt Townhouse Centre Dublin 2
Tel: 01 633 4477

Great simple Italian food from the Dunne & Crescenzi stable, at the top of the Powerscourt Townhouse shopping centre - classics like a superb minestrone, bruschetta worth climbing for, ultra fresh salads and coffee strong enough to set the weariest shopper back on course again. Simply smashing. **Directions:** Powerscourt Townhouse S.C.

CAFÉ   # La Maison des Gourmets

15 Castle Market Dublin 2 **Tel: 01 672 7258**

In a pedestrianised area handy to car parks and away from the hustle and bustle of nearby Grafton Street, this French boulangerie has a smart little café on the first floor and also a couple of outdoor tables on the pavement for fine weather. Home-baked bread is the speciality, made to a very high standard by French bakers who work in front of customers throughout the day, creating a wonderful aroma that wafts through the entire premises. The speciality is their award-winning sourdough bread, which is used as the base for a selection of tartines - French open-style sandwiches served warm - on the lunch menu (about €12): baked ham with thyme jus and smoked bacon cream; smoked salmon with crème fraîche, lemon confit & fresh dill and vegetarian ones like roast aubergine with plum tomato, fresh parmesan & basil pesto are all typical. Add to this a couple of delicious soups (French onion with Emmental croûtons, perhaps), a hot dish like classic beef bourguignon with potato purée, one or two salads - and a simple dessert like strawberries with balsamic reduction and fresh cream - and the result is as tempting a little menu as any discerning luncher could wish for. Portions are on the small side, which suits most lunch time appetites, and service can be a little slow; but everything is very appetising, the atmosphere is chic and you can stock up on bread and croissants from the shop as you leave

- just don't think in terms of a quick bite. **Seats 26**. Open Mon-Sat, 9-5.30 (L12-4). L special €9.50. A la carte. SC discretionary. House wine €16. Closed Sun, bank hols, 1 week Christmas. Amex, MasterCard, Visa, Laser. **Directions:** Pedestrianised area from Georges Street Arcade to Powerscourt Shopping Centre.

Ⓑ RESTAURANT   # La Mère Zou

22 St Stephen's Green Dublin 2 **Tel: 01 661 6669**
Fax: 01 661 6669 Email: merzou@indigo.ie

Eric Tydgadt's French/Belgian restaurant is situated in a Georgian basement on the north side of the Green. Although there are some concessions to current cuisine (especially on the lunch menu), their reputation is based on French/Belgian country cooking, as in rillette of pork with toasted baguette or confit duck leg with braised lentils, mashed potato & red wine jus; specialities include steamed mussels (various ways) with French fries and prices are reasonable - a policy carried through to the wine list too. The lunch menu - which offers a choice of three dishes on each course - also suggests six or seven more luxurious seafood dishes from the à la carte, so you can make a feast of it if time allows or, at the other extreme, they offer a range of Big Plates, with a salad starter and a main course served together on a king size plate which is great value and ideal if you're in a hurry. This is one of Dublin's pleasantest and most reliable restaurants. [*The associated business, Supper's Ready - an enlightened takeaway doing real food like navarin of lamb and potée paysanne - now has three outlets: 51, Pleasant Street, Dublin, 8. (Tel: 01-475 4556); 58 Clontarf Road, Dublin 3 (Tel: 01 853 3555) and Monread Avenue, Naas, Co. Kildare (Tel: 045 889554). Check the website for further details: www.suppersready.ie] **Seats 55**. L Mon-Fri, 12-2.30. D 6-11 (Sun to 9.30). Early L about €21.50 (6-7.30), Set L about €18.50; also à la carte. House wine from about €17.50. SC discretionary. Closed L Sat, L Sun, 24 Dec-6 Jan. Amex, Diners, MasterCard, Visa, Laser. **Directions:** Beside Shelbourne Hotel.

RESTAURANT/HOTEL   # La Stampa Hotel & Restaurant

35 Dawson Street Dublin 2 **Tel: 01 677 4444** Fax: 01 677 4411
Email: dine@lastampa.ie Web: www.lastampa.ie

Already well-established as a restaurant, La Stampa is now an hotel and development continues: three new suites, a new reception area and lift were all compelted recently - and the next project is a spa. There's an exotic lounge bar on the ground floor - to the right of the restaurant entrance - and the reception desk is upstairs, on the first floor. Rooms are very attractive, with an abundance of sumptuous fabrics, notably velvet, in rich colours echoing the ambience of the restaurant and bar below and neat en-suite bathrooms. No pets. **Rooms 30** (6 suites). Lift. 24 hour room service. Room rate €135. Open all year.

Restaurant: Reminiscent of a grand French belle époque brasserie, this is one of Ireland's finest dining rooms - high-ceiling, with large mirrors, wooden floor, candelabra, Victorian lamps, plants, flowers and various bits of bric-a-brac, the whole noisily complemented by a constant bustle. There's a small bar with a few comfortable seats where you can sip a drink while studying menus that encompass dishes from around the world. Menus are changed fairly often and, although prices can mount rather quickly for the style and quality of food and service, this is a fun and lively place, offering international brasserie-style food in delightful surroundings. No children under 12 after 8pm. Air conditioning. **Seats 230** (private room, 70). L daily, 12-3; D daily, 6-12.30am. Set menus offered; also à la carte. SC10%. ***Tiger Becs**, a mainly Thai restaurant downstairs, is under the same management. **Seats 130**, D Mon-Sat 6-12.30. *Sam Sara Bar and Café is also part of the La Stampa complex. Amex, Diners, MasterCard, Visa, Laser. **Directions:** Opposite the Mansion House.

RESTAURANT

Les Frères Jacques

74 Dame Street Dublin 2 **Tel: 01 679 4555** Fax: 01 679 4725
Email: info@lesfreresjacques.com Web: www.lesfreresjacques.com

One of the few genuinely French restaurants in Dublin, Les Frères Jacques opened beside the Olympia Theatre in 1986, well before the development of Temple Bar made the area fashionable. Most of the staff are French, the atmosphere is French - and the cooking is classic French. The restaurant has recently been renovated, and now has a soothing scheme of soft browns and creams, with comfortable leather chairs - all the better to enjoy seasonal menus that are wide-ranging and well-balanced but - as expected when you notice the lobster tank on entering - there is a strong emphasis on fish and seafood, all of it from Irish waters; game also features in season. Lunch at Les Frères Jacques is a treat (and good value) but dinner is a feast. West coast mussel risotto with a saffron cream, roast lamb tian with aubergine, courgette & thyme juices and strawberry tiramisu with a red fruit coulis are all typical. Finish with cheeses (including some Irish ones) or a classic dessert like warm thin apple tart (baked to order), with a rum & raisin ice cream. The wine list naturally favours France and makes interesting reading, notably the two pages of "recommendations du patron" (en rouge et blanc). **Seats 60** (private room, 40). L Mon-Fri, 12.30-2.30; D Mon-Sat, 7.15-10.30. Set L €22; Set D €35; D also à la carte. House wine €18.50. SC 12.5%. Closed L Sat, all Sun, 24 Dec-2 Jan. Amex, MasterCard, Visa, Laser. **Directions:** Next to Olympia Theatre.

ATMOSPHERIC PUB

The Long Hall Bar

51 South Great George's Dublin 2 **Tel: 01 475 1590**

A wonderful old pub with magnificent plasterwork ceilings, traditional mahogany bar and Victorian lighting. One of Dublin's finest bars and well worth a visit. Closed 25 Dec & Good Fri.

Ⓑ HOTEL/RESTAURANT

Longfields Hotel

10 Lower Fitzwilliam Street Dublin 2 **Tel: 01 676 1367**
Fax: 01 676 1542 Email: info@longfields.ie Web: www.longfields.ie

Located in a Georgian terrace between Fitzwilliam and Merrion Squares, this reasonably priced hotel is more like a well proportioned private house, furnished with antiques in period style - notably in elegant public areas. Comfortable bedrooms are individually furnished, some with four-posters or half-tester beds, although they vary considerably in size as rooms are smaller on the upper floors. The hotel's basement restaurant is open to non-residents and has a separate entrance from the street. Morning coffee and afternoon tea are available in The Drawing Room, which can also be used for private dining or small conferences (22). 24 hour room service. Children welcome (cots available). No pets. Lift. **Rooms 26** (2 junior suites, 19 shower only). B&B about €87.50pps, ss about €47.50 Special Breaks offered. Open all year. Amex, MasterCard, Laser, Visa. **Directions:** On corner of Fitzwilliam Street & Baggot Street.

PUB

M.J. O'Neill's Public House

2 Suffolk Street Dublin 2 **Tel: 01 679 3656** Fax: 01 679 0689
Email: mike@oneillsbar.com Web: www.oneillsbar.com

A striking pub with its own fine clock over the door and an excellent corner location, this large bar has been in the O'Neill family since 1920 and is popular with Dubliners and visitors alike. Students from Trinity and several other colleges nearby home into O'Neill's for its wide range of reasonably priced bar food, which includes a carvery with a choice of five or six roasts and an equal number of other dishes (perhaps including traditional favourites such as Irish Stew) each day; finish off with some home-made rhubarb pie, perhaps. There is also a well-presented sandwich/salad bar. Carvery 2pm - 3.30pm on Monday to Thursday, Friday 12pm - 6pm, Saturday 12pm - 8pm and Sunday 12pm - 10pm. An extensive à la carte bar menu takes over after the carvery, except on Fridays. Live traditional music every Sunday night at 8:30pm. Wheelchair access. No children after 6pm. Closed 25 & 26 Dec, Good Fri. Amex, MasterCard, Visa, Laser. **Directions:** Opposite the Dublin Tourist Centre.

RESTAURANT ## Mao Café Bar

2-3 Chatham Row Dublin 2 **Tel: 01 670 4899** Fax: 01 670 4993
Email: info@cafemao.com Web: www.cafemao.com

féile bia In simple but stylish surroundings, Mao Café Bar brings to the Grafton Street area the cuisines of Thailand, Malaysia, Indonesia, Japan and China - about as 'Asian Fusion' as it gets. The atmosphere is bright and very buzzy, and interesting food is based on seasonal ingredients; the standard of cooking is consistently good and so is value for money, although the bill can mount up quickly if you don't watch the number of Asian beers ordered. Chilli squid, Nasi Goreng and Malaysian chicken are established favourites, also tempura sole with stir-fried vegetables in a citrus sauce. No reservations. Wheelchair access. Children welcome. **Seats 95.** Air conditioning. Open daily, 12-11 (Sun to 10, Mon-Wed to 10.30). Menu à la carte. House wine from about €18; Asian beers from about €4.50. SC discretionary. Closed 25-26 Dec, Good Fri. MasterCard, Visa, Laser. **Directions:** City centre - just off Grafton Street.

BAR ## The Market Bar

Fade Street Dublin 2 **Tel: 01 613 9094**

In the Victorian redbrick block best known for the George's Street Market Arcade that runs through its centre, this is an attractive space with lofty ceilings (high enough to allow the addition of a mezzanine floor) and simple, stylish furnishings - a little too simple perhaps, as the wooden floor and hard surfaces bounce noise around and there's precious little to absorb it. It's a hit with young Dubliners however and the food, which is cooked in an open kitchen, is part of the attraction. The menu is loosely Spanish, offering nibbles like olives, smoked almonds and anchovies, and more substantial dishes which can be ordered as small or large portions (about €6-9 each) and include fairly faithful renditions of Spanish classics like tortilla and patatas bravas. Not perfectly authentic tapas, perhaps, but the right kind of food for this fashionable space, and a move in the right direction. Food daily: Mon-Sat 12-9.30; Sun 4-9.30. Closed 25 Dec, Good Fri. MasterCard, Visa.

ATMOSPHERIC PUB ## McDaids

3 Harry Street Dublin 2

Established in 1779, McDaids more recently achieved fame as one of the great literary pubs - and its association with Brendan Behan, especially, brings a steady trail of pilgrims from all over the world to this traditional premises just beside the Westbury Hotel. Dubliners, however, tend to be immune to this kind of thing and drink there because it's a good pub - and, although its character is safe, it's not a place set in aspic either, as a younger crowd has been attracted by recent changes. History and character are generally of more interest than food here, but sandwiches are available. Open Mon-Wed,10.30am-11.30pm; Thu-Sat, 10.30am-12.30am; Sun 12.30-11. Closed 25 Dec & Good Fri.

✓ RESTAURANT

The Mermaid Café

69-70 Dame Street Dublin 2 **Tel: 01 670 8236** Fax: 01 670 8205
Email: info.@mermaid.ie Web: www.mermaid.ie

Interesting decor and imaginative French and American-inspired cooking are to be found at Ben Gorman and Mark Harrell's unusual restaurant on the edge of Temple Bar. The two dining areas have recently been supplemented by a new wine lounge, which still hasn't transformed it into a big restaurant - but every inch of space has always been used with style here. Cooking at The Mermaid is among the best in the area - innovative, mid-Atlantic, seasonal and often memorable for inspired combinations of flavour, texture and colour - and service, although not always notable for swiftness, is invariably courteous and helpful. Menus change frequently but there would be public outcry if specialities like New England crab cakes with piquant mayonnaise, the Giant Seafood Casserole (which changes daily depending on availability) or pecan pie were taken off. Vegetables, always used imaginatively, are beautifully integrated into main courses - loin of lamb with beetroot and couscous is a good, colourful example, and there are many more like it on each day's menus. Then delicious desserts, wonderful Irish cheeses (like the deeply flavoured Gabriel and Desmond from West Cork, served with celery biscuits) and coffees with crystallised pecan nuts: attention to detail right to the finish. Sunday brunch is not to be missed if you are in the area: the extent and quality of the menu is amazing. Wines are imported privately and are exclusive to the restaurant. Children welcome. **Seats 60** (private room, 24). Reservations accepted. Air conditioning. Toilets wheelchair accessible. L 12.30-3 (Sun to 3.30), D 6.30-11 (Sun to 9). Set L €23.95; Set D €34.95; also à la carte. House wine €19.95. SC discretionary. Closed Christmas, New Year, Easter. * Next door, **Gruel** (Tel 01 670 7119), is a quality fast-food outlet under the same management, with a large & loyal following; open Mon-Fri 7.30-9.30; Sat & Sun 10.30-4.30.] MasterCard, Visa, Laser. **Directions:** Next door to Olympia Theatre.

✓ ⑬ HOTEL/RESTAURANT

Merrion Hotel

Upper Merrion Street Dublin 2 **Tel: 01 603 0600** Fax: 01 603 0700
Email: info@merrionhotel.com Web: www.merrionhotel.com

Right in the heart of Georgian Dublin opposite the Government Buildings, the main house of this luxurious hotel comprises four meticulously restored Grade 1 listed townhouses built in the 1760s and now restored to their former glory; behind them, a contemporary garden wing has been added, overlooking two private period and formal landscaped gardens. Inside, Irish fabrics and antiques reflect the architecture and original interiors with rococo plasterwork ceilings and classically proportioned windows - and the hotel has one of the most important private collections of 20th-century art. Public areas include three interconnecting drawing rooms (one is the cocktail bar with a log fire), with French windows giving access to the gardens. Elegant and gracious bedrooms have sumptuous Italian marble bathrooms, with a separate walk-in shower, pamper guests to the extreme. The six meeting/private dining rooms combine state-of-the-art technology and Georgian splendour, while the splendid leisure complex, **The Tethra Spa**, with classical mosaics, is almost Romanesque. Staff, under the excellent direction of General Manager Peter MacCann, are quite exemplary and courteous, suggesting standards of hospitality from a bygone era. Complimentary underground valet parking. Restaurant Patrick Guilbaud (see separate entry) is also on site. Conference/banqueting (50). Secretarial services. Leisure centre; swimming pool. Garden. Children welcome (under 4 free in parents' room, cots available free of charge, baby sitting arranged). No pets. Lift. Valet parking. **Rooms 142** (20 suites, 10 junior suites, 80 no-smoking, 5 for disabled). Room rate €370. Open all year.

The Cellar Restaurant: This elegant vaulted dining-room has a new entrance from Merrion Street, through a pleasing corridor decorated with flower arrangements. Warm, friendly staff seat arriving guests at beautiful classically appointed tables, and with everything of the best quality (including the lighting and ventilation), it is a very relaxing room - and the philosophy of sourcing the best ingredients and treating them with respect in a simple style makes a refreshing change from the multi-cultural menus in so many restaurants. Delicious flavours, excellent service and great value for the quality of food and surroundings - this fine restaurant is proving very attractive to those who value quality in a discreet atmosphere. A good wine list also offers value, including wines by the glass. Air conditioning. **Seats 60**. Reservations required. L 12.30-2 Sun-Fri, D 6-10 daily. Set L from €21.95. Early D from €24.50, (6-7pm). D also à la carte. House wine from €24. Closed L Sat. Amex, Diners, MasterCard, Visa, Laser. **Directions:** City centre, opposite Government Buildings.

RESTAURANT   **Milano**

38 Dawson Street Dublin 2 **Tel: 01 670 7744** Fax: 01 679 2717

This stylish contemporary restaurant at the top of Dawson Street is best known for its wide range of excellent pizzas (it's owned by the UK company Pizza Express), but it's more of a restaurant than the description implies. Children are welcome and they run a very popular crèche facility on Sunday afternoons (12-5). Branches also in Temple Bar, and Cork & Galway. **Seats 140** (private room 80). Air conditioning. Open daily,12 noon-12 midnight (Sun to 11.30). Menu à la carte. House wine about €17. SC discretionary (10% on parties of 7+). Closed Dec 25 & 26. Amex, Diners, MasterCard, Visa, Laser. **Directions:** Opposite Mansion House, just off Stephens Green.

B HOTEL   **Mont Clare Hotel**

Merrion Square Dublin 2 **Tel: 01 607 3800**
Fax: 01 661 5663 Email: montclareres@ocallaghanhotels.ie
Web: www.ocallaghanhotels.ie

féile bia A few doors away from the National Gallery, this well-located and reasonably priced hotel is in common ownership with the nearby Davenport and Alexander Hotels. The hotel is imaginatively decorated in contemporary style - except the old stained glass and mahogany Gallery Bar, which has retained its original pubby atmosphere. Compact bedrooms are well furnished and comfortable - and executive rooms for business guests have full marbled bathrooms and good amenities. Business centre; use of gym (at Davenport Hotel). Conference/banqueting. (200). Children welcome (Under 2s free in parents' room; cots available free of charge). No pets. **Rooms 80** (40 no-smoking). Lift. Room rate about €245. Open all year. Amex, Diners, MasterCard, Visa, Laser. **Directions:** Corner of Clare Street, just off Merrion Square.

RESTAURANT   **Montys of Kathmandu**

28 Eustace Street Temple Bar Dublin 2 **Tel: 01 670 4911**
Fax: 01 494 4359 Email: montys@eircom.net Web: www.montys.ie

féile bia At first glance this restaurant deep in the heart of Temple Bar seems ordinary enough, but the food here can have real character - and at agreeably low prices. The chefs are all from Nepal and although all the familiar dishes are represented there are definite undertones of Nepalese cooking throughout the menu. This is quite extensive and includes a platter of assorted starters which is a good choice for a group of four, allowing time to consider the rest of the menu without rushing; there's also a good choice of vegetarian dishes, including a traditional Nepali mixed vegetable curry which can be served mild, medium or hot. At its best, this is a really rewarding restaurant:

friendly staff are more than happy to offer suggestions or choose a well balanced meal for you; shish kebabs, for example, and other specialities like cochlea (raw minced lamb), Moo (Nepalese dumplings) and Tandoori butter chicken: moist pieces of tender tandoori chicken off the bone, cooked in a creamy measlier sauce. And, in addition to a very adequate wine list and drinks menu, they even have their own beer, 'Shiva', brewed exclusively for the restaurant. Children welcome. **Seats 60** (private room, 30) L Mon-Sat, 12-2.15; Set L €17, D from €20; D daily 6-11.30, (Sun to 11), Tasting Menu about €30-45. L&D à la carte available. SC discretionary. House wine from about €17. Closed L Sun, 25-26 Dec, 1 Jan & Good Fri. Amex, MasterCard, Visa, Laser. **Directions:** Temple Bar - opposite the Irish Film Centre(IFC).

B HOTEL   # Morgan Hotel

10 Fleet Street Temple Bar Dublin 2
Tel: 01 679 3939 Fax: 01 679 3946
Email: sales@themorgan.com Web: www.themorgan.com

In deepest Temple Bar, this unusual boutique hotel is characterised by clean simple lines and uncluttered elegance. Bedrooms have 6' beds in light beech, with classic white cotton bed linen and natural throws, while standard bedroom facilities include satellite TV and video, CD/hi-fi system, mini-bar, safe, voicemail and Internet access. The stylish Morgan Bar is open all day and offers an oasis of comfort and relaxation amongst the hustle and bustle of Temple Bar try an exotic Morgan Mai Tai, perhaps? Strangely, as it seems so much at odds with the cool, reserved style of the rest of the hotel, the brash All Sports Café next door is part of it. Children welcome (cots available without charge, baby sitting arranged). **Rooms 66** (1 suite, 1 junior suite, 15 executive, 30 shower only, 33 no-smoking). Lift. Room rate €220. Closed Christmas. Amex, Diners, MasterCard, Visa, Laser. **Directions:** off Westrmoreland Street.

ATMOSPHERIC PUB   # Neary's

1 Chatham Street Dublin 2 **Tel: 01 677 8596** Fax: 01 677 7371

This unspoilt Edwardian pub off Grafton Street has been in the present ownership for over half a century and is is popular at all times of day - handy for lunch or as a meeting place in the early evening and full of buzz later when post-theatre crowd, including actors from the nearby Gaiety Theatre, will probably be amongst the late night throng in the downstairs bar. Traditional values assert themselves through gleaming brass, well-polished mahogany and classics like smoked salmon and mixed meat salads amongst the bar fare. Open Sun-Thu 10.30-11.30 (to 12.30 Fri & Sat). Bar food: Mon-Sat, 10.30-2.45. Closed 25 Dec & Good Fri. MasterCard, Visa, Laser. **Directions:** Off Grafton St.

CAFÉ   # Nude Restaurant

21 Suffolk Street Dublin 2 **Tel: 01 672 5577**
Fax: 01 672 5773 Email: niamh@nude.ie

Nude offers fantastic very fresh food - organic whenever possible - in an ultra-cool, youthful environment. Just off Grafton Street, it's a great place for a quick snack, with plenty of room to sit down at long canteen-style tables. Queue up, order and pay at the till, then collect your food if it's ready or it will be delivered to your table. If you eat with your eyes, just looking at the fresh fruit and vegetables hanging or racked up in the open kitchen should revive you while you wait! A choice of soups includes seafood chowder, chunky vegetable and Thai chicken broth, all served with freshly baked breads; there are hot wraps - chicken satay or vegetarian Jumping Bean, for example - and paninis, including one with Gubeen cheese, or try the chill cabinet for salads like Caesar or tomato & mozzarella, and cold wraps such as hummus or spinach

& peppers, or soft bread rolls (e.g. smoked salmon & cream cheese). Freshly squeezed juices, smoothies and organic Fair Trade coffees, teas and herbal teas are all very popular (drinks can be made up to order) and the menu caters for vegetarians, people with nut allergies and other dietary requirements. **Seats 40.** Open Mon-Sat, 8am-9.30pm, Sun 11-7 MasterCard, Visa, Laser. **Directions** Near Dublin Tourism office.

GUESTHOUSE **Number 31**

31 Leeson Close Lr Leeson Street Dublin 2 **Tel: 01 676 5011**
Fax: 01 676 2929 Email: number31@iol.ie Web: number31.ie

Formerly the home of leading architect Sam Stephenson, Noel and Deirdre Comer's 'oasis of tranquillity and greenery' just off St Stephen's Green makes an excellent city centre base, with virtually everything within walking distance in fine weather. Warm hospitality, huge breakfasts and secure parking add greatly to the attraction and rooms have everything you could wish for, including phones, TVs and tea/coffee trays. Not suitable for children under 10. No pets. Rooms at the back are quieter. **Rooms 20** (all en-suite & no smoking). B&B from about €75, ss €25. Open all year. Amex, MasterCard, Visa. **Directions** From St. Stephens Green onto Baggot St., turn right on to Pembroke St. and left on to Leeson St.

ATMOSPHERIC PUB **O'Donoghue's**

15 Merrion Row Dublin 2 **Tel: 01 676 2807**

O'Donoghues has long been the Dublin mecca for visitors in search of a lively evening with traditional music - live music every night is a major claim to fame - but a visit to this famous pub near the Shelbourne Hotel at quieter times can be rewarding too. Closed 25 Dec & Good Fri.

BAR/CAFÉ **Odessa Lounge & Grill**

13/14 Dame Lane Dublin 2 **Tel: 01 670 7634**

Tucked away about 5 minutes from Grafton Street, this has long been a favourite haunt for Dublin's bright young things and it is to their credit that they have retained that niche while so many new rivals have entered the scene. It was one of the first places in Dublin to do brunch and the room downstairs is the perfect place to nurse a hangover, with no natural light, subdued lighting, comfy chairs with plenty of room to spread out and read the papers in peace. The food is basic brunch fare - Eggs Benedict or Florentine, huevos rancheros or a char-grilled steak sandwich (all around €12) - but the atmosphere is a major attraction. The service is relaxed and friendly even when they are very busy there's never a feeling of being rushed. At night is just right for those who want more than a fast-food burger, but who do not want to dress for dinner - and it's also perfect for large groups with something to celebrate. At the time of going to press development of a guesthouse and private club was reaching completion. **Seats 100.** Air conditioning. Sat & Sun open noon-midnight, brunch 12-4. D Mon-Wed 6-11, Thu & Fri 5-12. SC discretionary (10% on parties of 6+). Amex, MasterCard, Visa. **Directions:** Left off Dame Street onto George's Street, left onto Exchequer Street, then left again.

RESTAURANT **The Old Mill**

14 Temple Bar Dublin 2 **Tel: 01 671 9262**

Long before this area became trendy Temple Bar, Moroccan chef-patron Lahcen Iouani had a loyal following in the '80s, for his restaurant 'Pigalle'. The name change has relevance to local history (you can read all about it on the back of he menu) but other things have thankfully remained the same and Lahcen continues to offer admirably traditional French cooking at refreshingly modest prices. The place has a homely feeling, like stepping back in time to an old French restaurant - giving good value to the customer is something he feels strongly about. A blackboard menu offers traditional starters like paté de foie de canard and salade niçoise (around €9), while classic main courses such as boeuf Bourginonne and sole meunière are well-priced at around €18.50 each. Vegetarian dishes are around €10 and there's also an excellent value early menu. **Seats 50.** Reservations accepted. Air conditioning. Open Mon-Fri, 12.30-11.30; Sat-Sun, 5-11.30. L 12.30-4, D 5-11. Set L €16.95, also à la carte. House wine from about €18.50. SC discretionary except on parties of 8+ (12.5%). MasterCard, Visa, Laser. **Directions:** Above Merchants Arch on Temple Bar Square (behind Central Bank).

ATMOSPHERIC PUB

The Old Stand

37 Exchequer Street Dublin 2 **Tel: 01 677 7220**

This fine traditional pub, which is a sister establishment to Davy Byrnes, off Grafton Street, occupies a prominent position on the corner of Exchequer Street and St Andrew Street and lays claim to being "possibly the oldest public house in Ireland"! Named after the Old Stand at the Lansdowne Road rugby grounds, it has a loyal following amongst the local business community, notably from the 'rag trade' area around South William Street, and also attracts a good mixture of rugby fans and visitors, who enjoy the atmosphere. They offer no-nonsense traditional bar food (12.15-9 daily), but its warm and friendly atmosphere is a bigger draw than the food. Not suitable for children under 7. Closed 25-26 Dec & Good Fri. Amex, MasterCard, Visa, Laser. **Directions:** Off Grafton Street.

PUB/GUESTHOUSE

O'Neill's Pub & Guesthouse

37 Pearse Steet Dublin 2 **Tel: 01 677 5213** Fax: 01 832 5218
Email: oneilpub@iol.ie Web: www.oneillsdublin.com

Established in 1885, this centrally located pub on the corner of Pearse Street and Shaw Street is easily recognised by the well-maintained floral baskets that brighten up the street outside. Inside, this cosy bar has kept its Victorian character and charm (two bars have lots of little alcoves and snugs) and serves a good range of reasonably priced home-cooked food - typically steak champignon with red wine sauce, served with French fries and an attractive salad; lamb filo parcels with mint yoghurt and chilli con carne - all good value under €15). (Accommodation is available in en-suite rooms, with breakfast served in a pleasant room above the pub; about €45 pps midweek - a little more at weekends. Bar food: L 12.30-2.30, D 5.30-8. Closed Christmas & Good Fri. Amex, MasterCard, Visa, Laser. **Directions:** Opposite Pearse Street side of Trinity College.

B RESTAURANT

One Pico Restaurant

5-6 Molesworth Place Schoolhouse Lane Dublin 2
Tel: 01 676 0300 Fax: 01 676 0411
Email: eamonoreilly@ireland.com Web: www.onepico.com

féile bia In a magical location near St Stephen's Green, nicely tucked in a laneway just a couple of minutes walk from the Dáil (Parliament) and Grafton Street, Eamonn O'Reilly's One Pico is one of Dublin's most popular fine dining restaurants. The surroundings are elegant, with crisp white linen and top notch china and glassware, and the cooking is exceptionally good; the style is distinctly contemporary, with worldwide influences, and sophisticated, technically demanding dishes are invariably executed with confidence and flair. Eamonn has always based his menus on first class ingredients and it is their flavours that stand out, together with the precision of the cooking. Menus offered include a 2- and 3-course lunch which, as usual in restaurants of this calibre represents great value; equally, an early evening menu is good value although it may be a little rushed. A 'value' dinner menu is also offered (unrestricted time) as well as an à la carte, with about ten quite luxurious dishes offered on each course, plus optional side dishes which should not be necessary as each main course is individually garnished. There is an occasional small nod to Irish traditions, but this is mainstream European cooking, albeit based for the most part on the very best local ingredients (although these are not credited on the menu): a superb starter of shellfish risotto with Dublin Bay prawns, sweet peas and sorrel, for example, and a sophisticated main course of crispy duck confit with lightly pickled savoy cabbage, ballontine of duck foie gras with pomme maxime and sauternes dressing - a well-conceived dish beautifully executed. Be sure to sample an innovative and delicious cheese menu and/or beautifully presented desserts that taste as good as they look, some may have jokey names, but this is serious cooking. An 8-course tasting menu is also offered, for whole tables up to a maximum of six. Service is professional and friendly and a good wine list is generally fairly priced. *A sister restaurant is **Bleu Bistro Moderne** (see entry) and new establishments **Bleu Café Bar** and **Bam-Bou Grill Bar** are opening in Stepaside & Dundrum. **Seats 110** (private room, 45). Air conditioning. L& D Mon-Sat: L12-3, D 6-11 2/3 courses Set L €25/30, Early D €35 (6-7); Set D from €35, Tasting Menu €70, also à la carte. House wine €25. SC 10% (on food only). Closed Sun, ban hols, 25 Dec-6 Jan. Amex, Diners, MasterCard, Visa. **Directions:** 2 mins walk of St Stephens Green/Grafton Street.

RESTAURANT   **Pad Tha**

30 South Richmond Street Dublin 2 **Tel: 01 475 555**

While there may be little about this well-established restaurant near Portobello Bridge that would   draw you in by chance, it offers   flavoursome and largely authentic Thai cooking with an emphasis on spicing that is more than usually fearless. Menus give an indication of the heat level to expect (rated from one to three chililis), but there is generally plenty of punch - a refreshing change after the many dumbed-own versions on offer in Dublin - as well as the subtler flavours that give Thai food its wide appeal. All the key Thai trademark dishes are here - Pad Thai noodles, red, green and yellow curries - but there's also the opportunity to be more adventurous if you choose. MasterCard, Visa

---

ATMOSPHERIC PUB   **The Palace Ba**

21 Fleet Street Dublin 2 **Tel: 01 671 738**

Just around the corner from the Irish Times offices, The Palace has had strong connections with writers and journalists for many a decade. Its unspoilt frosted glass and mahogany are impressive enough but the special feature is the famous sky-lighted snug, which is really more of a back room. Many would cite The Palace as their favourite Dublin pub. Closed 25 Dec & Good Fri.

RESTAURANT   **Papaya**

8 Ely Place Dublin 2 **Tel: 01 676 004**
Fax: 01 288 0478 Web: www.papaya.i

One square room in a basement in Ely Place, Papya has a vaulted ceiling that lends character, to an elegant carpeted space with linen clad tables, soothing creamy tones and a sprinkling of Asian decorations. Welcoming staff swiftly offer menus that are quite extensive but clearly laid out by course and style the great Thai signature dishes are there, of course (the green, red and yellow curries are highlighted on the menu) but there are plenty of lesser known dishes to choose from too, and - with the exception of special ingredients like sea bass - most main courses are under €20. A Papaya Platter starter (€14 for two) is a good choice on a first visit, giving a selection of five appetisers to nibble on while familiarising yourself with the rest of the menu, which includes a good choice of seafood, and a separate vegetarian section. A pleasant, calm atmosphere, tasty food with well-balanced flavours and a reasonable bill all add up to satisfied customers - this is a restaurant that deserves to be better known. MasterCard, Visa

---

RESTAURANT/DELI   ## Pasta Fresca

2-4 Chatham Street Dublin 2 **Tel: 01 679 2402**
Fax: 01 668 4563 Email: info@pastafresca.ie

This long-established Italian restaurant in the Grafton Street shopping area specialises in fresh pasta, and their popular all-day menu is based on good home-made pastas, thin-based crispy Neapolitan pizzas, a wide range of interesting salads with well-made dressings. There are plenty of vegetarian dishes on offer - bruschetta rosso, with fresh tomatoes & mozzarella, for example, or fettucine al broccoli - and a speciality pasta salad (with Tuscan beans, sweetcorn, fresh vegetables, shaved Parmesan & house dressing). A shorter list of grills includes fish of the day and chicken dishes: such as Pollo Pasta Fresca - chicken breast filled with mozzarella cheese and spinach, wrapped in bacon the baked in its on juices and served with herby mashed potatoes and salad. Evening menus offer a wider choice and you can also buy Italian groceries, fresh pasta and sauces made on the premises from their deli counter. Children welcome. **Seats 150** (outdoors, 20). Air conditioning. Open all day Mon-Sat, 12-12, Sun 12.30 -10. Set L €9.95 (11-5); D also à la carte. House wine from €17.95. SC discretionary. Closed 25 Dec, 1 Jan. Amex, Diners, MasterCard, Visa, Laser. **Directions:** Off top of Grafton Street.

/ Ⓑ RESTAURANT/WINE BAR   ## Pearl Brasserie

20 Merrion Street Upper Dublin 2 **Tel: 01 661 3572** Fax: 01 661 3629
Email: info@pearl-brasserie.com Web: www.pearl-brasserie.com

Just a few doors away from The Merrion Hotel, this stylish basement restaurant has an open fire and colourful blue banquettes picking up tones from an aquarium that runs the length of the bar. It's run by Sebastien Masi and his partner Kirsten Batt, who is the restaurant manager, and the style is contemporary international, with a classic French base and a pleasing emphasis on clean flavours, highlighting the quality of ingredients. Menus lean towards fish, which Sebastien cooks with accuracy and flair - nearly half of the starters and main courses on the à la carte menu are seafood of some sort and very attractive they are too - who could resist a starter of clams & garden pea risotto with fresh white summer truffle, or a main course of pan-fried sea bass with fondue of spinach and provençal of fresh water crayfish? But there's plenty from the land too, with specialities including luscious pan-fried foie gras with roasted brioche and strawberry compôte, and a more homely main course of roasted round of Wicklow lamb, with gratin dauphinoise, broccoli & a mint jus - and there is also a separate vegetarian menu which is seriously tempting. Desserts are a highlight and include a delicious sorbet selection - light, refreshing and really luscious. A separate wine bar area - the **Oyster Bar** - offers a light supper menu with some interesting options, including Kilkee rock oysters with shallot vinaigrette, and a range of platters for two; a Fish Platter, for example, comprises a selection of squid tempura, crispy prawns, crab salad, salmon gravalax & dips - the perfect complement to an expanded list of wines available by the glass (and 'decadent cocktails'). Charming, efficient and well informed service complements Sebastien Masi's unusual and beautifully presented meals - and, as usual in restaurants of this calibre, lunch offers especially good value. The wine list is a good match for the food, favouring France and offering a good few champagnes and a fair choice of half bottles. Children welcome. **Seats 80** (private area, 10); Air-conditioning. L Tue-Fri 12-2.30, D daily 6-10.30. 'Value' L €25, D à la carte. House wine €19.50. SC discretionary. Closed bank hols, 1st 2 wks Jan. Amex, Diners, MasterCard, Visa, Laser. **Directions:** Opposite Government Buildings, near Merrion Hotel.

PUB   **The Pembroke**

31/32 Lower Pembroke Street Dublin 2 **Tel: 01 676 2980**
Fax: 01 676 6579 Email: info@pembroke.ie Web: www.pembroke.ie

This is a bright and spacious bar with some striking design features (notably lighting), the atrium/ conservatory area at the back brings the whole place to life and has space for a large number of outdoor tables for fine weather Meeting the needs of those who get in to work before the traffic builds up, bar food begins with an impressive breakfast menu offering everything from cereals or muesli to the Full Irish, with all sorts of more sophisticated treats like scrambled egg with smoked salmon and eggs benedict (ham) or florentine (spinach) in between. Later menus are appealing too, offering, for example hot sizzler dishes like strips of sirloin beef teriyaki, served with stir-fried noodles, peppers & beansprouts - and a range of bar snacks including grilled crostini or omelettes with fries and rocket leaves. **Seats 200** (private room 60, outdoor seating 80). Food served Mon-Sat, 7.30am-8pm. Closed Sun, Christmas & Good Fri. Amex, MasterCard, Visa, Laser. **Directions:** Off Lr Baggot Street.

✓ **B** RESTAURANT/WINE BAR   **Peploe's Wine Bistro**

16 St Stephen's Green Dublin 2 **Tel: 01 676 3144** Fax: 01 676 315·
Email: frederic@peploes.com Web: www.peploes.com

The brainchild of the well-named Barry Canny - who previously introduced boutique hotels to St Stephen's Green when he opened nearby Browne' Townhouse some years ago - this is a restaurant with a difference, as it location, long opening hours, flexible menus and weekend jazz all add up to relaxed place for a rendez-vous at any time - and he had the forethought to bring his team of head chef, Sebastien Scheer, and head waiter, Frederi Pelanne, to the new venture. It's in the basement of the Georgian terrace that runs along the north side of St Stephen's Green, making it very handy to both the Grafton Street area and the nearby offices - perfect territory for a laid-back wine bar (an extensive wine list includes a dozen or more champagnes and about thirty wines by the glass). Lunch and dinner menus are both informally arranged by style of dish - breads & savouries, soups, charcuterie, fish & shellfish, pasta, grills, roasts & pies - an approach which has found favour with customers. This is still pretty serious food, all the same - foie gras terrine with brioche, 1/2 grilled lobster with garlic butter, and Italian rabbit stew are random examples from a lunch menu, and dinner moves up a notch or two in the same style. Service is smart, the atmosphere is great and the cooking has style - all this and a reasonable bill too. Jazz at weekend, 8.30-midnight. **Seats 95.** Reservations required. Air conditioning. Toilets wheelchair accessible Children welcome. Open noon-11 daily; L 12-4, D 6-10; Set D €39.95, also la carte. Closed 25 Dec, Good Fri. Amex, MasterCard, Visa, Laser.

✓ ♣ PUB   **The Porterhouse**

16-18 Parliament Street Temple Bar Dublin
Tel: 01 679 8847 Fax: 01 670 9605 Email: porterh@indigo.·

Dublin's first micro-brewery pub opened in 1996 and, although several other have since set up and are doing an excellent job, The Porterhouse was at the cutting edge. Ten different beers are brewed on the premises and beer connoisseurs can sample a special tasting tray selection of plain porter (a classic light stout), oyster stout (brewed with fresh oysters, the logical development of a perfect partnership), Wrasslers 4X (based on a West Cork recipe from the early 1900s, and said to be Michael Collins' favourite tipple), Porter House Red (an Irish Red Ale with traditional flavour), An Brain Blasta (dangerous to know) and the aptly named Temple Brau. But you don't even have to like beer to love The Porterhouse. The whole concept is an innovative move away from the constraints of the traditional Irish pub and yet it stays in tune with its origins - it is emphatically not just another theme pub. The attention to detail which has gone into the decor and design is a constant source of pleasure to visitors and the food, while definitely not gourmet, is a cut above the usual bar food and, like the pub itself, combines elements of tradition with innovation: Carlingford oysters, Irish stew, beef & Guinness casserole are there, along with the likes of homemade burgers and and a good range of salads. This is a real Irish pub in the modern idiom and was a respected winner of our Jameson Pub of the Year award in 1999. No children after 9pm. **Seats 50**. Open noon - 11.30 daily (Thu-Sat to 12.30). Bar food served 12-9.30 daily (Sun from 12.30). Closed 25 Dec & Good Fri. [*The original Porterhouse is located on Strand Road on the seafront in Bray, Co. Wicklow and, like its sister pub in Temple Bar, it offers bar food daily from 12.30-9.30. Tel/Fax: 01 286 1839. There is also a Porterhouse in London, at Covent Garden, and a newer Dublin one, **Porterhouse North**, see entry.] MasterCard, Visa.

HOTEL

The Principal Hotel

19/20 Fleet Street Temple Bar Dublin 2 **Tel: 01 670 8122**
Fax: 01 670 8103 Email: principalhotel@eircom.net

Conveniently situated in the heart of Temple Bar, within easy walking distance of all the city's main attractions, this reasonably priced hotel is fairly small, allowing an intimate atmosphere and a welcome emphasis on service. Children welcome (under 12 free in parents' room; cots available without charge). No pets. **Rooms 71** (40 shower only, 35 no-smoking).B&B from about €50pps. Lift. Closed 24-26 Dec. Amex, Diners, Visa, MasterCard. **Directions:** Heart of Temple Bar, near Fleet Street.

CAFÉ

Queen of Tarts

4 Cork Hill Dame Street Dublin 2 **Tel: 01 670 7499**

Behind this quaint traditional shopfront near Dublin Castle lies an equally quaint traditional tea room, with friendly and efficient staff and wonderful smells wafting across the room as they struggle to make space for new arrivals to the comfortable, lived-in little room. Breakfast (including a vegetarian cooked breakfast) is served from 7.30 and the lunch/afternoon menu takes over at noon. Baking is a speciality, with home-made scones, buttermilk brown bread, hot savoury tarts, roast chicken & coriander tartlets, warm plum & cinnamon tarts, warm chocolate fudge cake, orange chocolate pinwheel cookies and much else besides taking their place on a surprisingly extensive menu, which includes some seriously good sandwiches and salads - most people pop in for a snack, but you could just as easily have a 3-course lunch. Inexpensive (there's not much over €7.95), consistently excellent food and great service - what more could anyone ask? [**Also at:** City Hall, Tel 01 672 2925. Open museum hours: Mon-Sat 10-4.30, Sun 2-5.] **Seats 25**. Air conditioning. Toilets wheelchair accessible. Children welcome.Open daily: Mon-Fri 7.30-6 (L12-6); Sat 10-6; Sun 10-6. Closed 24 Dec -3 Jan, bank hols. **No Credit Cards. Directions:** Opposite the gates of Dublin Castle.

RESTAURANT

Rajdoot Tandoori

26-28 Clarendon Street Dublin 2 **Tel: 01 679 4274** Fax: 01 679 4274
Email: info@rajdoottandoori.com Web: www.rajdoottandoori.com

A member of a small UK chain of restaurants specialising in subtle, aromatic
North Indian cuisine, this restaurant has had a fine reputation for its food and
service since it opened in 1984. Tandoori dishes are the main speciality, based
on a wide range of ingredients authentically cooked - this is possibly the only
restaurant in Ireland that still uses the traditional charcoal-fired clay oven
rather than gas. Speciality dishes include duck jaipur (with spring onions,
green peppers, mushrooms, garlic & red wine), chicken johl (a spicy Nepalese
dish with ginger, garlic, fresh coriander & fenugreek) and lamb chilli garlic.
There is also plenty of choice for vegetarians. Set menus include a keenly priced
3-course lunch and pre-theatre dinner. Children over 6 welcome until 7pm.
Seats 120. Air conditioning. L & D daily. Air conditioning. SC discretionary.
Closed 25-26 Dec. Amex, Diners, MasterCard, Visa, Laser. **Directions:** Parallel to
top of Grafton Street, behind Westbury Hotel.

RESTAURANT

Relax Café @ Habitat

6-7 St Stephen's Green Dublin 2 **Tel: 01 674 6622**

Relax Café is on the first floor at Habitat, overlooking St Stephen's Green. It is
a useful address to bear in mind when spending a day in town, as they're open
for breakfast (10-11.45am) and throughout the day, serving just the kind of
wholesome contemporary food that you'd expect of Habitat, in predictably chic
surroundings. Everything is freshly prepared using locally sourced ingredients -
gourmet sandwiches, salads, pastas are the style and, unlike many other
comparable places offering a degree of style, it is particularly family-friendly.
Licensed. Open daily: Mon-Wed & Fri 10-5.30; Thu 10-7.30; Sat 9.30-5.30; Su
12-5.30. **Directions:** Top of Grafton Street - north side of Stephen's Green.

✓ **Ⓑ** RESTAURANT

Restaurant Patrick Guilbaud

21 Upper Merrion Street Dublin 2 **Tel: 01 676 4192** Fax: 01 661 0052
Email: restaurantpatrickguilbaud@eircom.net

The capital's premier French restaurant occupies an elegant ground-floor
restaurant in the Main House of The Merrion Hotel, opening on to a terrace and
landscaped garden (with al fresco eating in fine weather). Although accessible via
the hotel, the main entrance is through the original front door to the 1760
Georgian townhouse. Works by Irish artists are a major decorative feature, making
a very fine setting for Ireland's most renowned restaurant. Head chef Guillaume
Lebrun has presided over this fine kitchen since the restaurant opened in its
original premises in 1982 and presents wide-ranging à la carte and set menus. The
table d'hôte lunch menu is changed daily - and a snip at about €30 - while, at
the other end of the spectrum an inspired, wonderfully creative 9-course 'Sea &
Land' Tasting Menu (about €130) celebrates traditional Irish themes - with Gallic
flair: Guinness & Oyster (a Carlingford oyster set in stout jelly and served with
oyster cream), Molly Malone cockle & mussel (marinière of shellfish from east
coast harbours, cooked in a cast iron pot with dulse) 'Bacon & Egg' (braised
crubeen, hock & bacon with a salad of white cabbage, poached quail egg and
crackling) lamb stew (loin of Wicklow lamb, slowly cooked in savoury scented
potatoes and root vegetables), Irish whiskey (cold coffee and Irish whiskey jelly
with a warm white chocolate mousse). Contemporary French cooking at its best,
consistent excellence is the order of the day. Cheeses are supplied by Sheridans
cheesemongers, breads are home-made, and the mostly French wine list includes
some great classics, with some reasonably-priced offerings. Service, under the
relaxed supervision of Stéphane Robin, is invariably immaculate and Patric

Guilbaud himself is usually present to greet guests personally and, discreetly working the tables, makes sure that all is well. Every capital city has its great restaurant and this is Dublin's: Restaurant Patrick Guilbaud sets the standard by which all others are judged. Children welcome. **Seats 85** (private room, 25; outdoor seating, 20). Air conditioning. L Tue-Sat 12.30-2.15, D Tue-Sat 7.30-10.15. Set L €30. Vegetarian Menu €24. 9-course Tasting Menu €130. L&D à la carte available. House wine from €32. SC discretionary. Closed Sun & Mon, bank hols, Christmas week. Amex, Diners, MasterCard, Visa, Laser. **Directions:** Opposite Government Buildings.

---

⑤ RESTAURANT   # Saagar Indian Restaurant

16 Harcourt Street Dublin 2 **Tel: 01 475 5060** / 5012
Fax: 01 475 5741 Email: info@saagarindianrestaurants.com
Web: www.saagarindianrestaurants.com

féile bia Meera and Sunil Kumar's highly-respected basement restaurant just off St Stephen's Green has a contemporary feel, with wooden flooring and restrained decor - and a music system featuring the latest Indian music. It s a hospitable place and you will be warmly welcomed - and probably offered a drink in the little bar while choosing from the menu. The cooking is consistently good, offering a wide range of speciality dishes, all prepared from fresh ingredients and considerately coded with a range of one to four stars to indicate the heat level. Thus Malai Kabab is a safe one-star dish, while traditional Lamb Balti and Lamb Aayish (marinated with exotic spices and cooked in a cognac-flavoured sauce) is a three-star and therefore pretty hot. Beef and pork are not served but this is balanced by a good vegetarian selection, and the side dishes such as Naan breads, which are made to order in the tandoori oven, are excellent. Customer care is a high priority here, and service is always knowledgeable and attentive. The Kumars also have restaurants in Athlone and Mullingar. Children welcome, but not very young babies (under 1), or after 10pm. **Seats 60**. Toilets wheelchair accessible. L Mon-Fri, 12.30-2.30; D 6-11 daily. L&D à la carte available. House wine about €16. SC discretionary. Closed L Sat, L Sun & Christmas week. Amex, Diners, MasterCard, Visa, Laser. **Directions:** Off Stephen's Green, opposite Children's Hospital.

RESTAURANT   # Salamanca

1 St Andrew's Street Dublin 2 **Tel: 01 670 8628**

John Harvey (always quick to spot a coming trend - he was one of the first to do a class coffee act) opened this atmospheric tapas bar and Spanish restaurant in the heart of Dublin a couple of years ago, and it has struck a chord with Dubliners, who enjoy the informality. It has no waiting space for new arrivals, but the entrance is pleasant - past a bar with flowers on the counter - and welcoming staff show you straight to a simple marble-topped table. The menu - which is in Spanish with English explanations - is flexible enough to suit anything from a light lunch to a full dinner and offers an embarrassment of good choices: three tapas plates will make a generous lunch for two. Decor is warm and bright, with interesting Spanish details to enjoy in the unlikely event that service might be slow. Although they might not pass on absolute authenticity with flying colours, Spanish staples are generally well-handled: garlic roast chicken, langoustines with serrano ham, squid in chilli butter and patatas bravas are all delicious and there are no short cuts on ingredients, including the quality of olive oil used for frying; presentation is simple and traditional, oval plates and shallow casseroles are used, and their lovely frothy-topped mocha served in a tall glass makes a great post-prandial reviver. Tasty food, delightful staff and good value (individual tapas from about

€4) have made this place a winner; food is served throughout the day and they don't take bookings - so be prepared to wait at peak times. Wine list includes a range of sherries by the glass - the traditional accompaniment for tapas. Meals: Mon-Thu, 12 noon-11 pm, Fri & Sat to midnight. Closed Sun. MasterCard, Visa. **Directions:** Near Dublin Tourism.

✓ **B** RESTAURANT   # Shanahan's on the Green

119 St. Stephen's Green Dublin 2 **Tel: 01 407 0939** Fax: 01 407 0940
Email: sales@shanahans.ie Web: www.shanahans.ie

féile bia Located on the west side of the Green, this opulent restaurant was Dublin's first dedicated American style steakhouse - although, as they will be quick to reassure you if required, their wide-ranging menu also offers plenty of other meats, poultry and seafood. However, the big attraction for many of the hungry diners who head for Shanahan's is their certified Irish Angus beef, which is seasoned and cooked in a special broiler, 1600-1800°F, to sear the outside and keep the inside tender and juicy. Their steaks range from a 'petit filet' at a mere 8 oz/225g right up to The Shanahan Steak (24 oz/700g), which is a sight to gladden the heart of many a traditionally-minded Irishman - and, more surprisingly perhaps, many of his trendier young friends too. Strange to think that steak was passé such a short time ago. There is much else to enjoy, of course: starters like a trio of Irish salmon (oak smoked, house cured and pastrami), with a giant blini, crème fraîche and caviar, or a main course of crisp pork shank and cracklings, with melted cabbage & leeks and a spiced apple sauce. Like everything else, side vegetables are different from other restaurants, and include a dramatic signature dish of onion strings with blue cheese dressing. Desserts are wonderful too - shared composition of desserts is probably a wise move, or you could just go straight for the hand rolled chocolate truffles with coffee. The cooking style is admirably simple, and dishes are skilfully executed but bring a good appetite - and a fat wallet (Portions tend to be very large, so regulars often order less courses than in other restaurants, which makes for better value.) The wide-ranging wine list includes many from the best of Californian producers; no house wine and little to choose from under €30, although a fair number by the glass. Less formal fare is served in The Oval Office bar, from 5pm daily. Not suitable for children **Seats 100.** Reservations required. Air conditioning. L Fri only (except for groups), 12.30-2. D daily, 6-10.30. Set L €45; otherwise à la carte. (S discretionary, but 15% on parties of 6+). Closed Christmas period. Amex, Diners, MasterCard, Visa, Laser. **Directions:** On the west side of St Stephen's Green, beside Royal College of Surgeons.

✓ **B** RESTAURANT/HOTEL   # Shelbourne Hotel

27 St Stephen's Green Dublin 2 **Tel: 01 663 4500** Fax: 01 661 6001
Email: shelbourneinfo@lemeridien-hotels.com Web: www.shelbourne.ie

The Irish Constitution was drafted here and this opulent 18th-century hotel overlooking St Stephen's Green (Europe's largest garden square) is still central to Dublin life today. Ranking among the world's great hotels, it has retained all its grandeur, and the entrance creates a strong impression with its magnificent faux-marble entrance hall and Lord Mayor's Lounge - a popular meeting place for afternoon tea. The Shelbourne Bar on Kildare Street is a relatively new initiative (food served 12-8 daily - may vary on Sun - includes 'traditional daily specials', some more traditional than others) but the Horseshoe Bar, renowned as a meeting place for local politicians and theatrical society, is nothing short of a Dublin institution. The best rooms and suites are very luxurious but accommodation varies somewhat due to the age of the building; however shortly before the Guide went to press, the hotle was bought by an Irish consortium and major investment is planned. The hotel has two restaurants, N

27 The Green (see below) and The Side Door At The Shelbourne (12-11 daily) which has a separate entrance from Kildare Street and, with its striking minimalist decor and Cal-Ital menus, provides a complete contrast to the ultra-traditional atmosphere of the hotel. **The Shelbourne Club**, a fine leisure complex with 18m swimming pool, and much else besides, is situated within the hotel complex. Conference/banqueting (400/320). Business centre. Valet Parking. 24 hour room service. Children welcome. Lift. **Rooms 190** (22 suites, 101 no smoking) Room rate from about €225ps, SC 15%. Open all year.

No 27 The Green: This elegant and lofty dining-room offers good cooking, combining the best of Irish produce with some traditional/continental flair and expertise. Alongside the daily-changing table d'hôte menus, an à la carte is offered at both lunch and dinner. Specialities, which are strongly seasonal, typically include the best Irish beef, in The Shelbourne Roast (sirloin on the trolley, with traditional garnish) and several other specialities on the evening menu: prime seafood such as No 27 Howth Seafood Caesar Salad and The Shelbourne Special (fricassée of lobster in its shell with tarragon leaves & bisque emulsion). The restaurant is a credit to the hotel, with fine food and service to match. **Seats 60.** L Sun-Fri,12.30-2.30; D 6.30-10.30 Mon-Sat, Sun 6-10. Set menus from about €35. L A la carte. House wine from about €20. SC15%. Closed L Sat. Amex, Diners, MasterCard, Visa. **Directions:** Landmark building on north side of St Stephen's Green.

CAFÉ
Silk Road Café
Chester Beatty Library Dublin Castle Dublin 2 **Tel: 01 407 0770**
Fax: 01 407 0788 Email: silkroadcafe@hotmail.com

In a fine location in the heart of the city centre, Dublin Castle provides wonderful gardens and historic architecture which greatly enhance the enjoyment of a visit to this unusual restaurant, which is situated in the clock tower beside the Chester Beatty Library (European Museum of the Year in 2002). Middle Eastern, Mediterranean, vegetarian and organic are the themes brought together by a dedicated small team who create inspired versions of classics like Greek moussaka, Moroccan cous cous, falafel and spinach & feta pie to the delight of their many returning customers. Fresh organic herbs are used in all dishes and, in line with halal/kosher rules, all dishes are made without the use of pork or beef. Prices are very reasonable - an average main course served with rice or salad is around €10. Children welcome. **Seats 65** (private room 25). Air conditioning. Open Mon-Fri, 10-5; à la carte. No service charge. Visa, Laser. **Directions:** Beside Chester Beatty Library in Dublin Castle.

ATMOSPHERIC PUB
The Stag's Head
1 Dame Court Dublin 2 **Tel: 01 679 3701**

In Dame Court, just behind the Adams Trinity Hotel, this impressive establishment has retained its original late-Victorian decor and is one of the city's finest pubs. It can get very busy at times - perhaps the volume of business makes it difficult to keep up with routine housekeeping, but this lovely pub is still worth a visit. Closed 25 Dec & Good Fri.

GUESTHOUSE
Stauntons on the Green
83 St Stephen's Green Dublin 2 **Tel: 01 478 2300**
Fax: 01 478 2263 Email: stauntonsonthegreen@eircom.net
Web: www.stauntonsonthegreen.ie

Well-located with views over St Stephen's Green at the front and its own private gardens at the back, this guesthouse - which is in an elegant Georgian terrace on the south of the Green and has fine period reception rooms - offers moderately priced accommodation of a good standard, with all the usual amenities.

Maintenance could be a little sharper and front rooms would benefit from sound-proofing from traffic noise, but it's in the heart of the business and banking district and the Grafton Street shopping area is just a stroll across the Green. Meeting rooms are available, with secretarial facilities on request - and there's private parking (valet parking service offered - it would be wise to phone ahead with your time of arrival to arrange this, as there is no parking at the door). Children welcome. No pets. **Rooms 38** (all en-suite, 24 shower only). B&B about €76 pps, ss €20. Closed 24-27 Dec. Amex, Diners, MasterCard, Visa, Laser. **Directions:** On south side of the Green.

Ⓑ HOTEL   ## Stephen's Green Hotel

St Stephen's Green Dublin 2 **Tel: 01 607 3600**
Fax: 01 661 5663 Email: stephensgreenres@ocallaghanhotels.ie
Web: www.ocallaghanhotels.ie

féile bia This striking landmark hotel on the south-western corner site overlooking St Stephen's Green is the newest of the O'Callaghan Hotels group (Alexander, Davenport, Mont Clare - see entries). Public areas include an impressive foyer and, in memory of the writer George Fitzmaurice who used to live here, 'Pie Dish' restaurant and 'Magic Glasses' bar - both named after titles from his work. It's a great location for business or leisure and bedrooms have exceptionally good facilities, particularly for business travellers. Small conference/meeting rooms. Business centre. Gym. Children welcome (Under 2s free in parents' room; cots available). No pets. **Rooms 75** (9 suites, including 2 studio terrace suites, 3 penthouse suites, junior suites; 40 no-smoking rooms, 2 for disabled). Lift. 24 hour room service. Room rate about €295, max. 2 guests). Open all year. Amex, Diners, MasterCard, Visa. **Directions:** Corner of HarcourtSt. and St. Stephen's Green.

RESTAURANT   ## Steps of Rome

1 Chatham Street Dublin 2 **Tel: 01-670 5630**

For some reason inexpensive little Italian places specialising in pizza have clustered around Balfe and Chatham Streets. Each has its following and this authentic little one-room café just beside Neary's pub is a favourite lunch spot for many discerning Dubliners. A good place to take a break. (**Branch at:** Ciao Bella Roma, Parliament St.) **Seats 18**. Open 12 noon-11pm Mon-Sat, Sun 1-10pm. House wine about €14. No service charge. **No Credit Cards. Directions:** Just off top of Grafton Street.

RESTAURANT   ## Tante Zoe's

1 Crow Street Temple Bar Dublin 2 **Tel: 01 679 4407** Fax: 01 670 7555
Email: tantezoes@eircom.net Web: www.tantezoes.com

Tante Zoe's is a dark, relaxing place - old posters and signs from the deep south on the walls. Cajun popcorn - a huge mound of juicy baby shrimps coated in crispy spiced breadcrumbs and served with a Marie Rose-style sauce or crab cakes, Shrimp Creole (spicy tomato sauce with plump jumbo shrimps) blackened chicken with spiced cream sauce are all typical and side dishes include Maque choux (sweetcorn cooked with peppers, onion and tomato). Bread pudding with whiskey sauce could make a great finale on a chilly night. But it is not so much the food as the outstandingly friendly and attentive waiting staff who contribute most to the relaxed atmosphere - and make informed suggestions - that make Tante Zoe's stand out from many other restaurants in the locality. Not suitable for children under 10. **Seats 150** (private room, 100). Open daily 12 noon-midnight, (Sun 12-4 & 6-12) Set L & early D (6-8pm). Also à la carte, L&D. SC discretionary (12.5% on parties of 6+). Closed 25 Dec & Good Fri. **Seats 160**. L daily, 12-4; D daily 5-12. Amex, Diners, MasterCard, Visa, Laser. **Directions:** Temple Bar, off Dame Street.

Ⓑ HOTEL   # Temple Bar Hotel

Fleet Street Temple Bar Dublin 2 **Tel: 01 677 3333**
Fax: 01 677 3088 Email: reservations@tbh.ie
Web: ww.templebarhotel.com

féile bia This pleasant hotel is relatively reasonably priced, and handy for both sides of the river. Spacious reception and lounge areas create a good impression and bedrooms are generally larger than average, almost all with a double and single bed and good amenities. Neat, well-lit bathrooms have over-bath showers and marble wash basin units. Room service menu (6-10pm). The hotel has an arrangement with a nearby car park. Conference/banqueting (80/70). Wheelchair access. Children welcome (Under 3s free in parents' room, cots available without charge). No pets. **Rooms 129** (10 no-smoking, 2 for disabled). Lift. B&B about €90pps, ss €55. Closed Christmas. Amex, Diners, MasterCard, Visa, Laser. **Directions:** Near Fleet Street car park.

✓ Ⓑ RESTAURANT   # Thornton's Restaurant

128 St Stephen's Green Dublin 2 **Tel: 01 478 7008**
Fax: 01 478 7009 Email: thorntonsrestaurant@eircom.net
Web: www.thorntonsrestaurant.com

Seriously good cooking in a seriously good restaurant is to be found at this lofty city-centre restaurant. Mounting the wide staircase, deep-carpeted in dark blue, conveys a sense of occasion; once inside, the decor leaves you in no doubt that the food is to be the star here: pale walls washed with reflected colour from heavy primrose silk curtains highlight a series of subtle oil paintings (commissioned from the Monaghan artist, Siobhán McDonald) while linen-clad tables each have a silver candlestick and a simple white candle, classical modern cutlery and glasses and restrained china with just a silver rim. A welcoming team of waiting staff set the tone from the outset, providing highly professional service to complement Kevin Thornton's superb cooking; you may be shown straight to your table to consider a menu which, literally, bears the hand of the master on the cover, in another stroke of understated originality. Menus offered include a concise 2 or 3-course lunch menu (which is great value), a vegetarian menu and a table d'hôte dinner menu, in addition to a shortish à la carte offering about eight luxurious choices on each course - Kevin Thornton has a name for generosity with truffles and he will not disappoint: a vegetarian first course of warm white asparagus is served with truffle hollandaise and green asparagus bavarois... a luxurious main course of poussin with foie gras, savoy cabbage and black truffle sauce. Seafood is well-represented in, for example, a signature dish of sautéed prawns with prawn bisque, and truffle sabayon, and another starter of fresh lobster with forest mushrooms, gnocchi, red chard leaves and lobster jus. Other signature dishes include braised suckling pig, and trotter served with glazed turnip and a light poitín sauce - and variations on these creations appear throughout an 8-course Surprise Menu (about €125) which is just that - there is nothing written and the menu created for each table is unique. This is creative cooking of the highest class, conceived with confidence to utilise first-rate seasonal ingredients, and beautifully (but not flamboyantly) presented with a perfectionist's eye for detail and a palate to match: this is extraordinarily intense, deeply flavoured food and it is far from the show-off creations commonly associated with top chefs: Kevin Thornton's cooking has soul. Service throughout is impeccable, from the moment a basket of breads arrive to the final presentation of assorted petits fours accompanying coffees and teas. An Irish and French cheese trolley deserves special mention (cheese supplied by Sheridan's cheesemongers) and there's also an excellent wine list, which includes many great bottles, a good collection of house wines and wines available by the half bottle or glass - and an extensive choice of dessert wines, ports and digestifs. Reservations required. Children welcome. Air conditioning. **Seats 65** (private area, 35). L Tue-Sat, 12.30-2; D Tue-Sat, 7-10.30. Set L €30. Set D €65; Set D €65, Surprise Menu €125, A la carte also offered. House wine from €28. SC discretionary. Closed Sun & Mon, Christmas & New Year. Amex, Diners, MasterCard, Visa, Laser. **Directions:** On St Stephen's Green (corner at top of Grafton Street); entrance beside Fitzwilliam Hotel.

ATMOSPHERIC PUB   **Toners**

139 Lower Baggot Street Dublin 2
Tel: 01 676 3090 Fax: 01 676 2617

One of the few authentic old pubs left in Dublin, Toners is definitely worth a visit (or two). Among many other claims to fame, it is said to be the only pub ever frequented by the poet W.B. Yeats. Closed 25 Dec & Good Fri.

✓ RESTAURANT   **Town Bar & Grill**

21 Kildare Street Dublin 2 **Tel: 01 662 4724** Fax: 01 662 3857
Email: reservations@townbarandgrill.com
Web: www.townbarandgrill.com

Warmly professional staff and a delicate hand with the decor - warm floor tiles, gentle lighting and smart but not overly-formal white-clothed tables with promising wine glasses - create a welcoming tone on arrival at Ronan Ryan and Temple Garnier's L-shaped basement restaurant under Mitchell's wine merchants. Although the name of the restaurant is quite meaningful (many would define 'town' as within walking distance of the nearby Dawson Street car park) it may not prepare first-time diners for the New York Italian style. Starters include a really excellent antipasti plate, and dishes rarely seen elsewhere, such as grilled fresh sardines, while classics like osso bucco Milanese with a pea and saffron risotto and gremolata may be among main courses which will also offer several interesting fish dishes and, in season, game such as crown of pheasant - served with confit leg, soft polenta and glazed shallots, perhaps. Moreish desserts may lean a little heavily on chocolate, but the combinations are unusual and tastes superb. Confident, accurate cooking, zesty flavours and simple presentation on plain white plates - all this is impressive, and interested, well-informed staff ensure a memorable meal. Don't expect bargain basement prices, but the cost is fair for the high quality of food and service offered. A concise, carefully selected wine list (mainly Italian) offers plenty of treats. **Seats 100.** Open Mon-Sat: L 12.15-3.15; short menu 3.15-6; pre-theatre menu 6-7.15 (excl Sat); à la carte 6-11. Closed Sun. MasterCard, Visa. **Directions:** Opposite side door of Shelbourne hotel, under Mitchell's Wines.

Ⓑ HOTEL   **Trinity Capital Hotel**

Pearse Street Dublin 2 **Tel: 01 648 1000** Fax: 01 648 1010
Email: info@trinitycapital-hotel.com Web: www.capital-hotels.com

A stylish hotel right beside the headquarters of Dublin's city centre fire brigade (inspiring the name 'Fireworks' for its unusual club-style bar) and opposite Trinity College. Very centrally located for business and leisure, the hotel is within easy walking distance of all the main city centre attractions on both sides of the Liffey and the lobby wine and coffee bar make handy meeting places. Rooms have a safe, interactive TV, phone, data ports, hair dryer, trouser press, tea/coffee trays, comfortable beds and good bathrooms -junior suites suites have jacuzzi baths, hi-fi system and mini-bar.

The Siena Restaurant offers an above-average experience for an hotel dining room, providing an appealing alternative for guests who prefer to dine in

(D daily, 6-9.30). Guests have free admission all the bars and clubs in the city centre owned by Capital Bars, including the adjacent Fireworks night club. Conference/banqueting 40/80. Meeting rooms; secretarial services. Children welcome (under 12s free in parents' room; cots available without charge, baby sitting arranged). Secure parking. **Rooms 82** (4 suites, 4 junior suites, 24 no-smoking, 3 shower only. Lift. 24 hour room service. B&B €106.50 pps, ss €30. (Room only €199). Amex, Diners, MasterCard, Visa, Laser.

Ⓑ GUESTHOUSE | **Trinity Lodge**

12 South Frederick Street Dublin 2 **Tel: 01 617 0900**
Fax: 01 617 0999 Email: trinitylodge@eircom.net
Web: www.trinitylodge.com

As centrally located as it is possible to get, this owner-run guesthouse offers a high standard of accommodation at a reasonable price just yards away from Trinity College. Six rooms - 3 deluxe twins and 3 standard doubles - were completely refurbished in 2004. Air-conditioned rooms have a safe, direct-dial phone, tea/coffee making facilities, multi-channel TV, trouser press and iron. Children welcome (under 12 free in parents' room; cots available free of charge). No pets. **Rooms 16** (3 superior, all shower only and no-smoking). Room service (limited hours). B&B €95pps, ss €50. Closed 22-27 Dec. Amex, Diners, MasterCard, Visa, Laser. **Directions:** Off Nassau Street, near Trinity College.

RESTAURANT | **Trocadero Restaurant**

3/4 St Andrew Street Dublin 2 **Tel: 01 677 5545**
Fax: 01 679 2385 Web: www.restaurants indublin.ie

The Dublin theatrical restaurant par excellence with deep blood-red walls and gold-trimmed stage curtains, black and white pictures of the celebrities who've passed through the place – dimly lit, intimate tables with individual beaded lampshades and snug, cosy seating, the 'Troc' is one of Dublin's longest-established restaurants and has presided over St. Andrew Street since 1956. It has atmosphere in spades, food and service to match. Comforting menus reminiscent of the Seventies offer starters like French onion soup, deep-fried brie, chicken liver pâté and avocado prawn Marie Rose, followed by ever-popular grills - fillet steak (with Cashel Blue cheese perhaps), Wicklow rack of lamb and sole on the bone are the mainstays of the menu, also wild Irish salmon and Dublin Bay Prawns from Clogherhead, naturally all with a sprinkling of freshly chopped parsley. Desserts include apple and cinnamon strudel and wicked chocolate and Baileys slice, and a better-value winelist will be hard to find. There's privacy too – sound-absorbing banquettes and curtains allow you to hear everything at your own table with just a pleasing murmur in the background. Lovely friendly service too: magic. **Seats 100**. Air conditioning. Children welcome (up to 9pm). D Mon-Sat, 5-12. D à la carte (pre-theatre D 5-7.30, about €18). House wine from about €18.50. Closed Sun, 25-26 Dec, 31 Dec, Good Fri. Amex, Diners, MasterCard, Visa, Laser. **Directions:** Beside Dublin Tourism Centre.

RESTAURANT | **Tulsi Restaurant**

17a Lr Baggot Street Dublin 2 **Tel: 01 676 4578** Fax: 01 6764579
Email: sharmin@gofree.indigo.ie Web: www.tulsi-indian.com

One of a small chain of authentic Indian restaurants, this bustling place has a compact reception area leading into a pleasingly elegant restaurant with echoes of the Raj in the decor. Tables are set up with plate warmers, fresh flowers, sauces and pickles and service is brisk so you will quickly be presented with menus offering a broad range of Indian styles - there's a slight leaning towards Punjabi style cooking, with its use of nuts and fruit in sauces, but also tandoori, tikka, biryani, balti and an extensive vegetarian menu. A selection of naan breads is offered and the food quality overall is consistently high; this, together with good value, make booking at both lunch and dinner advisable. A range of special menus offers variety and value; Indian beer available. **Seats 52.** L Mon-Sat, 12-2.15; D daily, 6-11.30 (Sun to 11). Set L €10.50. Set D €20/24. Also à la carte. House wine €16.95. Closed L Sun, L bank hols; 25-26 Dec, Good Fri. *Tulsi has a number of **branches**, including: Lr Charles Street, Castlebar, Co Mayo (Tel: 094 25066); Buttermilk Way, Middle Street, Galway Tel: 092-564831). **Sister restaurants** 'Shanai Indian' at Cornelscourt S.C. and Old Bray Road, Foxrock, Co Dublin. Amex, Diners, MasterCard, Visa, Laser. **Directions:** 2 minutes walk east from St Stephens Green (Shelbourne Hotel side).

RESTAURANT   **Unicorn Restaurant**

12B Merrion Court off Merrion Row Dublin 2 **Tel: 01 676 2182**
Fax: 01 662 4194 Email: unicorn12b@eircom.net

In a lovely, secluded location just off a busy street near the Shelbourne Hotel, this informal and perennially fashionable restaurant is famous for its buffet hors d'oeuvres selection, piano bar and exceptionally friendly staff. It's particularly charming in summer, as the doors open out onto a terrace which is used for al fresco dining in fine weather - and the Number Five piano bar, which extends to two floors, is also a great attraction for after-dinner relaxation with live music (Weds-Sat 9pm-3am). Good food (regional and modern Italian), efficient service and atmosphere all partially explain The Unicorn's enduring success - another element is the constant quest for further improvement. The "Unicorn Foodstore" Italian delicatessen on Merrion Row is a relatively recent addition to the enterprise, also the newer Unicorn Antipasto/Tapas Bar. Many of the Italian wines listed are exclusive to The Unicorn: uniquely, in Ireland, they stock the full collection of Gava wines and also the Pio Cesare range. Not suitable for children after 9pm. **Seats 85** (private room 16; outdoor 35). Reservations required. Air conditioning. Toilets wheelchair accessible. Open Mon-Sat, L12.30-4.30, D 6-11. A la carte. House wine about €21.90. SC discretionary. Closed Sun, bank hols, 10 days at Christmas. Amex, Diners, MasterCard, Visa, Laser. **Directions:** Near Shelbourne Hotel.

RESTAURANT   **Wagamama**

Unit 4B South King Street Dublin 2 **Tel: 01 478 2152**
Fax: 01 478 2154 Email: info@wagamama.ie Web: www.wagamama.ie

The Dublin branch of this popular London-based noodle bar is full of groovy young things, who find it cool - both for the food and the interior, which is a huge basement canteen, simple and functional, but strikingly designed with high ceilings. The generous portions of noodles consist of ramen (thread noodles), udon (fat noodles) or soba (a round buckwheat noodle) served in soups or pan-fried, well seasoned and colourfully decorated with South Asian ingredients. The large menu gives plenty of information about ingredients and dishes - and also explains how orders are taken (kids love the electronic notepads used by servers); it includes a few Japanese dishes such as teriyaki (little kebabs) and edamame (freshly steamed green soya beans, served sprinkled with salt), also a selection of fruit and vegetable juices, some rice dishes and plenty of vegetarian options. All food served in Wagamama noodle bars is GMO free, and Sake and interesting soft drinks such as kombucha take their place on the drinks menu alongside wines and coffees. Service is friendly and efficient. It's noisy, and not a place for those who value comfort - or privacy (not an intimate venue at all) - but kids love it. No reservations, but queues move quickly. Multi-storey carpark nearby. Children welcome. **Seats 136**. Air conditioning. Open daily, 12-11 (Sun to 10). A la carte. SC discretionary. Closed 25-26 Dec. Amex, Diners, MasterCard, Visa, Laser. **Directions:** Opposite Gaiety Theatre.

✔ **Ⓑ** HOTEL/RESTAURANT   # The Westbury Hotel

Grafton Street Dublin 2 **Tel: 01 679 1122** Fax: 01 679 7078
Email: westbury@jurysdoyle.com Web: www.jurysdoyle.com

féile bia Possibly the most conveniently situated of all the central Dublin hotels, the Westbury is a very small stone's throw from the city's premier shopping street and has all the benefits of luxury hotels - notably free valet parking - to offset any practical disadvantages of the location. Unashamedly sumptuous, the hotel's public areas drip with chandeliers and have accessories to match - like the grand piano on The Terrace, a popular first floor meeting place for afternoon tea and frequently used for fashion shows. Accommodation is similarly luxurious, with bedrooms that include penthouse suites and a high proportion of suites, junior suites and executive rooms. With conference facilities to match its quality of accommodation and service, the hotel is understandably popular with business guests, but it also makes a luxurious base for a leisure break in the city. Laundry/dry cleaning. Mini-gym. Conference/banqueting (220/200). Business centre. Secretarial services. ISDN lines. Children welcome (Under 12s free in parents' room; cots available). No pets. **Rooms 204** (3 suites, 4 junior suites, 24 executive rooms,160 no-smoking, 2 for disabled). Lifts. Room rate about €305. SC15%. Car park. Open all year.

Russell Room: After a drink in one of the hotel's bars - the first floor Terrace Bar and the Sandbank Bistro, an informal seafood restaurant and bar accessible from the back of the building - the Russell Room offers classic French dining, with some global cuisine and modern Irish influences. **Seats 100** (private room, 14). Air conditioning. SC 15%. L daily, 12.30-2.30; D daily 6.30-10.30 (Sun to 9). Set L from about €30, D à la carte. House wine about €20. Amex, Diners, MasterCard, Visa, Laser. **Directions:** City centre, off Grafton Street; near Trinty College & Stephens Green.

✔ **Ⓑ** HOTEL   # The Westin Dublin

College Green Dublin 2 **Tel: 01 645 1000** Fax: 01 645 1401
Email: sales.dublin@westin.com Web: www.westin.com

féile bia Two Victorian landmark buildings were more or less rebuilt to create this impressive hotel, and part of the former Allied Irish Bank was glassed over to create a dramatic lounging area, The Atrium, which has a huge palm tree feature and bedroom windows giving onto it like a courtyard (effective, if strangely airless). The magnificent Banking Hall provides the main conference and banqueting room and the adjacent Teller Room now makes an unusual circular boardroom, while the vaults have found a new lease of life as The Mint, a bar with its own access from College Street. It's an intriguing building, especially for those who remember its former commercial life, and it has many special features including a split-level penthouse suite, with views over Trinity College, which has a living room, board room and private exercise area; the business traveller's Westin Guest Office, designed to combine the efficiency and technology of a modern office with the comfort of a luxurious bedroom; and the so-called 'Heavenly Bed' designed by Westin and 'worlds apart from any other bed'. Very limited parking (some valet parking if it is arranged at the time of booking accommodation). Fitness room. **Rooms 164** (13 suites, 5 junior suites, 19 for disabled). Lift. Room rate from about €215.

Mint: An elegant, spacious room in 1930s style, the restaurant continues the banking theme and, with a welcome emphasis on comfort, it simply oozes luxury. Everything about it, from the classily understated decor in tones of cream and brown to the generous-sized, well-spaced tables and large carver chairs says expensive but worth it. And, in the Guide's experience, that promise generally follows through onto the plate in well-executed menus - a fairly contemporary style, and confident, unfussy cooking endear this restaurant to visitors and discerning Dublin diners alike. Westin Smart Dining options (moderate in calories and fat) and vegetarian options are highlighted on menus. Friendly service from knowledgeable young waiting staff. More extensive, luxurious evening menus are à la carte, except for a 3-course pre-theatre menu which (like Chapter One - see entry) allows you to return to your table for dessert after the performance. The Westin Sunday Brunch has become a bit of an institution, involving live jazz and all the traditional elements - an extensive buffet and a chef to cook omelettes and serve bacon, sausages and black pudding - and also dishes more usually attached to lunch, such as roasts and sophisticated fish dishes. and luscious desserts. A great way to deal with Sunday. **Seats 75.** Breakfast daily 6.30-10, L Mon-Fri 12-2.30, D daily 6.30-10 (Fri, Sat, Sun to 10.30). Sun Brunch 12-4.30, €40; live music (jazz). Restaurant closed L Sat. Hotel open all year. Amex, Diners, MasterCard, Visa, Laser. **Directions:** On Westmoreland Street, opposite Trinity College.

RESTAURANT

Yamamori Noodles

71 South Great George's Street Dublin 2
Tel: 01 475 5001 Fax: 01 475 5001

Good value speedy cooking with lots of flavour is the secret of Yamamori's success - and atmosphere too. It's just the kind of buzzy place that young people of all ages like to hang about in - a cool place for family outings. Specialities include Yamamori ramen, sushi and sashimi served in generous portions that give great value. Separate lunch and dinner menus are offered, with a more extensive choice in the evening. House wine (quarter bottles), about €5. **Seats 130.** Open daily, 12.30-11.30: L 12-5.30, D 5.30-11 (Sun-Wed 4-11). Closed Christmas, 1 Jan, Good Fri. Amex, MasterCard, Visa, Laser. **Directions:** City centre - 5 mins walk from Grafton Street.

DUBLIN 3

The fine residential area of **Clontarf** has an air of deep contentment about it - it's a very settled community and, until the arrival of the East Wall Business Park and the new DART station brought a new sense of bustle, it seemed an exceptionally quiet, self-contained kind of a place happy to gaze out over Dublin Bay and let the world go by. And, in many ways, it's still like that - as a browse around **Vernon Avenue** will quickly reveal. When you have stores like **Nolan's** Supermarket and **Tighe's** butchers on the doorstep, plus an informal Italian restaurant at **Picasso** (Tel: 01 853 1120) why go further than Vernon Avenue? Well, perhaps it's worth going along the seafront a bit, as there's a branch of **Oddbins** to visit - and other restaurants to note in the area include the smart modern **Bay Restaurant** (Tel: 01 853 2406) which is further out, on the main seafront road, and one of the small chain of upmarket Chinese restaurants, **Wongs** (Tel 01 853 2406), which is further along near St Anne's Park. At the Croke Park GAA Stadium (Jones Road) a new **Jurys Doyle Hotel** (Tel 01 607 0070; www.jurysdoyle.com) is under construction as we go to press. And, incidentally, visitors interested in architecture should make a point of visiting the 18th century neo-classical **Casino**, at Marino. (Tel: 01 833 1618)

Ⓑ HOTEL   # Clontarf Castle Hotel

Castle Avenue Clontarf Dublin 3 **Tel: 01 833 2321** Fax: 01 833 2279
Email: info@clontarfcastle.ie Web: www.clontarfcastle.ie

This historic 17th century castle is located near the coast, and convenient to both the airport and city centre. The hotel has been imaginatively incorporated into the old castle structure, retaining the historic atmosphere; some rooms, including the restaurant and the old bar, have original features and the atrium linking the old castle to the hotel is an impressive architectural feature. Clontarf Castle has extensive conference and banqueting facilities along with luxurious bedrooms furnished to a high standard and well equipped for business guests with ISDN lines, voicemail and US electrical sockets in addition to the usual amenities found in an hotel of this standard. Bathrooms are well designed, and all south-facing rooms have air conditioning. Welcoming, friendly staff contribute to the atmosphere - although it is a pity that so little of the original grounds now remain. Conference/banqueting (550/490). Secretarial services. Children welcome (Under 5 free in parents' room; cots available, baby sitting arranged). No pets. **Rooms 111** (3 suites, 2 junior suites, 4 executive rooms, 41 no-smoking, 3 for disabled). Lift. 24 hr room service. B&B €142.50 pps. Templars: D Mon-Sat, 6.30-10.30 (Sun 6-9); L Sun only, 1-3. Closed 24-25 Dec.* There is a sister hotel, the **Crowne Plaza, at Dublin Airport** (see entry). Amex, Diners, MasterCard, Visa, Laser. **Directions:** Take M1 from Dublin Airport, take a left on to Collins Avenue, continue to T junction, take left on to Howth Road. At second set of lights, take a right on to Castle Avenue, continue to roundabout, take right into hotel.

✓ RESTAURANT   # Kinara Restaurant

318 Clontarf Road Dublin 3 **Tel: 01 833 6759** Fax: 01 833 6651
Email: info@kinara.ie Web: www.kinara.ie

This smart two-storey restaurant specialising in authentic Pakistani and Northern Indian cuisine enjoys a scenic location overlooking Bull Island. Fine views - especially from the first floor dining room - are a feature at lunch time or on fine summer evenings, and there's a cosy upstairs bar with Indian cookbooks to inspire guests waiting for a table or relaxing after dinner. A warm welcome from the Sudanese doorman Muhammad ensures a good start as, with a mighty grin and a swirl of the traditional costume that has become the restaurant's trademark, he sweeps arriving guests into the little foyer. The restaurant has a very pleasant ambience, with soft lighting, some good antiques, interesting paintings, the gentlest of background music and streamlined table settings. The menu is unusual, beginning with a useful introduction to the cuisine that explains the four fundamental flavours known collectively as 'pisawa masala' - tomato, garlic, ginger and onions - and their uses, then offering a series of styles to choose from, opening with a range of traditional starters like kakeragh (local crab claws with garlic, yogurt, spices and a tandoori masala sauce) and main courses (such as Sumandari Badsha - lobster tails with cashew nuts, pineapple, chilli and spices). Each dish is described fully and there is a declared commitment to local produce - notably organic beef, lamb and chicken - and a section of the menu devoted to organic and 'lighter fare' main courses (typically Loki Mushroom, a vegetarian dish of courgettes and mushrooms in a light spicy yogurt sauce). The kitchen team team have over 80 years experience between them and the quality of both food and cooking is exemplary: dishes have distinct character and depth of flavour, and everything is appetisingly presented with regard for colour, texture and temperature - and fine food is backed up by attentive, professional service and fair prices. The care and attention that marks every aspect of this comfortable and attractive restaurant ensures that guests will return, time and again. [Kinara was the Guide's Ethnic Restaurant of the Year in 2004.}. Seats 75 (private room 30). Air conditioning. Children welcome. L Thu, Fri & Sun, 12.30-3; D daily, 6-11.30. Set L €14.95; early D about €19.95 (Mon-Thu, 6-7.30pm); also à la carte L&D. House wine about €17.25. Closed 25-26 Dec, 1 Jan. MasterCard, Visa, Laser. **Directions:** 1.5 miles north of city centre on coast road to Howth (opposite wooden bridge).

RESTAURANT

Ristorante Da Enzo

42a Fairview Strand Dublin 3 **Tel: 01 855 5274**

A Fairview cousin of the popular Blackrock restaurant, da Roberto, this basic little restaurant is wowing it to northsiders with its warm and friendly staff, great food and atmosphere - and terrific value. You'll be whisked to your table on arrival and presented with a complimentary mini-starter with the menu - a tomato and mozzarella bruschetta, perhaps - a lovely touch that really whets the appetite and sees you through what could be a longer time than anticipated deciding what to order, from a (very) long menu offering plenty to tempt, including many less usual dishes. Starters alone run to two pages - the second a range of pasta dishes, which you can have as a starter or main course - with each dish named in Italian and explained clearly in English. Fish, fowl, meat and so on each get their say - there really is a lot to choose from. Luckily the cooking follows through: authentic food - full of flavour and including a lot of fish, perfectly cooked, also a dozen or so dishes for vegetarians. And the best bit is the bill: the perfect neighbourhood restaurant. **Seats 45.** D Tue-Sun, 5-11, L&D Sun (1-10.30pm). Closed Mon. Diners, MasterCard, Visa, Laser. **Directions:** At Edge's corner.

DUBLIN 4

Large hotels, upmarket guesthouses and restaurants are typical of this, Dublin's "embassy belt". Business guests account for a high proportion of residential visitors to the area and amenities are provided accordingly - guesthouses tend to have private parking and spacious, well-appointed rooms with deskspace, comfortable residents' drawing rooms and perhaps even a bar, and some can also cater for small conferences. Restaurants in the area include a good selection suitable for business entertaining, but also a fair scattering of less formal restaurants for more relaxed outings - including several of the city's best ethnic restaurants.

Gourmets should allow time to browse a little, especially around **Donnybrook**, where there are several really interesting shops: on Main Street, in the "village", there's the **The Douglas Food Co**. where you can get all sorts of delicious ready-made foods (fit for a dinner party); then, for fresh fish and game in season (and some cooked fish dishes too), **Molloys of Donnybrook** is one of the city's finest shops and there's also an excellent wine shop, **O'Briens Fine Wines**. Just off the main road, you'll find all kinds of everything at **Roy Fox Gourmet Foods** - a surprising little shop and well worth a look even if you're only window-shopping. On Morehampton Road, there's a branch of Eileen Bergin's gourmet ready-made food outlet **The Butler's Pantry**, Dublin's most selective supermarket **Donnybrook Fair** (now with smart first floor café) and, best of all perhaps, is **Terroirs** - for its sheer elegance as well as the discernment with which its specialist French foods and wines are chosen.

B GUESTHOUSE

Aberdeen Lodge

53 Park Avenue Ballsbridge Dublin 4
Tel: 01 283 8155 Fax: 01 283 7877
Email: aberdeen@iol.ie Web: www.halpinsprivatehotels.com

Centrally located (close to the Sydney Parade DART station) yet away from the heavy traffic of nearby Merrion Road, this handsome period house in a pleasant leafy street offers all the advantages of an hotel at guesthouse prices. Elegantly furnished executive bedrooms and four-poster suites offer air conditioning and all the little comforts expected by the discerning traveller, there's a drawing room with comfortable chairs and plenty to read - and a room service menu (with wine list). Staff are extremely pleasant and helpful (tea and biscuits offered on arrival), housekeeping is immaculate - and you can also look forward to a particularly good breakfast. While breakfast is usually included in the overnight rate, guests can join residents for breakfast and there's an option of having the buffet (€10) or buffet plus a cooked breakfast (€15) - a useful service for early morning meetings. [Aberdeen Lodge was the Dublin winner of our Irish Breakfast Awards in 2004.] Boardroom, business and fitness facilities for business guests - and mature secluded gardens. Small conferences/banqueting (50/40). Children welcome. No pets. **Rooms 17** (2 suites, 6 executive rooms, 5 no-smoking). 24 hour room service. B&B €70 pps, ss €35. Residents' meals available: D about €30 + all-day menu. House wines from €25. SC 10%. Open all year. Amex, Diners, MasterCard, Visa, Laser. **Directions:** Minutes from the city centre by DART or by car, take the Merrion Road towards Sydney Parade DART station and then first left into Park Avenue.

B GUESTHOUSE

Anglesea Townhouse

63 Anglesea Road Ballsbridge Dublin 4
Tel: 01 668 3877 Fax: 01 668 3461

féile bia Helen Kirrane's guesthouse brings all the best 'country' house qualities to urban Dublin - a delightful building and pleasant location near Herbert Park, Ballsbridge; comfortable, attractive bedrooms; good housekeeping; a warm, welcoming drawing room with a real period flavour and wonderful breakfasts that prepare guests for the rigours of the most arduous of days. Thoroughly recommended for its creativity and perfectionism in redefining what a guesthouse can be, Anglesea Townhouse was the winner of our 1999 Irish Breakfast Award. Garden. Children welcome (Under 3s free in parents' room; cots available without charge). No pets. **Rooms 7** (5 shower only, all no-smoking). B&B about €65 pps, no ss. Closed Christmas and New Year. Amex, MasterCard, Visa, Laser. **Directions:** Located off Merrion Road, near the RDS; south of the city centre.

RESTAURANT

Baan Thai

16 Merrion Road Ballsbridge Dublin 4 **Tel: 01 660 8833**

Delicious aromas and oriental music greet you as you climb the stairs to Lek and Eamon Lancaster's well-appointed first floor restaurant opposite the RDS. Friendly staff, Thai furniture and woodcarvings create an authentic oriental feeling and intimate atmosphere - and, as many of the staff are Thai, it's almost like being in Thailand. A wide-ranging menu includes various set menus that provide a useful introduction to the cuisine (or speed up choices for groups) as well as an à la carte. The essential fragrance and spiciness of Thai cuisine is very much in evidence throughout and there's Thai beer as well as a fairly extensive wine list. D only, Sun-Thu 6-11, Fri & Sat to 11.30. Amex, Diners, MasterCard, Visa, Laser.

RESTAURANT

Bahay Kubo

14 Bath Avenue Sandymount Dublin 4
Tel: 01 660 5572 Fax: 01 668 2006

Don't be put off by trains rumbling overhead as you approach this unusual Filipino restaurant - once you get upstairs past the rather worn carpeted entrance and stairway, you will find yourself in a clean-lined modern room with pale beech flooring and matching panels on a vaulted roof space, which, together with fresh flowers at the entrance (and on each table), uncluttered decor in warm colours and crisp white linen on the tables, creates a spacious, airy and welcoming atmosphere. Friendly staff seat new guests immediately and bring iced water with menus that are well organised with explanations about dishes - which are probably very necessary as most guests will not be familiar with the cuisine, which is related to Chinese food, with Malaysian, Indonesian and Thai influences. Several set menus are offered (a good choice on a first visit, perhaps), and an à la carte which is, by oriental standards, quite restrained; anyone who likes Chinese food should enjoy the Filipino versions, which are similar but with generally fresher flavours of lemongrass, ginger, chilli and coconut; no MSG is used and soups are refreshingly free of cornstarch. As in some other oriental cuisines, the weakness is in the dessert menu, so make the most of the excellent savoury dishes instead. Service is attentive, making up in willingness anything it may occasionally lack in training. **Seats 80**. Reservations required. D Tue-Sat, 6-11 (Sun 5-10), L Thu & Fri, 12-2.30. Set Menu from €29, also à la carte Live music Thu & Sat. Closed Mon. Amex, MasterCard, Visa, Laser. **Directions:** Above Lansdowne Bar, at railway bridge.

RESTAURANT

Bella Cuba Restaurant

11 Ballsbridge Terrace Dublin 4 **Tel: 01 660 5539** Fax: 01 660 5539
Email: info@bella-cuba.com Web: www.bella-cuba.com

féile bia Juan Carlos & Larissa Gonzalez's bright and warm-toned restaurant is decorated with dramatic murals by a Cuban designer, bringing the atmosphere of that unique country to Dublin - and Juan Carlos's cooking demonstrates the Spanish, Caribbean and South American influences on Cuban food. It's a healthy cuisine, characterised by aromatic spices and herbs - predominantly garlic, cumin, oregano and bay - most dishes are slow cooked, with very little deep frying and no heavy sauces. It's well worth a visit to experience something genuinely different: begin with a famous Cuban cocktail like a Daiquiri or Mojito and then try a speciality of roast pork in Cuban dressing, perhaps, or chicken with chorizo stuffing. Seafood is well represented too and the wine list includes a pair of Cuban bottles. Unusually, the early evening 'Value Menu' allows you to choose from a limited selection on the à la carte. Not suitable for children after 7pm. **Seats 32**. D daily, 5 -10.30. L Thu & Fri, 12-3. Set L €15, Early D €20 (5-7). Also à la carte. House wine €18.50. SC discretionary. Closed Christmas. Amex, MasterCard, Visa, Laser. **Directions:** Near the RDS.

✓ Ⓑ HOTEL/RESTAURANT

Berkeley Court Hotel

Lansdowne Road Ballsbridge Dublin 4
Tel: 01 665 3200 Fax: 01 661 7238
Email: berkeley_court@jurysdoyle.com Web: www.jurysdoyle.com

féile bia Set in its own grounds yet convenient to the city centre, this luxurious hotel has long been a haunt of the rich and famous when in Dublin. The tone is set by an impressively spacious chandeliered foyer, which has groups of seating areas arranged around it, with bars, restaurants and private conference rooms leading off. The hotel has earned recognition for its high standards of service and accommodation. On-site facilities include health & beauty treatments, a barber shop and gift shop/newsagent. Conference/banqueting (400/380) Video-conferencing, business centre, secretarial services, ISDN lines. **Rooms 187** (1 penthouse suite, 6 luxury suites, 24 executive rooms, 35 no-smoking, 4 for disabled). Lift. B&B €190 pps, ss €148 SC15%. Open all year.

Berkeley Room: A fine hotel restaurant with very professional staff and some reliable specialities - seafood dishes are especially good and they are renowned for their roast beef. **Seats 60**. Air conditioning. L Sun-Fri,12.30-2.15; D Mon-Sat, 6.30-9.15. A la carte. SC 15%. Toilets wheelchair accessible. Restaurant closed L Sat, D Sun. Amex, Diners, MasterCard, Visa, Laser. **Directions:** Near Lansdowne Road rugby stadium; approx 13 Km from Airport.

ⒷRESTAURANT   **Berman & Wallace**

Belfield Office Park Beaver Row Clonskeagh Dublin 4
Tel: 01 219 6252 Fax: 01 219 6219
Email: bermanandwallace@eircom.net Web: www.bermanandwallace.com

This pavilion-style restaurant, in a courtyard surrounded by office buildings, supplies the local business community with wide-ranging high quality brasserie style daytime food. Choose from such all-time favourites as fish and chips, bangers and mash (made with Hicks sausages) and baguettes filled with chargrilled steak and garlic mayonnaise, to pasta dishes, lamb passanda, chicken piri-piri with herb risotto and a great deal more. There are also several revitalising or detoxing juices and smoothies for the diet conscious, and there is a daily health lunch special on offer. Wines by the glass or by bottle. Full breakfast; takeaway/corporate platters. Delivery and party menus available. Restaurant available for evening functions. **Seats 80**. Open Mon-Fri, 7.30-3.30; Sun 11.30-3. Closed Sat; Christmas, bank hols. MasterCard, Visa, Amex, Laser. **Directions:** From Donnybrook, turn at Bus Station up Beaver Road towards Clonskeagh. Turn left at second set of lights into business park and follow signs.

ⒷHOTEL/RESTAURANT   **Bewley's Hotel, Ballsbridge**

Merrion Road Ballsbridge Dublin 4 **Tel: 01 668 1111** Fax: 01 668 1999
Email: bb@bewleyshotels.com Web: www.bewleyshotels.com

This modern hotel is cleverly designed to incorporate a landmark period building next to the RDS (entrance by car is on Simmonscourt Road, via Merrion Road or Anglesea Road; underground carpark). Bedrooms are spacious and well-equipped with ISDN lines, iron/trouser press, tea/coffee facilities and safe, making a good base for business or leisure visits. Like its sister hotels at Newlands Cross and Leopardstown, you get a lot of comfort here at a very reasonable cost. Children welcome (free in parents' room up to 16; cots available without charge, baby sitting arranged). No pets. Garden; walking. Parking. **Rooms 304** (84 shower only). Lift. No room service. Room rate €99 (max. 2 adult guests, or 2 adults & 2 children). Closed 24-26 Dec. ***Restaurant:** See entry for **O'Connells in Ballsbridge**. Amex, Diners, MasterCard, Visa, Laser. **Directions:** At junction of Simmonscourt and Merrion Road.

ⒷGUESTHOUSE   **Blakes Townhouse**

50 Merrion Road Ballsbridge Dublin 4
Tel: 01 668 8324 Fax: 01 668 4280
Email: blakestownhouse@iol.ie Web: www.halpinsprivatehotels.com

One of Pat Halpin's small chain of quality guesthouses, Blakes is very handily situated for anyone attending exhibitions in Dublin, as it's directly opposite the RDS, and offers an attractive alternative to hotel accommodation. Comfortable bedrooms are well-equipped for business and professional travellers, and executive rooms and four-poster suites also have whirlpool spas. A high level of service for a guesthouse - and very good breakfasts. Drawing room and room service menu available all day (selection of quality wines, from €25); 24 hour room service. Children welcome (under 3 free in parents' room. No pets. Complimentary use of nearby leisure centre. Private parking. **Rooms 12** (2 suites,10 executive, 4 no smoking). B&B €70 pps, ss €35; SC 10%. * Short breaks, including golf breaks, offered. Open all year. Amex, Diners, MasterCard, Visa, Laser. **Directions:** Opposite the RDS in Ballsbridge.

Ⓑ HOTEL   # Burlington Hotel

Upper Leeson Street Dublin 4 **Tel: 01 660 5222** Fax: 01 660 8496
Email: burlington@jurysdoyle.com Web: www.jurysdoyle.com

féile bia Ireland's largest hotel, the Burlington has more experience of dealing with very big numbers efficiently and enjoyably than any other in the country. All bedrooms have been recently refurbished and banquets for huge numbers are not only catered for but can have a minimum choice of three main courses on all menus. Good facilities for business guests: a high proportion of bedrooms are designated executive, with ISDN lines, fax machines and air conditioning. Conference/banqueting (1200/1000). Business centre. Secretarial services. Video conferencing. No pets. Special offers often available. **Rooms 504**. B&B €143 pps, ss €113. Open all year. Amex, Diners, MasterCard, Visa, Laser.

Ⓑ GUESTHOUSE   # Butlers Town House

44 Lansdowne Road Ballsbridge Dublin 4
Tel: 01 667 4022 Fax: 01 667 3960
Email: info@butlers-hotel.com Web: butlers-hotel.com

On a corner site in Dublin's 'embassy belt' and close to the Lansdowne Road stadium, this large period guesthouse has been extensively refurbished and luxuriously decorated in a Victorian country house style and is a small hotel in all but name. Public rooms include a comfortable drawing room and an attractive conservatory-style breakfast room; an attractive all-day menu is also offered. Rooms are individually decorated and furnished to a high standard, some with four-poster beds. Private parking (guests checking in please note rear entrance for arriving with luggage). Wheelchair accessible. Not suitable for children. No pets. **Rooms 19** (3 superior, 1 disabled, all no smoking). 24 hr room service. Turndown service offered. B&B €95, ss €45; no SC. Closed 21 Dec-5 Jan. Amex, Diners, MasterCard, Visa, Laser. **Directions:** Corner of Lansdowne Road and Shelbourne Road.

RESTAURANT   # Canal Bank Café

146 Upper Leeson Street Dublin 4 **Tel: 01 664 2135**
Fax: 01 664 2719 Email: info@tribeca.ie Web: www.tribeca.ie

Trevor Browne and Gerard Foote's well-known almost-canalside restaurant meets the current demand for quality informal food or 'everyday dining'. Only the best ingredients are used - organic beef and lamb, free-range chicken and a wide variety of fresh fish daily. A user-friendly menu is divided by types of dish rather than by course, making it easy to choose depending on how hungry you are - tasters (bread & dips, olives), small plates (crispy fried calamari with lemon mayonnaise, serrano ham with celeriac slaw & rocket salad), soups, salads, gourmet sandwiches and pasta dishes look after the lighter options, and there are Large Plates for those who need a real feed: chargrilled steak lamb, or fish of the day, for example, or Brooklyn meatloaf with onion gravy & mashed potatoes. There's a good sprinkling of vegetarian dishes, classic desserts - and cheeses are supplied by Sheridan's cheesemongers, of South Anne Street. There's also a terrific separate breakfast menu, offering every possible variation on traditional combinations, plus a wide choice of lighter/healthy options and some classic county house specialities like eggs Benedict or Florentine. A carefully selected, compact wine list includes some interesting bottles - including the choice of house wines. Children welcome. **Seats 70.** Air conditioning. Open 8am-11pm daily (Sun from 11 am, Sun D 6-11). A la carte. House wine €20.95. SC 10% on parties of 6+. Closed 24-28 Dec & Good Fri. Amex, Diners, MasterCard, Visa, Laser. **Directions:** Near Burlington Hotel.

GUESTHOUSE   # Cedar Lodge

98 Merrion Road Ballsbridge Dublin 4
Tel: 01 668 4410 Fax: 01 668 4533
Email: info@cedarlodge.ie Web: www.cedarlodge.ie

Conveniently located near the RDS show grounds and conference centre, this owner-run guesthouse has been recently refurbished and is moderately priced for the area. All of the spacious rooms are double glazed and some are on the ground floor; everything is immaculately clean, and an iron and ironing board are supplied as well as tea and coffee facilities, but some rooms have only a shower and not much in the way of complimentary toiletries. Public rooms are comfortably furnished, with an emphasis on relaxation and creating a 'home from home'. Children over 3 welcome. No pets. **Rooms 15** (some shower only, all no-smoking, 1 for disabled). B&B from about €45pps, ss about €25. Closed 23-28 Dec. Amex, MasterCard, Visa, Laser. **Directions:** Directly opposite British Embassy on Merrion Road.

RESTAURANT   # Ciao Café

Victoria Buildings 1-2 Haddington Road Dublin 4
Tel: 01 799 6326 Fax: 01 799 6366

This smart modern cafe in a converted bank is useful to know for its location and long opening hours - easy to find, it makes a good meeting place. Expect competent contemporary café cooking with an Italian flavour - a signature dish is saffron, prawn & spinach risotto. The Vaughan Johnson wine shop next door is in the same ownership. **Seats 100.** Open Mon-Fri, 7am-10pm; Sat 11am-10pm. Closed Sun. **Directions:** On Baggot Street bridge.

ⓑ ♣RESTAURANT   # Ernie's Restaurant

Mulberry Gardens Donnybrook Dublin 4
Tel: 01 269 3300 Fax: 01 269 3260

féile bia Tucked away down a laneway and easy to miss, this famous restaurant is named after the late Ernie Evans and still owned by the family. The dining-room overlooks a pretty courtyard garden, floodlit at night, though its main feature is the fantastic art collection, mostly of Ernie's beloved Kerry, that over the walls entirely. Recent refurbishment has introduced a lighter, more contemporary tone, although there is still a generous nod to traditional values in both cooking and service. While based on the best local Irish ingredients where possible, the style is international - so you could begin with a Vietnamese spring roll, or Tuscan crostini, then move on to a main course house speciality of panseared Portavogie scallops & Clonakilty black pudding, served with a light curry sauce and spring onions. But the old favourites are still there too - grilled rib-eye steak with roasted vegetables, for example, or rack of Wicklow lamb. Desserts are seriously tempting romantic-sounding updated classics, like apricot and rosewater crème brulée or chocolate and star anise tart, served with with red orange ice cream. Competent cooking, refreshingly traditional presentation and professional old-style service add up to a different kind of experience from most contemporary restaurants, and make it worth seeking out this hidden restaurant; it also offers good value on the set menus, although the à la carte is expensive. Not suitable for children under 10 after 8pm. Air conditioning. **Seats 60**. Open Mon-Sat, L12-2, D 6.15-9.30. Set L from €15.50, Early D €22 (6.15-7.15); Set D €37. A la carte D also available. House wine from €21. SC discretionary. Closed Sun, Mon; 1 week Christmas. Amex, Diners, MasterCard, Visa, Laser. **Directions:** From city, first left after Victoria Avenue; to city, right turn opposite Ulster Bank in Donnybrook.

✓CAFÉ   # Expresso Bar Café

1 St Mary's Road Ballsbridge Dublin 4 **Tel: 01 660 0585**
Fax: 01 660 0585 Email: expressostmarys@hotmail.com

Colourful Cal-Ital food and classic brunches attract many a fan to Ann-Marie Nohl's clean-lined informal restaurant, which is renowned for diligently sourced ingredients that are well-prepared and carefully presented. The lively breakfasts for which they have become famous are served all morning and feature many of the best classic dishes, with a twist: thus a simple poached egg on toast comes with crispy bacon and relish, or cooked-to-order pancakes are served with crispy bacon and maple syrup, and French toast comes with bacon or winter berries and syrup. Lunch and dinner menus tend to favour an international style, but the same high standards apply: whether it's a warm expresso salad (with field mushrooms, crispy pancetta, mixed leaves, baby spinach and organic leaves), char-grilled fillet of black sole with minted new potatoes, watercress salad, shallot & caper butter or a vegetarian organic pasta dish, the concept is simple enough but it's the quality of the ingredient and cooking that make the difference. Weekend brunch is a must. Not suitable for children after 8pm. Air conditioning. ***Also at** IFSC and The Gables Foxrock Village (see entries). **Seats 60**. Open Mon-Fri, 7.30am-9.30pm (B'fst 7.30-11.30, L12-5, D 6-9.30), Sun brunch 10-5. Closed D Sun, D Mon, 25 Dec. Amex, MasterCard, Visa, Laser. **Directions:** Off Baggot Street.

✓ Ⓑ HOTEL   # Four Seasons Hotel

Simmonscourt Road Ballsbridge Dublin 4 **Tel: 01 665 4000**
Fax: 01 665 4880 Web: www.fourseasons.com

féile bia Set in its own gardens in the Royal Dublin Society's 42-acre show grounds, this luxurious hotel enjoys a magnificent site, allowing a sense of spaciousness while also being convenient to the city centre - the scale is generous throughout and there are views of the Wicklow Mountains or Dublin Bay from many bedrooms. Public areas are designed to impress, notably the foyer which is in the grand tradition; the original rather small, traditional cherrywood-panelled Lobby Bar was later joined by a second, larger bar called Ice: deliciously contemporary, it has been well received. Accommodation is very luxurious and the air-conditioned rooms are designed to appeal equally to leisure and business guests. There's great emphasis on service, with twice daily housekeeping service, overnight laundry and dry cleaning, one hour pressing and complimentary overnight shoe shine: everything, in short, that the immaculate traveller requires. Conference and meeting spaces can accommodate corporate events, business meetings and parties in groups from 5-500. But the Spa in the lower level of the hotel is perhaps its most outstanding feature, offering a wide range of amenities including a naturally lit 14m lap pool and adjacent jacuzzi pool, overlooking an outdoor sunken garden. **Rooms 259** (67 suites, 192 executive rooms, 4 floors no-smoking rooms, 1 rooms for disabled). Room rate from about €250 (max. 2 guests). SC included. Off-season special breaks available. Open all year.

Seasons Restaurant: Guests dining in Seasons Restaurant may have an aperitif in the Lobby Bar or the new contemporary Ice Bar - or, as there is no dedicated reception area/cocktail bar for the restaurant, you may go straight to your table - a situation which can make guests a little uncertain about procedures, although well-trained staff are generally very welcoming and attentive. No expense has been spared on the decor, and table settings are excellent, although the room does not perhaps have the elegance expected in a top hotel. A commendable commitment to sourcing the best Irish ingredients is stated on contemporary international menus - citing, for example, organic produce from a West Cork farm, as well as Irish farmhouse cheeses and other speciality foods - so the quality of ingredients is not in question, and the standard of cooking is generally high. While it may not rival the city's top independent restaurants as a cutting edge dining experience, this is a fine hotel restaurant with outstanding service, and a good pricing policy ensuring value for money in luxurious surroundings. An excellent wine list includes some very good wines by the glass. Air conditioning. **Seats 90** (private room, 12). Breakfast 7-11 daily, L 12-2.30 daily, D 6.30-10 daily. Set L from €27; Set D €55; à la carte also available L&D). House wine from €24. No SC.*Less formal dining is available in The Café, open daily 11 am-midnight. Amex, Diners, MasterCard, Visa, Laser. **Directions:** Located on the RDS Grounds on corner of Merrion and Simmonscourt Roads.

✔ WINE BAR/RESTAURANT   **The French Paradox**

53 Shelbourne Road Ballsbridge Dublin 4 **Tel: 01 660 4068**
Fax: 01 663 1026 Email: chapeauwines@eircom.net

On a busy road near the RDS, this inspired and stylish operation brings a new dimension (and a whiff of the south of France) to the concept of wine and food in Dublin. A warm welcome sets the tone for an experience characterised by caring service, knowledge of the (short) menu and - the main emphasis here - the wide range of wines available by the glass. A new ground floor wine bar has greatly increased the available space, and 65 wines are offered by the glass, using a wine sommelier, with inert gas, to keep wines in perfect condition once open. Food is, in theory, secondary here although the fact that a French chef joins the kitchen on an exchange from St Emilion for 4 months every year indicates the real seriousness of intent - and, limited as the choice deliberately is, the quality is exceptional and everyone just loves it. Food is simple - and superb: plates of charcuterie (cured meats from the Basque country and Spain); cured fish; pâtés (French style, with cornichons) and artisan cheeses, individual plates or shared ones for two, served with delicious crusty bread baked twice daily on the premises, and a green salad. If there is a signature dish it is probably the smoked duck breast salad, with quail's eggs, griottine and walnuts, with mixed leaves, but Salade Bill Hogan (Desmond and Gabriel cheese, mixed leaves & extra virgin oil dressing) is also a worthy contender. Given the simplicity of the food, bills can mount alarmingly fast - probably because the seductive atmosphere of the place makes it too tempting to linger over another glass (or two) of wine - but this is quality and worth paying for. Wines offered change regularly (the list is always growing), food can be purchased from the deli-counter to take home - and there's a more extensive menu in the evening, including tapas and, a wonderfully luxurious speciality: foie gras. Not suitable for children after 7pm. **Seats 25**. Air conditioning. Toilets wheelchair accessible. L&D Mon-Thu, 12-3 & 5-9.30; open all day Fri & Sat, 12-9.30. Set L €19.50; Set D €29. A la carte. House wines (4) change monthly. Closed Sun. Amex, Diners, MasterCard, Visa, Laser. **Directions:** Opposite Ballsbridge Post Office.

RESTAURANT

Furama Restaurant

G/F Eirepage House Donnybrook Dublin 4 **Tel: 01 283 0522**
Fax: 01 668 7623 Email: info@furama.ie Web: www.furama.ie

In the sleek black interior of Rodney Mak's long-established restaurant, Freddie Lee, who has been head chef since the restaurant opened in 1989, produces terrific food with an authenticity which is unusual in Ireland. Even the menu does not read like other Chinese restaurants - dishes aren't numbered, for a start, and they are also presented and described individually. They do offer Set Dinners, which are more predictable - and many traditional Chinese dishes on the à la carte menu - but the option is there to try something different. Specialities include steamed seafood, roasted duck and Chinese vegetables. Service, under the supervision of Rodney Mak and manager Stephen Lee, is friendly and efficient. A Special Chinese Menu can be arranged for banqueting with one week's notice (up to 30 people) and outside catering is also available. Parking. **Seats 100** L Sun-Fri, D daily: Various set menus from about €35. A la carte available. House wine from about €17. Air conditioning. SC 10%. Closed 24-26 Dec & Good Fri. Amex, Diners, MasterCard, Visa, Laser. **Directions** Opposite Bective Rugby Ground in Donnybrook, near RTE.

GUESTHOUSE

Glenogra House

64 Merrion Road Ballsbride Dublin 4 **Tel: 01 668 3661**
Fax: 01 668 3698 Email: glenogra@indigo.ie Web: www.glenogra.com

Seamus and Cherry McNamee make a point of providing personal service and good breakfasts at their comfortable Ballsbridge guesthouse. Old and new are carefully combined to create a homelike atmosphere and three new rooms were recently added. Conveniently located for the RDS and within 3 minutes walk of the Sandymount DART station, they also offer good value for the location Children welcome (cots available free of charge). No pets. **Rooms 12** (2 shower only, all no-smoking). B&B €57.50 pps, ss €27.50. Closed Christmas week MasterCard, Visa, Laser. **Directions:** Opposite Four Seasons Hotel, RDS.

✓ Ⓑ HOTEL

Herbert Park Hotel

Ballsbridge Dublin 4 **Tel: 01 667 2200** Fax: 01 667 2595
Email: reservations@herbertparkhotel.ie Web: www.herbertparkhotel.ie

féile bia This large, privately-owned contemporary hotel is attractively located in an 'urban plaza' near the RDS and the public park after which it is named. It is approached over a little bridge, which leads to an underground carpark and, ultimately, to a chic lower ground foyer and the lift up to the main lobby. Public areas on the ground floor are impressively light and spacious, and the bright and modern style is also repeated in the bedrooms, which have views over Ballsbridge and Herbert Park and are stylishly designed and well-finished with a high standard of amenities, including air conditioning and individual temperature control. Snacks and light lunches are available all day in The Terrace lounge (8am-10pm). Team building, jazz events, golf packages and special breaks are all offered, and this hotel is also reasonably priced for the standard of accommodation and facilities offered. Conference/banqueting (120/150). Business centre. Secretarial services. Video conferencing. Gym. Garden. Children welcome (under 2 free in parents' room, cots available free of charge, playground). Pets by arrangement. **Rooms 153** (2 suites, 1 junior suite 27 executive rooms, 65 no-smoking, 7 disabled). Lift. B&B €90pps. SS €90 No SC. Open all year.

Pavilion Restaurant: In a bright, elegant, contemporary room overlooking garden terrace (where tables can be set up in fine weather), wide-ranging international menus are offered with, perhaps, a slight leaning towards fish and seafood: herb roasted seabass with spiced green lentil stew & cabernet sauvignon beurre blanc is a signature dish. Prices are reasonable, when seen in comparison with nearby competition, and the lunch menu offers particularly good value. **Seats 150**. Breakfast 7-10 (Sat & Sun to 10.30, Sun from 8); L 12.30-2.30 (Sun to 3); D Tue-Sat 5.30-9.30). Set L €23.50 (Sun L €33); 2-course D €19.70, otherwise à la carte. House wine €21. Closed D Sun, D Mon; also D on Good Fri & bank hols. Amex, Diners, MasterCard, Visa. **Directions:** Shortly before RDS heading out of city.

B HOTEL   # Jurys Ballsbridge Hotel

Pembroke Road Ballsbridge Dublin 4 **Tel: 01 660 5000** Fax: 01 660 5540
Email: ballsbridge@jurysdoyle.com Web: wwwjurysdoyle.com

féile bia Centrally located in the Ballsbridge area, and always busy, Jurys has the distinction of being both an international hotel providing high levels of service to business and leisure guests, while remaining a popular local hotel for Dubliners. Rooms and service are of a high standard, and the facilities offered by the hotel generally are excellent - Jurys was the first Dublin hotel to have a swimming pool; the leisure centre currently also has a whirlpool, sauna and gym and there's a health & beauty salon, hairdresser and newsagent on site. There are two restaurants, **Raglans** (Seats 120. Air conditioning. Open for L&D daily. Toilets wheelchair accessible.) and the informal **Coffee Dock**; two bars: the larger **Dubliner Bar** is a popular meeting place. Conference/banqueting (850/600). Business centre, secretarial services. No pets. Special offers often available. **Rooms 303** (3 suites, 300 executive rooms, 150 no-smoking, 2 for disabled). Lifts. B&B from about €155pps, ss about €120. SC12.5%. Open all year. Amex, Diners, MasterCard, Visa, Laser. **Directions:** About 11 km from the airport & 1 km from city centre.

B HOTEL   # Jurys Ballsbridge The Towers

Lansdowne Road Dublin 4 **Tel: 01 667 0033** Fax: 01 660 5540
Email: towers@jurysdoyle.com Web: www.jurysdoyle.com

féile bia The Towers is a quieter, more exclusive section of the main Jurys Hotel in Ballsbridge, a hotel within a hotel located to the rear of the main block with its own entrance on Lansdowne Road and a high level of security - entry to the inner foyer and thus to accommodation is by card key. Business and corporate guests are well looked after and constant maintenance and upgrading, plus a high level of service from a committed and well-trained staff, keep this hotel up with the leaders in an increasingly competitive market. The many little extras that make The Towers especially desirable for business guests include complimentary tea, coffee and biscuits, served all day in a seating area known as the Hospitality Lounge, where guests can avail of a complimentary light breakfast (included in the room rate), and complimentary drinks are served, 6-7pm Monday-Thursday. Rooms are spacious, with queen/king size beds, dedicated work desk and lamp, luxurious bathrooms and all the usual 'executive' extras. There is direct access to the main hotel from The Towers, and use of all its amenities. Business centre. **Rooms 107** (4 suites, 103 executive, 50 no-smoking, 2 for disabled). Lift. B&B from about €175 pps, ss about €140, C12.5%. Open all year. Amex, Diners, MasterCard, Visa, Laser. **Directions:** Approx 11 km from the airport, 1 km from city centre.

B HOTEL   # Jurys Montrose Hotel

Stillorgan Road Dublin 4 **Tel: 01 269 3311** Fax: 01 269 1164
Email: montrose@jurysdoyle.com Web: www.jurysdoyle.com

féile bia This south-city hotel near the University College campus has undergone extensive refurbishment, including completely updating the exterior; more rooms are now offered to executive standard, and some are wheelchair friendly. All rooms have quite good facilities and there's 12 hour room service and also laundry/dry cleaning services. Executive rooms also have a modem line and complimentary newspaper and business magazines. Although conference facilities are not extensive (max. 70 delegates), there's a business centre, seven meeting rooms and free parking, making this an attractive venue for small events. Children welcome (cots available) **Rooms 180** (35 executive). B&B from about €100pps, ss about about €75; weekend specials available. Open all year. Amex, Diners, MasterCard, Visa. **Directions:** On Stillorgan dual carriageway near RTE studios.

RESTAURANT   # Kites Restaurant

15-17 Ballsbridge Terrace Ballsbridge Dublin 4
Tel: 01 660 7415 Fax: 01 660 5978 Email: kites@eircom.net

Lots of natural light with white painted walls, dark wooden fittings and a rich, dark carpet create a good first impression at this split-level Ballsbridge restaurant, and a mix of diners (Chinese and non-Chinese, business and pleasure) gives the place a nice buzz. The cuisine is a combination of Cantonese, Szechuan, Peking and Thai - predominantly Cantonese - and menus range from the standard set meals to a decent list of specials. For the indecisive, a house platter of appetisers makes a good beginning. Duckling and seafood are specialities: half a crispy aromatic duck comes with fresh steaming pancakes, while a combination dish of salt & pepper jumbo king prawns and a stir-fry is interesting. Stir-fried lamb with ginger & spring onion (one of the few Peking dishes) is to be recommended. Desserts are not a strong point, but courteous, good humoured and charming service adds considerably to the experience. **Seats 100** (private room, 100). Air conditioning. L daily 12.30-2, D daily 6.30-11.30. Set L €18,50, set D €35; also à la carte. House wine from €18.40. SC 10%. Closed 25-26 Dec. Good Fri. Amex, Diners, MasterCard, Visa, Laser. **Directions:** In the heart of Ballsbridge.

RESTAURANT   # Langkawi Malaysian Restaurant

46 Upper Baggot Street Dublin 4 **Tel: 01 668 2760**
Fax: 01 668 2760 Email: hosey@indigo.ie

Proprietor-chef Alex Hosey uses genuine imported ingredients at this long-established restaurant, to produce dishes with authentic Malaysian flavours. Three distinct national cuisines - Malay, Chinese, and Indian - influence Malaysian cooking, and the result is an usual range of dishes which can be seriously hot and fiery, or much more subtle. Wheelchair access. Children welcome. **Seats 50.** L & D Mon-Sat. Closed Sun. Amex, Diners, MasterCard, Visa, Laser. **Directions:** Beside Searsons pub.

Ⓑ RESTAURANT   # The Lobster Pot

9 Ballsbridge Terrace Ballsbridge Dublin 4 **Tel: 01 660 9170**
Fax: 01 668 0025 Web: www.thelobsterpot.ie

On the first floor of a redbrick Ballsbridge terrace, conspicuously located near the Herbert Park Hotel - and just a few minutes walk from all the major Ballsbridge hotels - this long-established restaurant has lost none of its charm or quality over the years. The whole team - owner Thomas Crean, restaurant manager (and sommelier) John Rigby and head chef Don McGuinness - have been working here together since 1980 and the system is running very sweetly. How good it is to see old favourites like dressed Kilmore Quay crab, home-made chicken liver pate and fresh prawn bisque on the menu, along with fresh prawns Mornay and many other old friends, including kidneys turbigo and game in season. The menu is a treat to read and there's also a daily fish tray display for specials - dishes are explained and diners are encouraged to choose their own combinations. All this and wonderfully old-fashioned service too, including advice from John Rigby on the best wine to match your meal. If only there were more places like this - long may it last. L Mon-Fri, 12.30-2, D Mon-Sat, 6.30-10.30. SC 12.5%. Closed L Sat, all Sun, 24 Dec-4 Jan, bank hols. Amex, Diners, MasterCard, Visa, Laser.

B GUESTHOUSE **Merrion Hall**

54 Merrion Road Ballsbridge Dublin 4
Tel: 01 668 1426 Fax: 01 668 4280
Email: merrionhall@iol.ie Web: halpinsprivatehotels.com

This Edwardian style townhouse opposite the RDS is handy to the DART (suburban rail) and makes a good base for business or leisure, offering great value in comparison with hotels in the area. Major renovation has taken place over the last year and an additional 12 rooms were added; some rooms have four-posters and the suites have air conditioning and whirlpool spa baths. There's a well-stocked library and a comfortable big drawing room where an all day menu is available (also 24 hour room service), with a wine selection to complement it. Off-street parking at the back. Small conference/private parties (50/50). Garden. Children welcome (under 3s free in parents' room, cots available free of charge). No pets. **Rooms 34** (6 suites,14 executive, 20 no smoking, 2 disabled). Lift. 24 hr room service. Turndown service. B&B €76 pps, ss €35. Drawing Room/room service menu available 7am-9pm daily; house wine €25. Open all year. Amex, Diners, MasterCard, Visa, Laser. **Directions:** Opposite the RDS in Ballsbridge.

BAR **Merrion Inn**

188 Merrion Road Dublin 4 **Tel: 01 269 3816**
Fax: 01 269 7669 Email: themerrioninn@o2.ie

féile bia The McCormacks are a great pub family (see separate entry for their Mounttown establishment) and this attractive contemporary pub on the main road between Dublin and Dun Laoghaire has always had a name for making an effort with food. At lunchtime, a buffet offers a selection of hot main courses as well as a wide range of salads; it's a well-organised operation and details (such as having chilled drinks to hand) are well-planned, although the standard can be inconsistent. In the evening the style moves up a notch or two, with a menu including the likes of warm crispy bacon & croûton salad, pastas and substantial main courses such as chargrilled sirloin steak (served with a choice of sauces and salads) as well as some good fish dishes, vegetarian options and the day's specials. Homely desserts always include home-made apple pie. A partially covered heated patio area is available for smokers. Bar food served daily 12-10 (L12-3, D 3.30-10). Buffet / à la carte. House wine from about €16.95. Closed 25 Dec & Good Fri. Amex, Diners, MasterCard, Visa, Laser. **Directions:** Opposite St. Vincent's Hospital.

B HOTEL **Mespil Hotel**

Mespil Road Dublin 4 **Tel: 01 488 4600** Fax: 01 667 1244
Email: mespil@leehotels.ie Web: www.leehotels.ie

féile bia This fine modern hotel enjoys an excellent location in the Georgian district of the city, overlooking the Grand Canal and within easy walking distance of St Stephen's Green and all the city centre attractions. Public areas are spacious and elegant in an easy contemporary style and bright, generously-sized bedrooms are comfortably furnished with good amenities including fax/modem connection and voicemail. Dining options include the 100-seater restaurant 'Glaze Restaurant, which is open for lunch and dinner daily and offers a well-balanced choice of traditional and contemporary fare based on carefully sourced ingredients at fair prices (main courses from about €12), and the Terrace Bar, where lunch and light snacks are served. The hotel takes pride in the friendliness and efficiency of the staff and is moderately priced for the area; special breaks offer especially good value. Small meeting and seminars (25). Children welcome (Under 12 free in parents' room; cots available free of charge, baby sitting arranged). No pets. **Rooms 256**. Lift. Room service (limited hours). Room rate €150 (max. 3 guests). Closed 24-26 Dec. Amex, Diners, MasterCard, Visa, Laser. **Directions:** At Baggot St. Bridge.

✓ Ⓑ ♣ RESTAURANT · **O'Connells Restaurant**

Bewleys Hotel Merrion Road Dublin 4 **Tel: 01 647 3304**
Fax: 01 647 3398 Email: info@oconnellsballsbridge.com
Web: www.oconnellsballsbridge.com

féile bia Located in a large semi-basement under Bewley's Hotel, this remarkable restaurant continues to strive for the highest standards: what you will get here is quality ingredient driven modern Irish cooking - simple food, with natural flavours, often emphasised by cooking in a special wood-fired oven. It has dark wood-panelled walls and floor to ceiling windows overlooking a courtyard used for al fresco dining in summer - arriving by the courtyard steps rather than through the hotel helps the ambience considerably. Recently Rosemary Kearney, author of 'Healthy Gluten Free Eating', has joined as a consultant, and the goal is for O'Connell's to become Ireland's most coeliac-friendly restaurant. Menus are a hymn to quality ingredients, stating that pork, beef, eggs and catering supplies are sourced using Bord Bia's Quality Assurance Schemes, and also naming a number of individual artisan producers and suppliers, often in dishes that have become house specialities - typically a starter salad is made with Fingal Ferguson's Gubbeen smoked bacon, from Schull in Co. Cork, an East Cork smoked fish plate comprises a selection from Frank Hederman's smokery in Cobh and smoked salmon from Bill Casey at Shanagarry (both Co. Cork) and beef comes from the Irish Hereford Prime Beef Society, Co. Offaly and Slaney Foods, Co. Wexford. Irish farmhouse cheese matured on the premises, is served with home-made biscuits and excellent classic desserts range from deliciously homely sugar crust apple tart served with lightly whipped cream to a light summery strawberry délice or (genuinely home-made ice creams. A highly informative wine list, which includes an extensive selection of by-the-glass and 24 house wines, reflects the same philosophy and gives details of vintage, region, grape, grower/shipper, merchant, taster's notes, suggested food partnership, bottle size (including some magnums) and price - invariably moderate for the quality offered - for every wine on the list; even the house water, Tipperary, (served by the carafe at Ireland's lowest price, €1.50 per litre) gets 'the treatment' (region, taster' notes...) Service can seem to be under pressure, even the cooking occasionally uneven, but this remains an amazing restaurant, offering meals based on the very highest quality ingredients at very reasonable prices. **Seats 172** (summer courtyard 60). Air conditioning. Buffet L daily 12.30-2.30 (Sun to 3). D daily 6-10 (Sun to 9.30). Early D from €19.75 (6-7pm). Set D from €25. Also à la carte D available. SC discretionary (10% on parties of 6+).Hpuse wines from €18.95. Closed 25-26 Dec. Amex, Diners, MasterCard, Visa, Laser. **Directions:** Off Merrion Road at Simmonscourt Road, opposite the Four Seasons Hotel.

BAR · **Ocean Bar**

Charlotte Quay Dock Ringsend Road Dublin 4 **Tel: 01 668 8862**
Fax: 01 6677435 Email: andyatocean@hotmail.com

Dramatically situated on the water's edge with lots of glass on two sides, an extensive outdoor patio seating to take full advantage of views over the Grand

Canal Basin, Ocean has great atmosphere and makes an excellent meeting place for people of all ages. The location, style and friendliness of the staff all make it a great place to relax - and a particularly good choice for visitors to the city. There's a choice of three bars and dining areas and, while menus offering a wide range of contemporary favourites may not contain many surprises, food is freshly prepared and competently cooked - and the ambience is exceptional. Ingredients are carefully sourced, and it would be interesting to see details on menus. Tables are laid as you order - simple cutlery, paper napkins - and food is served modern bistro style on big white plates. Food with an international tone is pleasant rather than outstanding, but what makes for a special feeling is the location - and the Sunday jazz brunches are a particular success. Conference/banqueting. Children welcome. **Seats 180** (private room, 80; outdoor seating, 80). Air conditioning. Toilets wheelchair accessible. Food served daily, 12 -10. House wine €21. Closed 25 Dec, Good Fri. Amex, MasterCard, Visa, Laser. **Directions:** On Pearse Street/Ringsend Road bridge.

RESTAURANT   # The Orchid Szechuan Restaurant

120 Pembroke Road Ballsbridge Dublin 4 **Tel: 01 660 0629**

This long established restaurant has a faithful following – not surprisingly, as the food is of very high quality and provides for both conservative and adventurous tastes, whilst the service is admirably efficient and friendly. Once you have braved the entrance (which would benefit from refurbishment) the interior is warm, welcoming and typically Chinese with smoky mirrors and black-painted walls decorated with simple floral designs. Fresh flowers and linen napkins set the tone for clearly presented menus that offer many Szechuan specialities but also Cantonese some and even a few Thai dishes. Try the light and crispy deep-fried scallops, served with a simple light soy dip, and follow with Yin-yang Prawn – two prawn dishes (one hot and spicy, the other a mild fresh flavoured stirfry) served side-by-side – both delicious and pretty – or popular roast duck in plum sauce, prettily garnished with an orchid.. 'House dinners' are good-value (each about €35; one is dedicated entirely to Dim Sum), and include some 8 dishes as well as jasmine tea or (very good) coffee... The wine list is on the pricey side, but offers a good choice. MasterCard, Visa. **Directions:** Pembroke Road leads onto Baggot St. On the right hand side going towards town.

B GUESTHOUSE   # Pembroke Townhouse

90 Pembroke Road Ballsbridge Dublin 4 **Tel: 01 660 0277**
Fax: 01 660 0291 Email: info@pembroketownhouse.ie
Web: www.pembroketownhouse.ie

féile bia Conveniently located close to the RDS and Lansdowne Road, this fine period guesthouse has all the amenities usually expected of an hotel. There's a drawing room and study for residents' use and comfortably furnished, individually designed rooms have a safe and fax facilities (on request) for business guests, as well as direct dial phone, cable television, tea/coffee facilities and trouser press (but no tea / coffee making facilities). Breakfast is the only meal served, but it offers dishes like sautéed lambs liver served on a bed of sautéed onions and topped with bacon as well as the traditional cooked breakfast. When arriving by car, it is best to go the carpark at the back, as you can then take a lift with your luggage (avoiding heavy traffic and steep steps to the front door). Private parking at rear. **Rooms 48** (7 suites, 41 executive, shower only, 4 disabled, 20 no smoking). Lift. 24 hr room service. B&B about €98 pps, ss €33. Amex, Diners, MasterCard, Visa, Laser. **Directions:** Pembroke Road leads onto Baggot St. On the right hand side going towards town.

✓ Ⓑ HOTEL/RESTAURANT   Radisson SAS St Helen's

Stillorgan Road Dublin 4 **Tel: 01 218 6000** Fax: 01 218 6030
Email: info.dublin@radissonsas.com Web: www.radissonsas.com

 Set in formal gardens just south of Dublin's city centre, with views across Dublin Bay to Howth Head, the fine 18th century house at the heart of this impressive new hotel was once a private residence. Careful restoration and imaginative modernisation have created interesting public areas, including the Orangerie bar and a pillared ballroom with minstrels' gallery and grand piano. Compact bedrooms, in a new four-storey block adjoining the main building, all have garden views (some of the best rooms also have balconies) and air conditioning, and are well-equipped for business guests. Rooms are comfortably furnished to a high standard in contemporary style, with neat bathrooms. Light meals are offered all day in the **Orangerie Bar**. Conference/banqueting (350/220). Fitness centre; beauty salon. Garden; snooker. Ample parking. Children welcome (Under 17s free in parents' room; cots available, baby sitting arranged). **Rooms 151** (25 suites, 70 no-smoking, 8 for disabled). Room rate from €165 (max. 3 guests). Open all year.

Talavera: In four interconnecting rooms in the lower ground floor, this informal Italian restaurant is decorated in warm Mediterranean colours and, with smart wooden tables dressed with slips, modern cutlery, fresh flowers and Bristol blue water glasses, it is atmospheric when candle-lit at night. A well-balanced menu offers a balanced choice of dishes inspired by tradition and tailored to the modern palate. Head chef Cian Carlo Anselmi is producing very good food here; he specialises in authentic dishes from Tuscany and Basilicata, and a fine antipasti buffet sets the tone for an unusually pleasing dining experience, where skilful cooking is matched by a good atmosphere and caring service from friendly, efficient staff. Risotto - so popular, yet rarely cooked correctly - is a speciality; a rather exotic version with asparagus & truffle scent is quoted as a signature dish and another, with smoked chicken breast, butter squash and fresh sage, was singled out for praise on a recent visit by the Guide. The wine list offers a strong selection of regional Italian bottles to match the food. **Seats 110**. Air conditioning, toilets wheelchair accessible. D daily 7-10.30. Set menus from €35; also a la carte. Amex, Diners, MasterCard, Visa, Laser. **Directions:** Just 3 miles south from the city centre, on N11.

✓ Ⓑ GUESTHOUSE   Raglan Lodge

10 Raglan Road Ballsbridge Dublin 4
Tel: 01 660 6697 Fax: 01 660 6781

Helen Moran's elegant mid-19th century residence is peacefully situated near the US embassy, yet convenient to the city centre - and reasonably priced too. Well-proportioned, high-ceilinged reception rooms are reminiscent of more leisurely times and the en-suite bedrooms are exceptionally comfortable. Raglan Lodge is renowned for the high level of comfort and service provided, and particularly for outstanding breakfasts: a white-clothed sideboard displays freshly squeezed orange juice, fresh fruits and compôtes, home-made muesli and cereals, creamy porridge, yoghurt and cheeses, then a choice of kippers, scrambled eggs with smoked salmon or a fine traditional breakfast delivered piping hot under silver dome covers - a great start to the day. (Raglan Lodge was the Dublin winner of our Denny Irish Breakfast awards in 2001). Theatre reservations can be arranged. Children welcome (under 3s free in parents' room; cot available without charge). No pets. Garden. **Rooms 7** (3 shower only, 3 no smoking). B&B €69.85 pps, ss €12.80. Closed 1 week Nov, Christmas/New Year, Easter week. Amex, Diners, MasterCard, Visa. **Directions:** Follow signs for South city to Baggot Street, turn right on to Raglan Road, Raglan Lodge is on the left.

✓ Ⓑ ♣ RESTAURANT

Roly's Bistro

7 Ballsbridge Terrace Ballsbridge Dublin 4
Tel: 01 668 2611 Fax: 01 660 8535
Email: ireland@rolysbistro.ie Web: www.rolysbistro.ie

féile bia This bustling Ballsbridge bistro has been a smash hit since the day it opened. Chef-patron Colin O'Daly (one of Ireland's most highly regarded chefs) and head chef Paul Cartwright present imaginative, reasonably priced seasonal menus at lunch and an early dinner, and also an evening à la carte menu. A lively style is based on Colin's classical French training but it also gives more than a passing nod to Irish traditions, world cuisines and contemporary styles. Carefully sourced ingredients are the sound foundation for cooking that never disappoints - Dublin Bay Prawns are always in demand and may be served Neuberg (a speciality that comes with a tian of mixed long grain and wild rice), or in prawn cocktail, when using fresh Dublin Bay prawns moves that old favourite up into a different class - or, eventually, in the house prawn bisque. Traditional Kerry lamb pie is another favourite, served with celeriac and thyme (a lovely dish although, it must be admitted, some way from its rural origins) but the cooking is always innovative, colourful and appealing. Wholesomely delicious puddings are worth saving a little space for, and they always have a great cheese board, served with pickled vegetables. Service is efficient but discreet, cooking is invariably excellent, everyone loves the buzz, and Rolys has always given great value for money - they were the first to offer a good range of wines at an accessible price, for example, and famously ran a whole selection at £10; now they offer a House Selection at €20.95 which doesn't have quite the same ring to it but it's a good deal all the same. Offering quality with good value has been the philosophy of the restaurant from the outset and it continues to fulfil this promise well. **Seats 140.** Air conditioning. L daily 12-3, D daily 6-10 Set L €18.50; Early D (Mon-Thu, 6-6.45); L&D also à la carte. SC10%. Closed 4 days at Christmas. Amex, Diners, MasterCard, Visa.

Ⓑ HOTEL/RESTAURANT

Schoolhouse Hotel

2-8 Northumberland Road Ballsbridge Dublin 4 **Tel: 01 667 5014**
Fax: 01 667 5015 Email: reservations@schoolhousehotel.com
Web: www.schoolhousehotel.com

féile bia Dating back to its opening in 1896 as a school, this canalside building at Mount Street Bridge has seen many changes, culminating in its opening in 1998 as one of Dublin's trendiest small hotels. The Inkwell Bar is always a-buzz with young business people of the area, and the classroom theme continues to the restaurant, Satchels. The dining style is informal at the Schoolhouse, but executive chef Kevin Arundel and his team are delivering very good contemporary cooking here. Rooms are finished to a high standard, with air conditioning, power showers and the usual amenities expected of a quality hotel. Small conference (20). Wheelchair access. Parking. Children welcome (Under 5s free in parents room; cots available). No pets. Lift. **Rooms 31** (15 no-smoking, 2 for disabled). B&B from about €90ps. SC discretionary. Closed 24-26 Dec. Amex, Diners, MasterCard, Visa. **Directions:** Southbound from Trinity College, at the end of Mount St. across the Grand Canal.

RESTAURANT

The Courtyard Café

1 Belmont Avenue Donnybrook Dublin 4
Tel: 01 283 0407

Donnybrook restaurants have a tendency to discretion and The Courtyard is typical - entered through an arched gateway, then a courtyard which is set up with tables in fine weather, the restaurant itself is cocooned away at the back of the site and seems a long way from the nearby roads. Having been the home

91

of several quite prominent establishments in recent years, it seems now to have found favour with a steady local clientele who appreciate the surroundings - spacious, quite plush - good cooking in the international style, and fairly reasonable prices. **Directions:** Behind Madigan's pub.

 GUESTHOUSE   # Waterloo House

8-10 Waterloo Road Ballsbridge Dublin 4
Tel: 01 660 1888 Fax: 01 667 1955
Email: waterloohouse@eircom.ie Web: waterloohouse.ie

Evelyn Corcoran has combined two Georgian townhouses to make a luxurious and reasonably priced base in a quiet location very convenient to the city centre and also Lansdowne Road (rugby), RDS (equestrian & exhibitions) and some of the city's most famous restaurants. With ISDN lines, a conservatory and garden, Waterloo House is equally attractive to the business or leisure traveller. Excellent breakfasts are a high point of any stay. Wheelchair access. Own parking. Children welcome (under 4 free in parents' room, cot available). No pets. **Rooms 17** (1 disabled). Lift. B&B about €60 pps, ss about €20. Closed Christmas. MasterCard, Visa, Laser. **Directions:** South on Stephens Green or Merrion Row for 1 mile. First turn right after Baggot Street Bridge.

DUBLIN 6

Dublin 6 - a densely populated series of villages south of the Grand Canal - is a fascinating place to stay, or visit for a meal, and especially well-endowed with restaurants, interesting delicatessens and food-to-go. In Rathgar, take time call in to **The Vintry** wine shop and also Thomas Cronin's delightful shop **The Gourmet Store** (497 0365; the window display will draw you in anyway especially coming up to Christmas). In nearby Rathmines, there's also plenty of interest to food-lovers: **Bombay Pantry** offers great Indian food, while, over towards Ranelagh, **Mortons** "Fresh Food Emporium" on Dunville Avenue is a supermarket with a difference, offering only the best - and with service to match - and there's **The Best of Italy**, for Italian foods, including a deli; also on Dunville Avenue, there's an outstanding wine shop, **Brechin Watchorn** resist this if you can! Loversl of Chinese food will find a branch of the upmarket Chinese restaurant chain, **Wongs**, nearby at 7 Sandford Road (Tel 01 496 7722) Locals also swear by **Ruen Thai** ("authentic - best value in Ireland"), and a new branch of the popular **Café Bar Deli** (Tel 01 496 1886) opened just before the Guide went to press (see Dublin 2 entry). On a slightly different tack, garden lovers should make a point of visiting **The Dillon Garden** (45 Sandyford Road Ranelagh; Tel 01 497 1308) open March-September; days vary.

*Nearby **Dublin 6W** is a peculiarity of the city's postal system which might be unremarkable except that two exceptional butchers shops are in the district **Downey's** of Terenure Cross (organic meats, duck, geese and unusual meats are all to be found here) and **O'Toole's**, of Terenure Road North, who spearheaded the organic campaign and are the city's leading suppliers of organic meat; they have a second shop in Glasthule (see South County Dublin).

RESTAURANT   # Antica Venezia

97 Ashfield Road Ranelagh Dublin 6 **Tel: 01 497 411**

A real throw-back in time and refreshingly so: this entirely Italian-run restaurant has a classic Italian 70's interior with stained wooden floors and ceiling beams, Venetian trompe-l'oeil scenes on the walls and candlewax-dripped Chianti bottles on every table. The food is also traditional Italian, with a menu that could easily date back to the Seventies too: old-fashioned favourites like stuffed mushrooms and antipasto misto of Italian meats are followed by classics like chicken breast with mushroom and white wine sauce, salmon with lemon butter sauce, pork with marsala sauce and a choice of pasta dishes and pizzas, with predictable but good desserts such as banoffi, tiramisu and cassata as well as a selection of ice creams. Consistently good food, with service that is laid back but attentive - a perfect recipe for a popular neighbourhood restaurant. **Seats 45**. Reservations advised. Air conditioning. Children welcome. D daily, 5-11.30, L Fri only 12-2.30. A la carte. House wine €18.50. SC discretionary, but 10% on parties of 6+. MasterCard, Visa, Laser.

RESTAURANT **Bijou Bistro**

47 Highfiield Road Rathgar Dublin 6 **Tel: 01 496 1518**
Fax: 01 491 1410 Email: bijourestaurant@eircom.net

An intimate restaurant with four smallish rooms on two floors and a distinctly French atmosphere with curtained doorways, colourful turn-of-the-century style paintings, frilled lampshades and vases of lilies - and charming, efficient staff. Well made breads accompany an innovative menu with a dozen or so choices on each course and several fish specialities each evening (typically chargrilled loin of swordfish with chive mash and spiced chickpea salsa); other specialities include risotto of spiced cajun chicken with parmesan herb salad, while more traditional tastes will welcome dishes like pork fillet with sage & bacon potato cake, apple & raisin chutney and Vermouth cream, cooked with accuracy and style - and served on plates decorated with a colourful art deco flourish. Finish with classic desserts or an Irish cheese selection with muscat grapes. A good wine list, plus a couple of weekly specials. Booking at this popular neighbourhood restaurant is essential. Children welcome. **Seats 70** (private room, 14). Air conditioning. D daily, 5-11, L Sun only 12-3. Set Sun L about €20, early D about €20 (Mon-Fri, 5-6.45); wines from about €16. SC discretionary. Closed Christmas/ New Year. MasterCard, Visa, Laser. **Directions:** Rathgar crossroads.

RESTAURANT **Diep Noodle Bar**

19 Ranelagh Dublin 6 **Tel: 01 497 6550** Fax: 01 497 6549
Email: info@diep.net Web: www.diep.net

Younger sister to Diep le Shaker off Fitzwilliam Square, this colourful little place quickly gained a reputation as the in place for discerning young things to meet. It has a great atmosphere, chic, clean-lined decor and - as if a mixture of Thai and Vietnamese food weren't fashionable enough - a cocktail bar too. Closely packed tables reach a long way back down the long narrow room, and you can be fairly sure it will be packed, any night of the week, which adds to the ambience. Service is a strong point from the moment you arrive and the menu - which offers plenty of noodle dishes, and much else besides - points out that no monosodium glutamate is used and that food arrives, Asian style, just as soon as it's ready, rather than in courses. Eschewing MSG is a big bonus, allowing lots of different natural flavours and textures to come through in very fresh food that seems to be made for sharing. Whether the freefall attitude to meal structure works is, perhaps, more a matter of luck - if you order well, it's fine and adds to the fun, but you could end up with too much or too little of one thing, or a feeling that dishes are arriving in the wrong order. Individual dishes are not expensive - a classic Phad Thai, for example, is around €13.50, Tom Yaam Goong (hot & sour soup with prawns) €6.50, Vietnamese noodle soups all around €9-10, and curries and stir-fries in the €15-16 region; but by the time you've had a couple of cocktails, ordered a bit of everything and had an Asian beer or a bottle of wine with your food it can add up surprisingly fast. There's a sense of excitement to this little restaurant - it's a place to have fun; so first time out, order carefully - old hands know how to work the menu. Open 7 days: L 2.30-5.30, D 5.30-11.30. 2/3 course Set L. €11.50/14.50. Early D from €24.50 (5.30-7.30); also à la carte. Wine from €17.50. Closed Mon to 5.30, 24-31 Dec (re-opens 1 Jan at 5.30). Amex, MasterCard, Visa, Laser.

RESTAURANT   **The Glass Onion**

25 Dunville Avenue Dublin 6 **Tel: 01 496 5445** Fax: 01 496 5442
Email: reservations@glassonion.ie Web: www.glassonion.ie

The Glass Onion quickly earned a loyal local following in this well-heeled residential area. Fashionably dark walnut and neutral shades of beiges and aubergines, quality furniture and discreet lighting create a pleasant and welcoming ambience - and the restaurant (which is on two levels) opens onto a south-facing patio with water feature at the back. Head chef and part-owner Grainne Walsh's menus offer admirably simple, well sourced food with natural flavours, and modern renditions of traditional dishes such as rack of lamb with a minted broad bean purée and a simple jus, or char-grilled calf's liver with caramelised onions and sweet potatoes with a thyme jus) sit comfortably beside more contemporary dishes like seared scallops with papardelle, artichoke hearts and gremolata. Desserts tend to be classic and comforting: bread and butter pudding with raspberries, crumbles (with cranberries, perhaps), crème brulées, chocolate cakes... Attention to detail combined with generally excellent cooking of quality ingredients, generous portions and professional, charming service, make this restaurant a popular and good-value choice. Its popularity ensures a good buzz at all times, even on weekdays, but dinner service kicks off as early as 6pm, so there's still a fair chance of getting a last minute reservation. **Seats 54.** Open all day Mon-Fri (Breakfast 8-11.30, L 12-5); D Tue-Sat 6-10. Sat Brunch 9-5, Sun Brunch 10-5. Amex, MasterCard, Visa, Laser. **Directions:** Heart of Ranelagh village.

✓ Ⓑ RESTAURANT   **Mint**

47 Ranelagh Village Dublin 6 **Tel: 01 497 8655** Fax: 01 282 7018

This striking, glass-fronted restaurant is stylish and minimalist, with a view of the busy street and décor in a mixture of dark wood, pale walls, glass and polished steel that works well with small square tables and contemporary metal and leather - a small area used well, giving a feeling of spaciousness. Friendly, attentive staff are very professional, immediately bringing you to a very smart table with white linen and quality glassware, cutlery and beautiful crockery. There is no room for a reception area, which is a small downside, but all the niceties are observed and a tasty little amuse-bouche from the chef quickly settles new arrivals in. Head chef Oliver Dunne is one of the most exciting younger chefs in Ireland today and his menus - which include set lunch and early dinners which are exceptionally good value - are ambitious yet simply stated, and offer about half a dozen choices per course on the à la carte; many are luxurious, but this chef also takes inexpensive everyday ingredients and creates something wonderful with them, which takes great skill. A starter of confit duck, foie gras and root vegetables, served with a wild mushroom and bean salad and fig jelly, is a good example of the style- also an unusual main course of braised lamb neck, with pomme purée, red pepper purée and red pepper jus. Desserts - which, refreshingly, tend to favour fruit - include a number of the intriguing trios based on a single ingredient beloved of top chefs: caramelised mango, with mango and pineapple salad and mango sorbet is a pretty example here. A cheeseboard is also offered - surprisingly, restricted to French cheeses; this is a pity considering the range of wonderful Irish artisan cheeses to choose from, even though 'modern French cuisine' is the declared house style. With excellent service and a wine list well matched to the aspirations of the establishment, Mint now takes its place as one of Dublin's leading restaurants. Children welcome, until 8pm. **Seats 45.** Reservations advised. L Tue-Sun, 12-3; D Tue-Sun, 6-10. Set 1-3 course L €15-25; Early D €27 (6-6.45); D also à la carte. Wines from €19.Closed Mon, all bank holidays. Amex, MasterCard, Visa, Laser. **Directions:** Centre of Ranelagh Village.

RESTAURANT
Ouzo

1 Sandford Road Ranelagh Dublin 6
Tel: 01 491 2253 Fax: 01 667 0780

The entrance to Ouzo is not obvious as it's somewhat concealed beside the doors to McSorley's pub. Once found however, you're in for a treat. Two large rooms, basically furnished and decorated, make up the buzzing restaurant: no frills, but this is reflected in the price list. Though steaks are equally popular, it is the high quality and superfresh fish (caught by their own Dingle-based, 21-foot fishing boat MFV Phoenix) that draws the attention: everything that comes out of head chef Shaun Paul Brady's kitchen is cooked to perfection, and served at very reasonable prices. But there's even more: the service reflects that genuine (but today not always observed) 'old-fashioned' Irish hospitality. Brilliant. ***Also at** 11, Upper Baggot Street, Dublin 4 (Tel 01 667 3279). **Seats 80.** Children welcome - children's menus available. Wheelchair access difficult. Open 12-"late" daily. Closed Good Fri & 25-26 Dec. Amex, Diners, MasterCard, Visa, Laser. **Directions:** Above McSorleys pub.

Ⓑ RESTAURANT
Poppadom Indian Restaurant

91a Rathgar Road Dublin 6 **Tel: 01 490 2383**
Fax: 01 411 1155 Web: www.qualityfoodonline.ie

féile bia Behind a neat but unremarkable frontage in a row of modern shops lies a treat: colourful and airy, with linen-clad tables, comfortable chairs and a bar, this new wave Indian restaurant demonstrates the delicious diversity of Indian cooking and offers some appealingly unusual dishes. Complimentary poppadoms with fresh chutney dips are brought before menus which offer regional specialities including a starter of Karwari Prawns - deep-fried jumbo prawns marinated in ginger, garlic, yoghurt, garam masala and barbecued in the tandoor, then served with a fresh mint chutney - and main courses ranging in heat from Chicken Avadh, a mild and creamy dish with nuts that was a speciality of the erstwhile Avadh empire of central India, to Lamb Chettinad, a fiery festive dish of the Chettiyar clan in Tamil Nadu. Vegetarians are spoilt for choice, with plenty of dishes available as main courses or side orders, and a new range of beef dishes is planned. Variations like garlic, onion & coriander naan and lime rice offer a subtle change from the standard accompaniments, food presentation is contemporary and service solicitous. Make a point of trying the masala tea, made with leaf tea and cardamom pods. The wine list helpfully begins with some advice on the styles that partner spicy food well, wisely suggesting Alsace wines, notably Gewurtztraminer as the best all-rounder. **Seats 45.** Reservations advised. Air conditioning. D daily, 6-12. A la carte. Wines from about €17. SC discretionary. Closed 25 Dec. Amex, MasterCard, Visa, Laser. **Directions:** A minute away on the same side as Comans Pub, Rathgar.

RESTAURANT
TriBeCa

65 Ranelagh Village Dublin 6 **Tel: 01 497 4174** Fax: 01 491 1584

An outpost of the Canal Bank Café (see entry), this New York style restaurant was a hit from the start for its good fast food and relaxed, casual feel, with bright and airy decor and wooden floors and tables. It's just right for food like carefully sourced burgers (made from 100% organic beef), salads, omelettes and chicken wings, which take their place beside the fusion inspired dishes that keep the more adventurous diners happy. It's not cheap, but it is wholesome fare - and portions are generous so it works out as quite good value for money. Children welcome. **Seats 70** (outside seating 16). Reservations advised. Air conditioning. Toilets wheelchair accessible. Open daily, 12-11. Set L €9.50/15 (12-5); otherwise à la carte, plus daily blackboard specials. House wine €17.50. Closed Dec 24-26, Good Fri. MasterCard, Visa, Laser. **Directions:** Heading southbound from city centre, halfway along Ranelagh main street, on right.

RESTAURANT   **Vermilion**

94-96 Terenure Road North Terenure Dublin 6W
Tel: 01 499 1400 Fax: 01 499 1300
Email: mail@vermilion.ie Web: www.vermilion.ie

This purpose-built restaurant on the first floor above the Terenure Inn pub opened to some acclaim in 2001 and the decor - a contemporary, smart interior in soft primary colours - reflects a forward-looking food philosophy, which offers colourful, beautifully presented and updated versions of many Indian favourites. The menu includes specialities from Kerala, Tamil-Nadu and Goa and pride is generally taken in every aspect of the operation from the quality of the ingredients and cooking, to a good wine list and friendly service. A small selection of desserts is much more tempting than is usual in oriental restaurants (although only the kulfi is an Indian speciality). Each summer, from June to September, Vermilion hosts an Indian Summer Festival, following a culinary trail around India - from the fiery southern dishes and curries with cooling coconut, to the Punjabi and Kashmiri styles of the north, and from western hot and spicy dishes to the rich and creamy dishes from the central Mogul region - and the ethnic experience is brought to life through Bollywood movie clips and performances by a popular belly dancer. Although the wide-ranging menu gives detailed explanations of each dish, some of which are well known, this is not a traditional Indian restaurant and it is necessary to come with an open mind rather than in the expectation of the usual, familiar experience of 'popular' Indian food. **Seats 90** (private area 35). Reservations advised. Air conditioning. D daily 5.30-10, L Sun only, 1-3.30. Set Menu, €20 (available L Sun Sep-May & D 5.30-7 Sun-Thu & to 6.30 Fri & Sat). D also à la carte. Indian Summer Menu €38 inc 1/2 bottle wine). House wine from €17.50. Closed 25-26 Dec, Good Fri. Amex, Diners, MasterCard, Visa, Laser. **Directions:** 200 yards from Terenure crossroads.

DUBLIN 7

Nowhere are the dramatic changes taking place in Dublin more evident than in this old area of the city to the north of the Liffey, just across from Christchurch and St Patrick's cathedrals. The corporation **wholesale markets** are here, in fine Victorian redbrick buildings which were allowed for years to go without so much as a lick of paint but have recently undergone overdue renovation, on the outside at least, while their future is debated. Meanwhile, a youthful new residential population is growing up around them and an unprecedented number of visitors now come to this part of the city. The main thrust of development in this area is around **Smithfield**, home to the **Old Jameson**

Distillery: the main elements of Smithfield Village - at ground level at least - are residential apartment blocks and Chief O'Neill's Hotel - but perhaps the most imaginative component is **The Chimney**, a huge tower which was once a part of the old distillery and now takes visitors soaring up 175 feet above Smithfield in a glass-walled lift, to experience a unique birds-eye view of the city. On returning to earth visitors tend to feel the need of a drink - luckily there's no lack of it next door, at the Old Jameson Distillery. An unusual contemporary restaurant, **Hanley at the Bar** (01 878 0104) is at The Distillery Building in May Lane; open 8am-5pm Mon-Fri during the Law Term (more variable hours at other times), it has earned a reputation with legal eagles at the nearby Four Courts for great cooking at smart prices.

Ⓑ HOTEL   # Chief O'Neill's Hotel

Smithfield Village Dublin 7 **Tel: 01 817 3838** Fax: 01 817 3839
Email: reservations@chiefoneills.com Web: www.chiefoneills.com

This unusual hotel is central to the developing complex around Smithfield Village - and the on-going upgrading of the areas along Dublin's north quays. Accommodation is a strikingly modern style which guests will either love or loathe - the bathroom arrangements, for example, are perhaps more sculptural than practical - all bedrooms have good facilities, while penthouse suites also have jacuzzis and rooftop balconies. Lines are simple, colours strong and there's a distinctly youthful air about the place. State of the art conference facilities and meeting rooms attract corporate guests and, for relaxation, Chief O'Neill's Café Bar features live traditional music at weekends and offers a combination of traditional and contemporary Irish food. Unusual attractions incorporated into the hotel complex include The Chimney Viewing Tower, reached by a glass-walled lift. It's open every day and panoramic views over the city can be spectacular on a good day (also available for private parties of up to 50 guests). Video-conferencing. Conference/banqueting (120/150). Children welcome (under 12 free in parents' room; cots available free of charge, baby sitting arranged). **Rooms 73** (3 suites, 63 shower only, 18 no-smoking, 5 disabled). Lift. Room service (limited hours). Room rates from about €180. Closed 24-26 Dec. Amex, MasterCard, Visa, Laser.

♣PUB   # The Hole in the Wall

Blackhorse Avenue Phoenix Park Dublin 7 **Tel: 01 838 9491**
Fax: 01 868 5160 Email: h/w.eircom.net

PJ McCaffrey's remarkable pub beside the Phoenix Park is named in honour of a tradition which existed here for around a hundred years - the practice of serving drinks through a hole in the wall of the Phoenix Park to members of the army garrison stationed nearby. Today the Hole in the Wall also claims to be the longest pub in Ireland - and it is certainly one of the most interesting. They do good food too - there's a carvery lunch, and a bar menu available throughout the day offers a wide choice including traditional Irish dishes like Beef & Guinness Pie, Dublin Coddle and Irish Stew. Children welcome. Music nightly and all day Sun. Wheelchair access. Parking. Bar menu served daily (12-9). Closed 25 Dec & Good Fri. Amex, MasterCard, Visa, Laser. **Directions:** Beside Phoenix Park.

RESTAURANT   # Kelly & Ping, Bar & Restaurant

Smithfield Village Dublin 7 **Tel: 01 817 3840** Fax: 01 817 3841
Email: info@kellyandping.com Web: www.kellyandping.com

In common ownership with **Chief O'Neill's Hotel**, but with its own entrance from Duck Lane, this colourful, glass-fronted restaurant has established its own separate identity and is now serving a growing local population - both business and residential - well. The style is broadly Asian, mainly Thai, and many of the popular dishes are offered - chicken satay, vegetable spring rolls, Thai style sweet & sour pork, Nasi Goreng - along with many less well-known dishes, and a range of Kelly & Ping Thai curries which can be ordered red (hot), green (medium) or yellow (mild). There's also a sprinkling of international bistro dishes like goats cheese & home-dried tomato salad, baked salmon with caramelised onion mash and smoked chicken & mango quesadilla, all offered in generous portions and well- priced. As well as a moderately priced wine list, there's a good choice of Asian beers. **Seats 100** (outdoor, 50). Open Mon-Sat 12-11 (L12-3, D 4-11). Closed Sun, bank hols. Amex, MasterCard, Visa, Laser. **Directions:** Behind the Four Courts, beside Old Jameson Distillery.

♣PUB   **The Old Jameson Distillery**

Bow Street Smithfield Dublin 7 **Tel: 01 807 2355** Fax: 01 807 2369
Email: reservations@ojd.ie Web: www.whiskeytours.com

While most visitors to Dublin will visit the restored Old Jameson Distillery to do the tour (which is fascinating), it's also a good spot for a bite to eat. There are special menus for groups (including evening functions, when the Distillery is not otherwise open) but the café style **Stillroom Restaurant** is also open to individuals - light food served all day and lunch, featuring Irish specialities like John Jameson beef casserole, roast loin of pork with apple & Jameson sauce, and Jameson farmhouse whiskey cake - and the standard of cooking is generally high. Downstairs, the **1780 Bar** is open from 12 noon daily, with bar food (mainly modern international - chicken Caesar, paninis etc) available at lunchtime (12.30-3). Restaurant **Seats 103**. Reservations accepted. Open 9-5 daily; L 12.30-2.30. House wine €18. Closed 25 Dec, Goood Fri. Amex, MasterCard, Visa, Laser. **Directions:** On northside of Quays, off Arran Quay, near Four Courts. Well signed.

DUBLIN 8

The exception to the rule that unevenly numbered districts of Dublin are north of the Liffey and even ones on the south, Dublin 8 stretches from the Grand Canal right across the ancient districts of The Coombe, Christchurch and Wood Quay and "leaks" over the river to the western quays and the south-eastern corner of Phoenix Park. By any standards it covers some of the most historic and fascinating areas of the city - and, by a happy chance, it also encompasses some fine restaurants along the Grand Canal (look out for the latest branch of **Dunne & Crescenzi** which is due to open at **Portobello** shortly after the guide goes to press, in the previous Thornton's premises, near Locks) and, in the heart of Viking Dublin, there's a a goodly selection of characterful pubs. The **Francis Street** area is renowned for its **antiques** and, should you feel the need of wholesome sustenance while browsing, Sarah Webb's famous bakery and cafe, **The Gallic Kitchen**, could be just the spot. For the thirsty, or just plain curious, the most spectacular pint of Guinness in Dublin awaits you in **Gravity**, the panoramic bar atop the **Guinness Storehouse**, while visitors with no head for heights but an interest in gardens and architecture should visit the **War Memorial Gardens** at Islandbridge, designed by Sir Edwin Lutyens.

CAFÉ/RESTAURANT

Bar Italia

Lr Exchange Street Essex Quay Dublin 8
Tel: 01 679 5128 Email: acrobat_ltd@yahoo.it

In a modern office block on the edge of Temple Bar and close to the Civic Offices known disparagingly to Dubliners as 'The Bunkers', this little Italian café has floor-to-ceiling glass to make the most of a splendid view across the Liffey towards the magnificent Four Courts - and there's plenty of space outside to enjoy lunch 'al fresco' when the weather's right. Attentive Italian waiters quickly seat new arrivals, service throughout is quick and professional and the banter lends a relaxed atmosphere - matched by colourful, flavoursome food, simply presented. The minestrone soup can be memorable, paninis and pasta dishes are the business, and it's a place worth seeking out for their espressos alone. And it's great value too. **Seats 25.** Outdoor seating. Open every day: Mon-Fri, 8-6, Sat 9-6, Sun 12-6. A la carte. Closed Christmas/New Year. **Also at:** Bar Italia, 26 Lower Ormond Quay, Dublin, 1 (Tel 01 874 1000); La Corte 5a Custom House, Dublin 1 (Tel 01 672 1929) & Powerscourt Town House, Dublin 2. MasterCard, Visa. **Directions:** South quays, west end of Temple Bar (near Dublin Corporation head office).

♣ATMOSPHERIC PUB

Brazen Head

20 Lower Bridge Street Dublin 8 **Tel: 01 677 9549** Fax: 01 670 4042
Email: info@brazenhead.com Web: www.brazenhead.com

Dublin's (possibly Ireland's) oldest pub was built on the site of a tavern dating back to the 12th century - and it's still going strong. Full of genuine character, this friendly, well-run pub has lots of different levels and dark corners. Food is wholesome and middle-of-the-road, at reasonable prices - visitors will be pleased to find sound renditions of traditional favourites like beef & Guinness stew and Irish stew, but there are also more contemporary dishes like stuffed breast of chicken with sage & sausage meat, wrapped in bacon - and a lot of seafood. Live music nightly in the Music Lounge. **Seats 80** (private room 40, outdoor seating 40). Open every day,12-10: L12-6 & D 6-10 daily (Bar meals 12-9). Closed 25 Dec & Good Fri. Amex, MasterCard, Visa, Laser. **Directions:** Opposite the Four Courts.

CAFÉ

Chorus Café

Fishamble Street Dublin 8 **Tel: 01 616 7088** Fax: 01 616 7088

A small restaurant with a big heart, this bright and friendly little place is near the site of the first performance of Handel's Messiah, hence the name - and some features of the decor. Interesting breakfasts (Danish pastries, home-made scones and bagels with imaginative fillings, for example, as well as the 'full Irish'), are followed by an all-day procession of good things. Gourmet ciabatta and panini, and old favourites like tuna melts, jostle for space alongside wonderful salads: a great daytime place to know about if you're visiting anywhere in the Christchurch area. **Seats 24.** Open Mon-Fri, 7am-5pm, Sat 10-6. Closed Sun, Christmas, New Year. **No Credit Cards. Directions:** Opposite Dublin Corporation Offices, at Christchurch end of Fishamble Street.

CAFÉ

Gallic Kitchen

49 Francis Street Dublin 8 **Tel: 01 454 4912**
Fax: 01 473 3972 Email: galkit@iol.ie

This little spot in Dublin's "antique" district has been delighting locals and visitors alike for some years now. Patissière Sarah Webb is renowned for quality baking (quiches, roulades, plaits, tartlets, wraps) and also salads and delicious little numbers to have with coffee. A judicious selection from an extensive range is offered to eat in the shop: sourcing is immaculate, cooking skilful and prices reasonable, so you may have to queue. Outside catering offered (with staff if required). Open Mon-Sat, 9-5. *Sarah also has a stall at several markets: Temple Bar (Sat, 9-5); Dun Laoghaire (Thu, 10.30-5); Leopardstown (Fri, 11-5); Laragh, Co Wicklow (one Sun each month). MasterCard, Visa, Laser.

♣ BAR/RESTAURANT   # Guinness Storehouse

St Jame's Gate Dublin 8 **Tel: 01 453 8364** Web: www.guinness.com

The most spectacular pint of Guinness in Dublin - indeed, in all Ireland - awaits you in Gravity, the modern glass-walled bar providing panoramic views of the city from its unique position atop the impressive Guinness Storehouse, a handsome 1904 building. The Storehouse is commodious - with 170,000 square feet of floor space, it is one of the choicest pieces of real estate in Dublin. The space is imaginatively used to house the Guinness Museum, the story - told with fascinating high tech exhibits - of the famous company's 250-plus years in business. It also includes (on Level 5) the traditional Brewery Bar, serving nourishing Irish fare (seafood chowder, beef & Guinness stew, Guinness white & dark chocolate mousse) and the contemporary-style Source Bar. Slightly more formal evening menus, including a short children's menu, are available in Jul-Aug. Opened in the autumn of 2000, the Guinness Storehouse has long since welcomed its millionth visitor: it has so much to offer that some folk spend an entire day there. The Storehouse is open daily, 9.30-5. **Entrance fees apply.** Bureau de Change. Free parking. Brewery Bar **Seats 150**. Food served 11-4 daily. Closed 25-26 Dec, 31 Dec, 1 Jan, Good Fri.

CAFÉ   # Havana Tapas Bar

3 Camden Market Grantham Street Dublin 8 **Tel: 01 476 0046**
Email: info@havana.ie Web: www.havana.ie

This smashing little tapas bar is tucked away on a little street off Camden Street and, although understandably extremely popular with locals and people working in the area, it's otherwise one of Dublin's best kept secrets. Prices are very reasonable and lunch is a real bargain. Home-cooked food freshly made on the premises is the philosophy: Spanish tortilla, paella, Serrano ham and delicious breads from the famous Bretzel Bakery is the kind of food you'll get, along with tapas like marinated jumbo prawns. Don't miss the chorizo & lentil stew. * A new Havana is due to open in **Temple Bar West** as we go to press. For music, be there on Friday and Saturday nights at 10 o'clock (until "late") for salsa music. **Seats 60** (private room 20). Open Mon-Sat 12-11.30 (Fri-Sat to 2 am, last orders 1.30). Tapas from about €6.50. Set Menu €13 (available all day Mon-Wed). House wine about €15. SC 12%. Closed Sun, bank hols, 1st 2 weeks Aug. Amex, MasterCard, Visa, Laser. **Directions:** Adjacent to Cassidy's Pub, Camden Street.

HOTEL   # Jurys Inn Christchurch

Christchurch Place Dublin 8 **Tel: 01 454 0000** Fax: 01 454 0012
Email: info@jurysdoyle.com Web: www.jurysdoyle.com

féile bia Jurys Inn Christchurch is well placed for both tourist and business travellers, offering reasonably priced accommodation within walking distance of the main city centre areas on both sides of the Liffey and close to Dublin Castle and attractions in Temple Bar. Rooms are comfortable and spacious, with large, well positioned work desks and practical bathrooms with economy baths and overbath showers. A large multi-storey car park at the rear has convenient access to the hotel. **Rooms 182**. Room rate from €108 (up to

3 adults or 2 adults & 2 children); weekend rate €117, rising to €225 on rugby weekends. Breakfast from about €10. Closed 24-26 Dec. Amex, Diners, MasterCard, Visa, Laser. **Directions:** Follow signs to city centre; opposite Christchurch Cathedral.

✓ Ⓑ RESTAURANT

Locks Restaurant

1 Windsor Terrace Portobello Dublin 8
Tel: 01 454 3391 Fax: 01 453 8352

féile bia In an old building with a lovely canal-side setting, Claire Douglas's long-established two-storey restaurant is furnished and decorated in a warm and elegant style with soft lighting, open fires and a soothing atmosphere. There's a timelessness about the place which is extremely refreshing in contrast to the ubiquitous minimalism that has hit Dublin recently: classically laid tables are beautifully appointed with crisp white tablecloths and napkins, lovely wine glasses, silver cutlery and white china - and now that head chef, Alan Kinsella, has had time to settle in fully, the cooking has real heart. He offers a (slightly daunting) range of menus including a Table d'Hôte and an extensive (and pricey) à la carte dinner menu, a set lunch (which is a real snip) and also a Tasting Menu on some evenings - you can opt to have anything from five to eight courses, and it is invariably booked out. Mainly local and quality Irish ingredients are used and, despite occasional mis-spellings, it is good to see Greystone crab, Lough Shinny lobster and meats from Meath, Carlow and Roscommon credited on the menu, providing the base for a cooking style that is predominantly contemporary French/Irish, although other influences do creep in - a starter of 'Kinsella Sushi' for example, and a house speciality '3 Way Rabbit': a stylish dish of loin of rabbit with chorizo mousse, rillette and spring roll, served with with a fig compôte & rosemary jus. Desserts tend towards the sophisticated - a pyramid of white chocolate & coffee mousse, with Earl Grey anglaise froth and pistachio ice cream, perhaps. Accomplished cooking, caring service and a warm ambience make this a lovely restaurant, and the dining experience should be memorable. The wine list favours France, notably Bordeaux, and is reasonably priced for the quality; several house choices (all French) are offered by the glass. Children welcome. **Seats 60** (private room, 30). L Mon-Fri,12.15-2; D Mon-Sat, 6-10. Set L €28.95, Set D 3-5 course €28.95-39.95; 5-8 course Tasting Menu, €49-79. L&D à la carte also available. House wine from €23.50. SC 12.5%. Closed L Sat, all Sun, bank hols, Christmas week, last week Jul. Amex, Diners, MasterCard, Visa, Laser. **Directions:** Half way between Portobello and Harold's Cross Bridges.

♣ RESTAURANT/ATMOSPHERIC PUB

The Lord Edward

23 Christchurch Place Dublin 8 **Tel: 01 4542 420**
Fax: 01 4542 420 Email: ledward@indigo.ie

Dublin's oldest seafood restaurant/bar spans three floors of a tall, narrow building overlooking Christchurch Cathedral. Traditional in a decidedly old-fashioned way, The Lord Edward provides a complete contrast to the current wave of trendy restaurants that has taken over Dublin recently, which is just the way a lot of people like it. If you enjoy seafood and like old-fashioned cooking with plenty of butter and cream (as nature intended) and without too many concessions to the contemporary style of presentation either, then this could be the place for you. While certainly caught in a time warp, the range of fish and seafood offered is second to none and the fish cookery is excellent, with simplest choices almost invariably the best. There are a few non-seafood options - traditional dishes like Irish stew, perhaps, or corned beef and cabbage and desserts also favour the classics. Bar food is also available Mon-Fri, 12-2.30. Children welcome. **Seats 40.** L Mon-Fri, 12-3. D 6-10.30 Mon-Sat. Set menu from about €35; also à la carte. Reservations required. Closed Sun, 24 Dec-2 Jan, bank hols. Amex, Diners, MasterCard, Visa, Laser. **Directions:** Opposite Christchurch Cathedral.

PUB   # Nancy Hands

30-32 Parkgate Street Dublin 8 **Tel: 01 677 0149** Fax: 01 677 0187
Email: nancyh@indigo.ie Web: www.nancyhands.com

A sister establishment to The Hole in the Wall (see entry), Nancy Hands is a newish pub with an old feel, but far from being a theme pub. It's a characterful place for a drink and the selection stocked is unusually extensive: it includes an unusualy good choice of wines, also a cocktail menu and a wide range of vodkas and whiskeys. Food was an important aspect of Nancy Hands from the outset and, on the whole, it is well done with menus successfully straddling the divide between traditional bar food (seafood chowder, steaks; lunchtime carvery) and lighter international fare. Children welcome. Live music on occasion. Air conditioning. Toilets wheelchair accessible. Restaurant: **Seats 120**. Meals available from 10am; L&D menus daily. Closed 25-26 Dec & Good Fri. Amex, Diners, MasterCard, Visa. **Directions:** 100 metres from gates of Phoenix Park going towards Heuston Station.

PUB   # Ryan's of Parkgate Street

28 Parkgate Street Dublin 8 **Tel: 01 677 6097** Fax: 01 677 6098

Ryan's is one of Ireland's finest and best-loved original Victorian pubs, with magnificent stained glass, original mahogany bar fixtures and an outstanding collection of antique mirrors all contributing to its unique atmosphere. Bar food is available every day except Sunday and, upstairs, there's a small restaurant, Ryan's Kitchen & Bakery, serving food which is a step up from bar meals. Ryan's changed hands just before the guide went to press, but major changes are unlikely. Street parking only (can be difficult, but Pay & Display nearby). Pub food: Mon-Fri, 3-11.30, Fri & Sat, 12-10. Restaurant: L Fri & Sat from 12 noon; D Mon-Sat 5-9.30 (last orders). Closed 25 Dec, Good Fri, first 2 wks Jan & bank hols. MasterCard, Visa, Laser. **Directions:** On the quays - across the river from Heuston Station.

CAFÉ   # The Grass Roots Café

Irish Museum of Modern Art Royal Hospital Kilmainham Dublin 8
Tel: 01 612 9900

This self-service café is a pleasant place for an informal meal, whether or not you are visiting the museum - it has good parking facilities and the spacious room, which is attractively located overlooking a garden area, has a pleasingly cool modern ambience. An appetising small menu offers home-made soup, salads and quiches, tarts and cakes plus several hot dishes - tortellini with pesto cream, perhaps, or tasty pork tacos, generously served - and about half the daily selection is vegetarian. Food quality and presentation is good (large white plates), cafeteria style service is efficient - and it's a handier choice for a quick lunch than city centre venues, perhaps. Wine choices are restricted to a few quarter bottles. Open: Mon-Sat 10-5, Sun 12-5. MasterCard, Visa **Directions:** At Royal Hospital Kilmainham museum.

This northern suburb entered the latest phase of a Cinderella-like transformation in 2002, when the President of Ireland formally opened **The Helix**, the large and stylish performing arts centre at the heart of the vigorous **Dublin City University**. With facilities including a superb 1260-seat concert hall, The Helix plays a central role in re-defining the area, and re-shaping the cultural map of the city.

In times past, perhaps the most useful feature of this somewhat workaday northern suburb for visitors was its convenience to the airport. But, as well as The Helix, it is also home to the **National Botanic Gardens**. The gardens, which date from 1795, have more than 20,000 varieties of plants, a rose garden, magnificent herbaceous borders, a vegetable garden and - the masterpiece - the Curvilinear Range of 400-feet-long greenhouses designed and built by the Dublin iron-master Richard Turner through the mid 19th-century and the Palm House, added in 1884. The greenhouses, which had been allowed to fall into disrepair, were restored in 1995 and replanted in 1997 - and work is continuing on new glasshouses, built to the original design. The wooded areas of the gardens are also delightful and full of interest - and a walk along the **River Tolka**, which flows along the edge of the grounds, can very pleasant.

♣PUB   **Addison Lodge**

Botanic Road Glasnevin Dublin 9 **Tel: 01 837 3534**
Fax: 01 837 5942 Email: addison@eircom.net

A very useful place to know about if you're visiting the Botanic Gardens, just across the road: this friendly family-run pub with accommodation is just the spot for wholesome, freshly-prepared food. Snacks like soup and sandwiches are available from opening time onwards and lunch-time brings hot food with a home-made flavour that is rare in carveries; traditional favourites like Irish stew and bacon & cabbage are especially welcome. Not suitable for children after 7pm. Food served daily,12.30-8 (Sun to 6). Closed 25 Dec, Good Fri. Amex, MasterCard, Visa. **Directions:** Opposite entrance to the Botanic Gardens.

✓WINE BAR/DELI   **Andersons Food Hall & Café**

3 The Rise Glasnevin Dublin 9 **Tel: 01 837 8394** Fax: 01 797 9004
Email: info@andersons.ie Web: www.andersons.ie

This wonderful delicatessen, wine shop and continental style café is quietly situated on a side road so the unexpected sight of jaunty aluminium chairs and tables outside - and a glimpse of many wine bottles lining the walls behind the elegant shopfront - should gladden the hearts of first-time visitors sweeping around the corner from Griffith Avenue. Noel Delaney and Patricia van der Velde opened this little gem in 2003, after refurbishing and extending the premises - previously a butchers shop, and still with its original 1930s' tiled floor, high ceiling and façade. Oak fittings have been used throughout, including the wine displays, and the chic little marble-topped tables for lighter bites suit the old shop well - in the extension behind it, there are larger tables and space for groups to eat in comfort. Now, where cuts of meat were once displayed, there's a wonderful selection of charcuterie and cheese from Ireland and the continent: an Irish Plate offers a selection of ham, pastrami, Irish stout cured beef and Irish farmhouse cheeses, for example, while The Iberian Selection comprises Serrano ham, chorizo salamis, Mediterranean vegetables, olives and Manchego sheep's milk cheese - all served with speciality breads - and a Children's Selection educates the younger palate with the likes of hot panini with Elliotts award-winning ham and Cheddar cheese. A short blackboard menu of hot dishes and specials (penne pasta with tomato, spicy meat & aubergine for example), plus a daily soup, a range of salads, gourmet sandwiches, wraps, hot paninis, pastries and classic café desserts (and ice creams from Murphys of Dingle) complement the charcuterie and cheese which have the gravitas to balance the collection of 160 wines lining the walls - and, in addition to the wine list, which changes regularly, you can choose any bottle to have with your food at a €6 corkage charge. There's also an extensive drinks menu, offering speciality coffees and teas, and some unusual beverages, like Lorina French lemonade. **Seats 40** (outside seating 18). No reservations. Children welcome, Toilets wheelchair accessible. Open daily: Mon-Wed, 9am-7pm; Thu-Sat, 9am-8.30pm, Sun 10am-7pm (last food orders half an hour before closing). 23 House Wines (€15.95-€35.95) & 160 wines available from the wine shop at €6 corkage. Amex, MasterCard, Visa. MasterCard, Visa, Laser. **Directions:** Off Griffith Avenue, near junction with Mobhi Road.

HOTEL
Crowne Plaza Dublin Airport Hotel
Northwood Park Santry Demesne Dublin 9

See entry in County Dublin, Dublin Airport Area.

GUESTHOUSE
Egans House
7-9 Iona Park Glasnevin Dublin 9 **Tel: 01 830 5283** Fax: 01 830 3312
Email: info@eganshouse.com Web: www.eganshouse.com

Within walking distance of the Botanic Gardens and convenient to the airport, north Dublin golf clubs, the Helix, Dublin port and the city centre, the Finns' family-run guesthouse offers comfortable, well-maintained accommodation at a reasonable price. All rooms are en-suite, with full bath, phone, tea/coffee trays. Writing desk, internet access, secretarial services. Wine licence. Wheelchair access. Parking. Children welcome (Under 3s free in parents' room; cots available, baby sitting aranged). No pets. Garden.**Rooms 23** (22 shower only, 18 no-smoking). B&B €50, ss€10. Closed 20-28 Dec. MasterCard, Visa, Laser. **Directions:** North of city centre - Dorset Street - St. Alphonsus Road- Iona Park.

RESTAURANT
Independent Pizza Company
28 Lr Drumcondra Road Dublin 9
Tel: 01 830 2044 Fax: 01 830 3952

A sister restaurant of the popular **Gotham Café** just off Grafton Street (see entry - menus are similar), the Independent Pizza Company is in smart new premises and the menu includes many of the Gotham favourites, so you can expect to find designer salads and contemporary pasta dishes, for example, alongside the excellent range of gourmet pizzas for which they are well known. Family-friendly (crayons, colouring books provided) and a handy place for a meal on the way to the airport. Lunchtime specials are good value and there's a good drinks menu, including speciality coffees. Air conditioning. Wheelchair friendly. **Seats 50** (Max table size 8). Open daily, 12 noon-midnight (Mon-Thu to 11). House wine €15; beer licence. A la carte; sc discretionary (except 10% on groups of 6+ adults). House wine €15. Closed Christmas, Good Fri. Amex, MasterCard, Visa, Laser. **Directions:** Under bridge at Drumcondra railway station.

ATMOSPHERIC PUB
John Kavanagh (Grave Diggers)
1 Prospect Square Glasnevin Dublin 9
Tel: 01 830 7978 Email: antokav@gofree.indigo.ie

John Kavanagh's lays claim to being the oldest family pub in Dublin - it was established in 1833 and the current family are the 6th generation in the business. Also known as "The Gravediggers" because of its location next to the Glasnevin cemetery and its attached folk history, this is a genuine Victorian bar, totally unspoilt - and it has a reputation for serving one of the best pints in Dublin. No music, "piped or otherwise". No food. Theme pub owners eat your hearts out. No children after 7pm. Closed Good Fri & Christmas. **No Credit Cards. Directions:** Old Glasnevin Cemetery Gate, off Botanic Road.

PUB
Porterhouse North

Cross Guns Bridge Glasnevin Dublin 9 **Tel: 01 830 9922**
Fax: 01 830 9920 Web: www.porterhousebrew.com

Originally the Iona Garage, owned by the Cahill family (who were also associated with the aviation industry), Porterhouse North is a large white canalside building with a copper sign above the door - hard to miss, although parking nearby may not be so easy in this busy area. It has been redeveloped to retain some of the original art deco features - notably the stepped badge detail in the middle of the pediments, which have been preserved, stripped back to the original plaster and clad with black and white terrazzo and copper banding. Inside it is a very trendy pub - on four different levels, with outdoor seating at the back and side - and the building's history is echoed in materials associated with the era (terrazo flooring, leather on the counter, rippled glass walls with copper banding and ceramic column castings). A large flat screen TV, an open kitchen with pizza oven on the first floor and a buzzy atmosphere all give it obvious youth appeal. Menus offer a range of popular dishes but, although interesting as a bar, the food to date has been disappointing so, perhaps with the exception of pizzas, it is more a place to drop in for a drink. Wheelchair accessible. Open usual pub hours (to 12.30am Fri & Sat). Food served daily: Sun-Fri, 12-10pm; Sat 12-9.30. Closed 25 Dec, Good Fri. **Directions:** At Cross Guns Bridge.

RESTAURANT
The Washerwomans Hill Restaurant

60a Glasnevin Hill Glasnevin Dublin 9 **Tel: 01 837 9199**
Fax: 01 837 9492 Email: washerwomanrestaurant@eircom.net

féile bia Situated on a busy road, just across from the Met Office and convenient to the Botanic Gardens and the airport area, first impressions of this popular neighbourhood restaurant may be a little dusty but prompt welcome and (if you are lucky) the offer of a choice of tables should help new arrivals warm to it. Traditional, even slightly old-world in style, the restaurant is quite dimly-lit, with simply-laid darkwood tables - place mats, pre-pack butter, a peppermill - and the work of a local artist displayed on the walls. Well-balanced traditional table d'hôte and à la carte menus offer the popular dishes that people of all ages feel comfortable with, sometimes with a contemporary twist - 'Fishysoisse' (leek & potato soup with smoked salmon & croûtons), deep-fried mushrooms (tossed in tandoori spices & serving with raita), pan fried fillet of pork garnished with apple strudel and served with an orange & ginger jus and char-grilled steak are all typical, and the cooking style is quite homely. Some suppliers are listed on the menu and special diets can be accommodated, but bought-in desserts are a weak point. The ambience on the ground floor is warmer and more relaxed than a first floor room, which has rather gimmicky decor. Not suitable for children after 9pm. **Seats 80.** Reservations required. Air conditioning. L Wed-Sun 12.30-3.30 (Sun 1.30-4.30); D daily 6-10.30. Set L €20, early D €26 (6-8). Set D €35; also à la carte. House wine €15.50. Closed 25-26 Dec, Good Fri. Amex, MasterCard, Visa, Laser. **Directions:** Past Bon Secours hospital, opposite the Met Office.

DUBLIN 14

Due south of the city, this pleasant residential suburb is poised on rising ground at the edge of the scenic Dublin mountains. **Marlay Park,** at Rathfarnham, marks the start of the 85 mile **Wicklow Way** walking route and is interesting for its famous **craft courtyard**; a **farmers' market** is held here every Saturday. At the time of going to press, huge developments are in progress in the area, at **Dundrum,** selected by **Harvey Nicholls** for their first site in Ireland, and a branch of Eamonn O'Reilly's city centre restaurant, **Bleu Café Bar**, is due to open in Dundrum shortly (details from Bleu Bistro Moderne, 01 676 7015; or One Pico, 01 676 0300).

RESTAURANT
Indian Brasserie
Main Street Rathfarnham Dublin 14 **Tel: 01 492 0260**

Samir Sapru's Indian Brasserie is just a minute's walk from Rathfarnham Castle, at the Butterfield Avenue end of the village. The restaurant, which is run as a buffet, offers freshly prepared wholesome food, aiming to make it the nearest to home cooking that can be achieved in a restaurant. The selection usually includes around eight starters, five or six salads and seven or eight main courses, with each dish individually prepared from scratch and the selection worked out so that all the dishes complement each other. Breads - which are baked quickly at a very high temperature - are cooked to order. The hospitality is intended to make each guest feel as if they are visiting a private house - customers are encouraged to try a little of everything that has been prepared on the night. Own parking. No children after 7pm. **Seats 50.** Air conditioning. D 5-11 daily. House wine about €14. SC discretionary. Toilets wheelchair accessible. Closed 25-26 Dec. Amex, Diners, MasterCard, Visa. **Directions:** At the Butterfield Ave. end of Rathfarnham village, under TSB Bank.

ATMOSPHERIC PUB
The Yellow House
1 Willbrook Road Rathfarnham Dublin 14
Tel: 01 493 2994 Fax: 01 494 2441

Named after the unusual shade of the bricks with which it is built, the landmark pub of Rathfarnham makes a perfect rendezvous, with no chance of confusion. The tall and rather forbidding exterior gives little hint of the warmth inside, where pictures and old decorative items relevant to local history repay close examination. (Traditional bar food is served in the lounge and there's a restaurant upstairs serving evening meals and Sunday lunch.) Closed 25-6 Dec & Good Fri. Amex, Diners, MasterCard, Visa, Laser. **Directions:** Prominent corner building in Rathfarnham Village.

DUBLIN 15

With the huge expanse of Phoenix Park right on its doorstep on the city side and easy access to the M50 and main routes to the north, west and south on the other, this fast developing suburb has a lot going for it. Useful addresses in the area include **The Vineyard Pub & Restaurant**, Main Street Blanchardstown (01 821 3109), **Travelodge Castleknock** (01 820 2626; www.travelodge.ie) for affordable accommodation charged at room rates. **Farmleigh** is nearby in the Phoenix Park (see page 11). **Castleknock Hotel & Country Club** (01 873 0199; www.towerhotelgroup.com) is due to open shortly.

after the Guide goes to press. Golfing gourmets likely to be in this area should check out **Luttrellstown Castle** at Clonsilla, renowned for its golf but also good food for groups and functions.

COUNTRY HOUSE ## Ashbrook House

River Road Ashtown Castleknock Dublin 15 **Tel: 01 838 5660**
Fax: 01 838 5660 Email: evemitchell@hotmail.com

Although it is only a 15 minutes drive from the airport (and a similar distance from the city centre), Eve Mitchell's lovely Georgian country house is in a countryside location beside the Tolka River. Set in 10 acres of grounds, with a grass tennis court, walled garden and many garden paths to wander, it is also just beside the Phoenix Park and within a few minutes' drive of seven golf courses. There are two magnificent drawing rooms, and the large beautifully furnished bedrooms are very comfortable, with phone, tea/coffee facilities and en-suite power showers; two family rooms have a single bed as well as doubles. TV lounge. Children welcome (baby sitting arranged) No pets. B&B €45 pps. Single supplement €15. Closed Christmas/New Year. MasterCard, Visa, Laser. **Directions:** Off N3, 15 minutes from airport; similar distance from city centre.

HOTEL/BAR/RESTAURANT ## The Twelfth Lock

Castleknock Marina The Royal Canal Castleknock Dublin 15
Tel: 01 860 7400 Fax: 01 860 7401
Email: info@twelfthlock.com Web: www.twelfthlock.com

Approaching by road, The Twelfth Lock may seem a little plain and institutional - and you have to walk up a sloping path from the carpark, like going into a station - but it looks better from the canal, and better again when you are inside and feel the building coming to life. The hotel reception is on your left (the rooms are downstairs) and, to the right is a cosmopolitan, light-filled open planned bar with stylish furnishings and a trendy bar with a huge mural behind it depicting work on the lock, and an al fresco dining area beyond it. Staff are exceptionally friendly and helpful, quickly taking orders from the cute filofax menus on the tables - food such as pastas, home made burgers, steak sandwiches and hot dishes of the day. Typically delicious samples include warm smoked salmon salad with walnut brown bread, dill & caper sauce, and 'Big Fat Greek salad' - a generous portion of feta cheese, olives, roasted peppers, onions and mixed leaves. As well as serving good bar food, there's also a separate bistro bar serving evening meals. The canalside location is lovely, the staff are just great and the food is good - sounds like a winner. Bar Meals Mon-Thu, 12 noon-9pm; Fri-Sat 12-8; Sun 12-9. Outside seating. Wheelchair accessible. Bistro Bar open Wed-Sat from 7pm (to 11.30 midweek, 12.30 on Fri & Sat).

Accommodation: Guest rooms are on the lower ground floor and a little dark, but furnished to executive standard and reasonably priced. Children welcome but not allowed in bar after 7pm. No pets. **Rooms 10** (1 disabled). Lift. Room service (limited hours). Room rate €115 (with breakfast); weekend rates available. Amex, MasterCard, Visa, Laser. **Directions:** On the Royal Canal, at the Twelfth Lock.

RESTAURANT ## Wongs Chinese Restaurant

Ashley Centre Main Street Castleknock Dublin 15
Tel: 01 822 3330

The darkly dramatic decor - ornate carved panelling, formal white-clothed tables - may come as a surprise to first-time visitors to this first-floor restaurant, but it will soon seem incidental in the the whirl of entertainment provided by their teppanyaki chef, who skilfully flambés everything in front of you with style and panache. Forget about chafing dishes, this is light years away from any such sedate culinary practice and well worth the pretty high prices charged (set menus start at around €50). Meals, which consist of several small courses, are very different from the usual Chinese dining experience and outstanding for variety, quality of ingredients, accuracy of cooking and good saucing - and, in the case of teppanyaki, entertainment is as important a part of the experience as the food: this, together with the high prices, mean it is very much a night out. The weak point, as usual in oriental restaurants, is dessert - better to settle for Chinese tea and be done with it. Pleasant staff, efficient service and consistently good food make this a place to remember when planning a big night out. Castleknock is generally recognised as the culinary flagship of the Wongs group but other restaurants are **also at:** 436 Clontarf Road Dublin 3. Tel: 01 833 4400; 7 Sandford Road, Dublin 6. Tel: 01 496 7722; 5a The Crescent, Monkstown. Tel: 01 230 1212. MasterCard, Visa **Directions:** Castleknock village - Ashley Centre carpark signposted on right.

DUBLIN 18

This desirable residential area has some good neighbourhood restaurants and an excellent store, **Thomas's** (greengrocery, deli and wines), in Foxrock - and **Leopardstown Race Course** is on the doorstep; a **farmers' market** is held here every Friday, 11am-7pm. Good value, contemporary accommodation too, at the new **Bewleys Hotel Leopardstown** (01 293 5000; www.BewleysHotels.com).

RESTAURANT   **Bistro One**

3 Brighton Road Foxrock Village Dublin 18 **Tel: 01 289 7711**
Fax: 01 207 0742 Email: bistroone@eircom.ie

féile bia This popular neighbourhood restaurant can get very busy but there is a bar on the way in, where guests are greeted and set up in comfort and the attitude throughout is laid back but not without care. Ingredients are carefully sourced - fresh produce comes from organic farmers' markets, cheese from Sheridan's cheesemongers, smoked fish from Frank Hederman's smokehouse in Cobh, Co Cork. Seasonal menus - which considerately indicate dishes containing nuts or nut oil - offer eight or ten tempting choices per course. Starters will almost certainly include the ever-popular Bistro One's salad with pancetta, rocket & pine nuts - while the pasta and risotto selection can be starter or main course as preferred: typically, spaghetti with organic meatballs & fresh basil, perhaps, or Carnaroli risotto with green pea and organic mint. Main courses include classics - in seafood dishes, maybe, or roast duck - and organic meats, perhaps in an old fashioned dish like pan fried lamb liver & organic streaky bacon with a red onion mash. There are generous side vegetables and a choice of French and Irish cheese; home-made ice creams or classic puddings to finish. Children welcome. **Seats 72.** D Tue-Sat 6-10, L 12-3. A la carte. House wine €22. SC 10%. Closed Sun, Mon & Christmas/New Year. **Directions:** Southbound on N11, first right after Foxrock church.

RESTAURANT   **The Gables Expresso Bar & Café**

The Gables Foxrock Village Dublin 18
Tel: 01 2892174 Fax: 01 289 2167
Email: value@mccabeswines.ie Web: www.mccabeswines.ie

A younger sister to Expresso Bar cafés in Ballsbridge and the IFSC, this is an imaginative joint venture with McCabes Wines, whose shop is part of the restaurant. So, in addition to the brunches and stylish contemporary food for which they are well known, the wine experience is now a major part of the attraction: the wine list (which begins at about €14) offers quality wines at an unusually low mark-up - and you can have any wine from about 800 available in the shop at a corkage charge of just €8 (half bottles, €5). A novel 'try before you buy' offer, would be hard to resist: you taste a wine before ordering it and, if you like it, you can add it to your bill and have a case put into your car (at a very favourable price) while dining at The Gables: easy peasy. A new head chef, Chris Allen, joined The Gables shortly before the Guide went to press - with experience at Harrods and The Ivy under his belt, this is one to watch. **Seats 70.** Open 9am-9.30pm daily. L daily, 12.30-5 (Sun brunch 10-5); D daily 6-9.30. A la carte. House wine €14. SC discretionary. Closed bank hol evenings. MasterCard, Visa, Laser. **Directions:** Travelling into the city on N11, turn off left for Foxrock Village.

DUBLIN 22 & 24

On the hub of the city's major exit point for the south and west of Ireland (N7) and convenient to Dublin airport via the M50, this area is characterised by a proliferation of industrial estates and business parks - and the associated business ensures high standards of accommodation and some good eating places. Conference facilities are much in demand and business guests are generally well looked after, even in budget accommodation. **Tallaght's Plaza Hotel** (01 462 4200; www.plazahotel.ie) on Belgard Road is the hospitality star of the area; conveniently located just off the M50, it has secure car parking, extensive conference facilities and food well above average hotel fare. The city centre is 8 miles away, but now easily accessible on the new Luas (tram) line. At Clondalkin, the **Green Isle Hotel** (Tel: 01 459 3406) is building a six storey penthouse extension and leisure centre.

Ⓑ HOTEL   **Bewley's Hotel at Newlands Cross**

Newlands Cross Naas Road Dublin 22
Tel: 01 464 0140 Fax: 01 464 0900
Email: res@bewleyshotels.com Web: www.bewleyshotels.com

The lobby gives a good first impression at this large and stylish budget hotel just off the N7. Bedrooms will confirm this feeling, especially at the price - a very reasonable room rate offers a large room with double, single and sofa-bed, a decent bathroom and excellent amenities including a trouser press, iron and ironing board and fax/modem lines. Many more expensive hotels might take note of these standards. Good business facilities too. The adjacent restaurant provides very acceptable food and there is free parking for 200 cars. Small conferences (20). Wheelchair access. Parking. Children welcome. (under 16 free in parents' room; cots available). No pets. Lift. **Rooms 260** (5 shower only, 183 no-smoking, 7 for disabled). Room rate about €79 (max 3 adults). Closed Dec 24-26. Amex, Diners, MasterCard, Visa, Laser.

Ⓑ ♣ RESTAURANT WITH ROOMS   **Kingswood Country House**

Naas Road Clondalkin Dublin 22 **Tel: 01 459 2428**
Fax: 01 459 2207 Email: kingswoodcountryhse@eircom.net
Web: www.kingswoodcountryhouse.com

Just off the Naas Road and very close to the industrial estates around Newlands Cross, the country house ambience of this guesthouse and restaurant comes as a very pleasant surprise. The restaurant has a lovely cosy atmosphere (with open fires, which is always a treat) and a loyal following, for service and friendliness as well as the food. This is an interesting combination of classic French and traditional and new Irish styles, using top quality ingredients - the policy is to use as much local and free range produce as possible, and both the cooking - which has a pleasing 'good home cooking with style' feel to it - and the ambience are invariably enjoyable. Private rooms are available for groups and small business meetings. Small conference/private parties (20/30). Garden. Children welcome (under 3 free in parents' room, cots available). Seats 80 (private room, 30). L daily, 12.30 -2.30 (Sun to 3). Set L about €24. D daily 6.30-10.30 (Sun to 10). House wine about €19. SC 12.5%. Closed 25-26 Dec & Good Fri. Open on bank hols. **Accommodation:** Guest rooms, like the rest of the house, have an old-fashioned charm. **Rooms 7** (all en-suite). 24 hour room service. B&B about €65 pps, ss €25. Amex, Diners, MasterCard, Visa, Laser. **Directions:** 1.5 miles past Newlands Cross heading south on N7.

Ⓑ HOTEL   # Red Cow Moran's Hotel

Red Cow Complex Naas Road Dublin 22 **Tel: 01 459 3650**
Fax: 01 459 1588 Email: info@morangroup.ie
Web: www.moranhotels.com

féile bia Strategically located close to the motorway and known as a pub for many years, the Red Cow Hotel has a grand staircase sweeping up from the marble lobby to give an indication of the style to follow and, although it may also be of interest to private guests, this is definitely a location to check out if you are considering visiting the area on business or wish to organise conferences or meetings. Bedrooms are all of executive standard, with excellent amenities for business guests including voice mail and fax/modem lines. The purpose-built conference centre offers a wide range of facilities and ample car parking. Conference/banqueting (720/550). Video conferencing. Wheelchair access. Parking (450). Children welcome (under 3 free in parents' room; cots available). No pets. **Rooms 123** (3 suites, 6 junior suites, 44 no-smoking, 5 for disabled). Lift. 24 hour room service. B&B €110pps, ss €35. Closed 25-26 Dec. Amex, Diners, MasterCard, Visa, Laser. **Directions:** Exit No.9 from M50 motorway, on the N7.

NORTH COUNTY DUBLIN

As traffic at **Dublin Airport** increases, so do the accommodation choices nearby - and also conference and business facilities, which may make the trek into the city centre unnecessary for many conference delegates and business guests. **Dublin Airport Hilton** (01 877 5400; email david.webster@hilton.com) is under construction at the time of going to press, and a 450 room **Bewley's Hotel** (www.BewleysHotels.com) is also planned. Prices will be reasonable for airport hotels, and the location convenient, near the M50 and M1 intersection.

Dublin Airport	Crowne Plaza Dublin Airport Hotel

B HOTEL   Northwood Park Santry Demesne Dublin 9

An impressive new hotel less than 2 miles from Dublin Airport and with parkland views, the Crowne Plaza is a sister hotel to Clontarf Castle (see entry) and a welcome addition to business and leisure options in the area. Complimentary on-site parking and state-of-the-art conference facilities and meeting rooms make it a good choice for business meetings, to avoid the hassle of going into the city (5 miles). Spacious air-conditioned rooms are designed in a simple, contemporary style and have king size beds, and high speed internet access as well as the more usual traveller's requirements of trouser press, iron & ironing board, tea/coffee facilities and mini-bar. Complimentary parking (200); 24 hour courtesy coach to and from the airport. Conferences (200); business centre; secretarial services. **Rooms 204** (2 suites, 3 junior suites, 34 executive, 10 disabled, 164 no smoking). Lift. 24 hr room service. Turn down service offered. Children welcome (under 18 free in parents' room; cot available without charge). B&B €130) pps, ss €110. Restaurant open L Sun-Fri, D daily. Bar meals available 12-9.30 daily. Amex, Diners, MasterCard, Visa, Laser. **Directions:** From MI out of Dublin, take Santry exit; right at 2nd set of lights. Continue to next lights, turn left to Santry Demesne.

Dublin Airport	Great Southern Hotel

B HOTEL   Dublin Airport Co Dublin **Tel: 01 812 7290** Fax: 01 844 6003
Email: res@dubairport-gsh.ie Web: www.gshotels.com

féile bia This spacious modern hotel in the airport complex is just two minutes drive from the main terminal building (with a coach service available); rooms are all double-glazed and include a high proportion of executive rooms 12 of which are designated lady executive). It's a good choice for business guests and, should your flight be delayed, the large bar and Potters Bistro on the ground floor could be a welcome place to pass the time. Conference/banqueting (400/320); video conferencing; business centre; secretarial service. Children welcome (under 2s free in parents' room; cots available free of charge). **Rooms 229** (2 suites, 4 junior suites, 82 executive rooms, 5 no-smoking floors, 11 rooms for disabled) Lifts. Room service (limited hours). Room rate about €250 (1 or 2 guests). Closed 24-25 Dec. Amex, Diners, MasterCard, Visa, Laser. **Directions:** Situated in airport complex.

Dublin Airport	Holiday Inn Dublin Airport

B HOTEL   Dublin Airport Co Dublin **Tel: 01 808 0500**
Fax: 01 844 6002 Email: reservations-dublinairport@6c.com
Web: dublinairport.holiday-inn.com

This large, comfortable hotel makes an ideal meeting place and guests may use the ALSAA Leisure Complex swimming pool, gymnasium and sauna free of charge. Bedrooms all have TV and pay movies, mini-bar. Well-equipped meeting rooms/conference suites available for groups of up to 130, with secretarial and business services. Courtesy bus to and from the airport terminal (24 hr). Two restaurants (Bistro and Sampan) offer contrasting styles of cuisine. Live music in the bar at weekends. Parking. Children welcome (Under 12s free in parents' room; cots available without charge). Wheelchair accessible. **Rooms 249** (110 executive rooms, 102 no-smoking, 3 for disabled). Lift. 24 hour room service. Room rate from about €127. Closed 24-25 Dec. Amex, Diners, MasterCard, Visa, Laser. **Directions:** In airport complex, on the right when entering airport.

Dublin Airport Area

Roganstown Golf & Country Club Hotel

✓ Ⓑ HOTEL/RESTAURANT

Swords Co Dublin **Tel: 01 843 3118**
Fax: 01 843 3303 Email: indo@roganstown.com
Web: www.roganstown.com

Converted from the original Roganstown House and situated only a few minutes' drive from Dublin Airport, this recently opened hotel enjoys a country setting and is the only golf hotel in the area also offering gym / leisure facilties and beauty therapies - a great amenity for local residents and weekenders, and an appealing alternative for travellers who want to be convenient to the airport but not too near. Although new, the hotel feels well established and it has personality - notably in O'Callaghan's Bar, a spacious bar with a country club atmosphere and imaginative informal menu. The Christy O'Connor Junior designed course ('a masterpiece of skill and tactical design') is a major attraction - add a high level of comfort and a country house ambience and it's easy to see why this new hotel is already making a mark. Business and conference facilities available. **Rooms 52**. B&B from €85 pps. Midweek specials offered. Open all year.

McLouglins Restaurant: The wood panelled fine dining restaurant is attractively situated, and is receiving favourable attention, for head chef Lewis Bannerman's appealing menus and a high standard of cooking. With attentive service to match, this restaurant has already earned a following. Major Credit Cards. **Directions:** 5 minutes from Dublin Airport, near Swords.

HOWTH

Despite being so close to Dublin city, the Howth peninsula enjoys a unique away from-it-all atmosphere and, as it's easily accessible by DART, it's a good place fo a day out if you're staying in the city. There's an immediate feeling of being in the great outdoors - the **Hill of Howth** dominates the skyline and the mind turns to walks on hill, beach or the cliff path (which goes all the way from Sutton to the Baily lighthouse and round to Howth harbour), or sailing, and golf, golf golf... **Sutton Cross** (officially Dublin 13, but at the neck of Howth peninsula) is a very short drive indeed from several of the country's most famous courses including the links at Royal Dublin (on the bird sanctuary, Bull Island) and Portmarnock - and there are many other fine, if marginally less famous course to choose from nearby. The fishing port of **Howth** is an interesting place to wander around. The fish shops along the west pier attract a loyal clientèle (the very last one, **Nicky's Plaice**, is a local favourite) and for many a year it's been a tradition to come out from town after work on a Thursday to buy fish for the fast day on Friday - while that is largely a thing of the past, the shops still stay open later on Thursday evenings, which gives the place a special buzz in summer when people linger for a walk around the harbour or a bite to eat before going home. There are several other interesting food shops too: on the seafront, **Cib**

01 839 6271) is a great place for real home-cooked food to take home, and up
n the village, **Baily Wines** (01 832 2394) is not only an interesting owner-run
vine shop but also offers a carefully selected choice of deli products, including
ome of the finest Irish artisan foods. Then up beside the church, there's **Main
treet Flowers & Country Market** (01 8395575) for flowers, fresh produce and
ome specialist groceries. An ever-growing selection of restaurants includes **Deep**
01 806 3921), a smart new place on the west pier; the popular neighbourhood
win restaurants **The Big Blue** (first floor) and its much-liked little ground floor
ister, **Café Blue** (01 832 0565), which are up near the old abbey and overlook
ne harbour, and a couple of ethnic restaurants - the long-established **El Paso**
01 832 3334) and a stylish Indian, **The Green Chilli** (01 832 0444), which are
oth on the front. For accommodation: the village centre **Baily Hotel** (01 832
691; www.baily.com) is in energetic new management and currently being re-
tyled as a boutique hotel (the cool **Bá Mizu** next door gives a sense of the
merging style); up the hill - above Howth castle and with spectacular sea and
oastal views over Irelands largest public golf complex - is the **Deer Park Hotel**
018322624; www.deerpark-hotel.ie). For B&B accommodation, try the Holden
mily's home, **Edri** (01 839 3131), just above the church on Thormanby Road.

---

owth   Abbey Tavern
B ♣ ATMOSPHERIC PUB/RESTAURANT   Abbey Street Howth Co Dublin
                                   Tel: 01 839 0282 Fax: 01 839 0284
                    Email: info@abbeytavern.ie Web: www.abbeytavern.ie

ust 50 yards up from the harbour, part of this famous pub dates back to the
5th century, when it was built as a seminary for the local monks (as an addition
o the 12th century Chapter House next door). Currently owned by James and
thne Scott-Lennon - James' grandfather bought it in 1945 - the entire
stablishment was refurbished in 1998 but this well-run and immaculately
aintained pub retains features that have always made the Abbey special - open
rf fires, original stone walls, flagged floors and gas lights. In 1960 the Abbey
arted to lay on entertainment and this, more than anything else, has brought
e tavern its fame: it can cater for groups of anything between two and 200
nd the format, which now runs like clockwork, is a traditional 5-course dinner
llowed by traditional Irish music. It's on every night but booking is essential,
pecially in high season. Bar food such as Howth seafood chowder, smoked
lmon with home-made brown bread, a hot traditional dish such as corned beef
d cabbage, and ploughman's salad is available at lunchtime.

estaurant: In 1956 a restaurant was opened, quite a novel move in a pub at
e time; it is now called The Abbot and has its own separate entrance.
tractively and comfortably refurbished in keeping with the building, with
en turf fires at both ends of the main room, it makes a fine setting for food
hich is generally well-cooked and not over-complicated simpler dishes are
ually the wisest choice. **Seats 75.** (private room, 45). Reservations required.
r conditioning. D only 7-10.30 Tue-Sat, all menus à la carte, house wine €18.
discretionary. Children welcome; carpark on harbour. Restaurant closed Sun,
on; establishment closed 25 Dec & Good Fri. Amex, Diners, MasterCard, Visa,
ser. **Directions:** 9 miles from Dublin, in the centre of Howth.

---

owth   Aqua Restaurant
B RESTAURANT   1 West Pier Howth Co Dublin **Tel: 01 8320 690**
                    Fax: 01 8320 687 Email: dine@aqua.ie Web: www.aqua.ie

a stunning sea and harbourside location at the end of the west pier,
erlooking the island of Ireland's Eye and with views west towards Malahide,
is building was previously a yacht club and has been sensitively converted

by the current owners to make a fine contemporary restaurant with plenty o
window tables (now with even better views since a recent refurbishment ha
included the installation of new windows). Behind a glass screen, head che
Brian Daly and his team provide entertainment as well as zesty cooking c
colourful food that is thoughtfully but quite simply presented - a refreshin
change from the overworked presentation in many restaurants at the momen
What was once a snooker room is now a characterful bar - with an open fir
and comfortable seating, it has retained a cosy, clubby atmosphere. Bria
Daly's style of cooking is strong, simple and modern; he favours seafooc
notably lobster, but dry aged steak - with grilled peppers, roasted bab
potatoes, balsamic vinegar and extra virgin olive oil, perhaps - is also
speciality. Menus offer a pleasing repertoire of broadly Cal-Ital origin - crostin
of Serrano ham with rocket, asparagus & extra virgin oil, char-grilled breast c
chicken with roasted corn salsa, red pepper coulis, herb oil - although change
could be introduced more often with benefit, to give new choices to a loy
local clientèle. The waterside location, well-sourced ingredients, skilful cookin
and solicitous service all make dining at Aqua a pleasure; à la carte menus ar
pricey but well-balanced set menus (early dinner, lunch and the popular Sunda
jazz brunch), offer very good value. **Seats 100.** D Tue-Sat 5.30-10.30, Sun 6
9.30; L Sun 12.30-4 (Bar L Tue-Sat, 1-3). Early D from about €19.95, Set Su
L about €26.95. Also à la carte. House wine about €21. SC discretionar
Closed Mon, 25 Dec, Good Fri. Amex, MasterCard, Visa, Laser. **Directions:** Le
along pier after Howth DART Station.

Howth   **Casa Past**

RESTAURANT   12 Harbour Road Howth Co Dubl
Tel: 01 839 3823 Fax: 01 839 31C

Great atmosphere is what sets this first floor restaurant overlooking Howt
harbour apart and the secret of Casa Pasta's success is its universal appeal f
all age groups - it's the ideal place for family outings, with swift, goo
humoured young servers and blackboard menus featuring youthful internation
food (lots of pastas and salads) that is neither over-ambitious nor over-price
Regulars that locals happily order without even consulting the menu inclu
runny deep-fried brie with spicy chutney, big Caesar salads (possibly wi
slivers of chicken breast), home-made tagliatelle with mixed seafood in
creamy wine sauce - and desserts like gooey, boozy tiramisu and sticky bano
pie. Wines are not quite as cheap and cheerful (house wine about €19)
might be hoped, given the style of food and surroundings. Children welcom
on Thursdays "kids eat free" (1 child under 10 per adult; 6-8pm) Open daily
6-11, (Sun 12-10). A la carte, 10% SC on parties of 6+. Closed 25 Dec, Goo
Fri. **Also at:** 55 Clontarf Road, Dublin 3. Tel/Fax: 01 833 1402; Eirpage Hous
Donnybrook, Dublin 4. Tel: 01 2608108. Amex, MasterCard, Visa, Lase
Directions: Harbour front, overlooking Howth Yacht Club.

Howth   **El**

RESTAURANT   7 Main Street Howth Co Dubl
Tel: 01 839 6264 Fax: 01 839 62

Aoife Healy's chic restaurant on the main street has earned a loyal followin
clean-lined and warm-toned, with friendly, helpful staff and Juan Miguel Lop
accomplished cooking, it hits the spot. Compact menus offer balanced choic
of about five dishes on each course - the lunch menu is great value, especia
as main courses are also priced separately, and there are a few sandwiches
wraps too. The early dinner is similar, offering, for example: a starter tart of r
peppers, asparagus, courgette and Cooleeney camembert, followed by roast
cod fillet with garlic & white wine on tomato salad with a tomato, red onion
pepper salsa and a dessert like mixed berry crumble. A la carte evening mer

move up a gear and widen the choice slightly, but there is no need for a long menu in an intimate restaurant like Ella. People feel comfortable here - and enjoy the live jazz on Friday and Saturday nights. Not suitable for children after ..pm. **Seats 30.** Reservations advised. Toilets wheelchair accessible. D Tue- Sat, ..30-9.30; L Sun-Sat, 12-3. Set L €14, early D €19 (5.30-7). Also à la carte. MasterCard, Visa. **Directions:** On the main street - opposite the Baily Hotel.

King Sitric Fish Restaurant & Accommodation

Howth

/ Ⓑ RESTAURANT WITH ROOMS

East Pier Howth Co Dublin
Tel: 01 832 5235 Fax: 01 839 2442
Email: info@kingsitric.ie Web: www.kingsitric.ie

féile bia Aidan and Joan MacManus' striking harbourside restaurant is named after an 11th century Norse King of Dublin who had close links with Howth and was a cousin of the legendary Brian Boru. It is one of Dublin's longest established fine dining restaurants - and, from its East Pier site, chef-patron Aidan MacManus can keep an eye on his lobster pots in Balscadden Bay on one side and the fishing boats coming into harbour on the other. Completely re-built in the recent past, this traditional restaurant has blossomed into a fine contemporary space, with first floor dining to take full advantage of the views (notably at lunch, which is especially good value too). Aidan's reputation for cooking seafood (and the excellent sauces that accompany) is of course what brings most people to The King Sitric, and lovers of game also wend their way here in winter, when it is likely to feature on both lunch and dinner menus. Always interested in using the best of local produce, informative notes on menu covers state the restaurant's commitment to local producers, some of whom are named, and gives a listing of Irish fish in six languages. Some specialities worth making a bee-line for include a luscious red velvet crab bisque, crab mayonnaise, and calmar frites with tartare or tomato sauce; less well known seafood, such as locally fished razor shell clams in garlic butter, often shares the menu with classics like sole meunière and Dublin lawyer (lobster with whiskey sauce) - and make sure you leave room for the house dessert, meringue Sitric. But wine interests Aidan MacManus every bit as much as food; he has long had one of the country's finest wine lists, with an especially fine selection of Chablis, magnificent burgundies and a special love of the wine of Alsace. Hence a very special feature of the King Sitric: a temperature controlled wine cellar on the ground floor, where tastings are held. The house wine, Pinot Blanc Cuvée Les Amours Hugel (a special reserve for the King Sitric) is outstanding for both quality and value. The King Sitric received the Guide's Wine List of the Year award in 2001 and the restaurant operates a Food & Wine Club off-season. Banqueting (70). **Seats 70** (private room, 30). Air conditioning. L Mon-Fri,12.30-2.15; D Mon-Sat, 6.30-10. Set L from €24. 'Value' D €30/35 (Mon-Thu all year, no time restrictions); 4-course Set D €52; also à la carte; house wine from €21; SC discretionary. Closed L Sat, all Sun, bank hols.

Accommodation: There are eight lovely rooms, all with sea views and individually designed bathrooms. **Rooms 8** (2 superior, all no-smoking). B&B from €69 pps, ss €30. Amex, MasterCard, Visa, Laser. **Directions:** Far end of the harbour front, facing the east pier.

The Waterside & The Wheelhouse Restaurant

Howth

RESTAURANT/PUB

Harbour Road Howth Co Dublin
Tel: 01 839 0555 Fax: 01 839 3632

The ground floor of this attractive premises overlooking the harbour front is, at quiet times, one of the pleasantest bars in the area - well-run, comfortable and full of character (although it can be very busy, especially at weekends). Upstairs, on the first floor, the **Wheelhouse Restaurant** is friendly and welcoming, with a cosy ambience and moderately priced middle-of-the-road food. They offer a wide choice on menus that naturally include a large selection of local fish dishes - but they're also especially known for good steaks and meat dishes; specialities include rack of Kildare lamb with honey & mustard crust, so non-fish eaters will be well looked after too. Main course dishes are consistently reliable and helpful staff want everyone to have a good time, so this is a popular neighbourhood restaurant: a relaxed family night out. Children welcome. Car parking nearby. **Seats 60**. Air conditioning. D only (in restaurant) 6.30-10 daily. Bar Food also available. Closed 25 Dec, Good Fri. Amex, Diners, MasterCard, Visa. **Directions:** On Howth harbour front.

Howth/Sutton Area   # Marine Hotel

Ⓑ HOTEL   Sutton Cross Co Dublin **Tel: 01 839 0000** Fax: 01 839 0444
             Email: info@marinehotel.ie Web: www.marinehotel.ie

Well-located on the sea side of a busy junction, this attractive hotel has ample car parking in front and a lawn reaching down to the foreshore at the rear. Recently renovated public areas give a good impression: a smart foyer and adjacent bar, an informal conservatory style seating area overlooking the garden and a well-appointed restaurant. Bedrooms, some of which have sea views, have recently been refurbished. A popular venue for conferences and social gatherings, especially weddings, the Marine is also the only hotel in this area providing for the business guest. Business centre; secretarial services; Conference/banqueting (80/190). Golf nearby. Indoor swimming pool. Garden. Children welcome (under 4 free in parents' room; cots available without charge; baby sitting arranged). No pets. **Rooms 48** (1 junior suite, 6 shower only, 3 executive rooms, 12 no-smoking, 2 disabled). Lift. 24 hour room service. B&B €95 pps, ss €30. Meridian Restaurant: L&D daily; bar meals available, 5-8pm daily. Closed 25-26 Dec. Amex, MasterCard, Visa, Laser. **Directions:** Take coast road towards Howth from city centre, on right at Sutton Cross.

MALAHIDE

The attractive coastal town of Malahide has an abundance of bars, cafés and restaurants. In New Street, **Gibneys** pub (01 845 0863) is a first port of call for many; it is a characterful place with a large beer garden at the back for fine weather, and offers contemporary bar food and an interesting wine selection (including a blackboard menu by the glass). In a first floor premises on The Green, and overlooking the marina area, **Ciao Ristorante** (01 845 1233) is a relaxed restaurant and can claim one of the best views in town - although corner windows at the more recently opened first floor Greek restaurant **Cape Greko** (01 845 6288), at the bottom of New Street, also command views across the green towards the marina. **Hush** (01 806 1928) was previously known as Restaurant 12a; now more casual, with longer opening hours. it's a good spot for lunch as well as dinner. A visit to **Malahide Castle** (01 846 2184) is a must, if only for a walk in the extensive parkland or to see the Fry Model Railway, and there is also an informal restaurant/tea rooms. Gardening enthusiasts will enjoy visiting the **Talbot Botanic Garden** and an excellent garden centre, **Gardenworks** (01 8450 110; opposite the back entrance to the castle grounds), which has a good daytime café (Mon-Sat 10-5, Sun & bank hols, 12-5). There's a **Farmers' Market** at Church Road in Malahide (Saturday, 11-5), and there are several shops in the town to interest lovers of food and wine, notably **The Foodware Store** (01 845 1830), at the bottom of Old Street, and **Cheers** wine shop, which is at Gibneys pub on New Street. And, a few miles along the coast towards Howth, at Portmarnock, an exceptional wine shop, **Jus de Vine** (01 846 1192) is well worth a visit.

Malahide

✓ **Ⓑ** RESTAURANT

Bon Appetit

9 St James Terrace Malahide Co Dublin
Tel: 01 8450 314 Fax: 01 8450 314
Email: info@bonappetit.ie Web: www.bonappetit.ie

féile bia In a Georgian terrace near the marina, Patsy McGuirk's highly-regarded basement restaurant is warmly decorated in shades of red and gold, enhanced by a collection of local watercolours - and there's a welcome emphasis on comfort. Patsy McGuirk is a very fine chef in the classic French style, sometimes tempered by Mediterranean and modern Irish influences; many years dedication in the kitchen have resulted in a long list of specialities, each as tempting as the next, although if a choice had to be made it is probably his fish cookery that would top the bill - seafood, mostly from nearby Howth, predominates on menus although steaks, Wicklow lamb, farmyard duckling and ostrich, which is farmed nearby, also feature. Fresh prawn bisque with cognac is a regular, and a long-established house speciality is Sole Creation McGuirk (whole boned black sole, filled with turbot and prawns, in a beurre blanc sauce), a dish so gloriously old-fashioned that it's now come full circle, while simple sole on the bone is presented whole at the table, then re-presented bone-free and neatly reassembled. Delicious roast crispy duckling Grand Marnier on a potato & herb stuffing is another speciality, also ostrich - medallions, perhaps, served on red cabbage champ with onion marmalade and port wine jus. It's worth leaving room for pretty desserts, usually including some with fruit: fresh seasonal fruit cream pavlova is typical, served with a mango & raspberry coulis, or there's a platter of Irish and continental cheeses - and petits fours with your coffee. A fine wine list has its heart in France; there are helpful tasting notes and a special selection, as well as six fairly priced house wines. While not inexpensive, prices have held steady at the Bon Appetit, and the set lunch menu is particularly good value. The more streamlined, contemporary restaurants there are in Ireland, the more precious places such as this become. Long may it remain to restore us. Not suitable for children after 9pm. Booking essential, especially for dinner. Small weddings catered for. **Seats 60** (private room, 24). Air conditioning. L Mon-Fri.12.30-2, D Mon-Sat 7-10; Set L €25, Set D €48, also à la carte; house wine from €22; SC discretionary. Closed Sun, bank hols & several days at Christmas. Amex, Diners, MasterCard, Visa, Laser. **Directions:** Coming from Dublin go through the lights and turn left into St James's Terrace at Malahide Garda Station.

Malahide

ESTAURANT

Cruzzo Bar & Restaurant

The Marina Malahide Co Dublin **Tel: 01 845 0599**
Fax: 01 845 0602 Email: info@cruzzo.ie Web: www.cruzzo.ie

féile bia Built on a platform over the water, this attractive bar and restaurant is large and stylish in Florida style, with views over the marina. Approaching from the carpark over a little bridge creates a sense of anticipation, and the interior is dashing, with a large piano bar on the lower floor and a rather grand staircase rising to the main dining areas above, which are comfortable and well-appointed, with well-spaced tables in interesting groupings - although it is worth ensuring a table with a view when booking, as there is always something interesting going on in daylight, and the seawater all around is impressively lit at night; an elevated section at the front has the best tables in the house. Contemporary menus hold no great surprises but offer a varied choice of perhaps eight or ten dishes on each course, including attractively presented starters like tian of avocado with Boston prawn, marinated shaved cucumber and citrus dressing, or simple Irish rock oyster with shallot vinegar. Main courses are not over-ambitious, offering many popular choices - panfried chicken breast, steaks, supreme of salmon - dressed with less usual accompaniments. Cooking has tended to be a little uneven, but the Guide's most recent experience was enjoyable, and the location and ambience always give a sense of occasion - especially at weekends, when a band or pianist playing downstairs adds to the atmosphere. Although prices on the à la carte are quite high (and vegetables are charged extra), the early dinner menu is good value. **Seats 290**. Reservations required.Lift; wheelchair friendly. L Tue- Fri, 12.30-2.45, Sun 12.30-4; D Tue-Sun 6-10 (Sun 6.30-9.30). Early D € 19 (Mon-Fri, 6-7pm); L & D also à la carte. Live music, weekends House wine from €19.50. SC discretionary. Closed L Mon, L Sat, 25-26 Dec, 1 Jan, Good Fri. Amex, MasterCard, Diners, Laser, Visa. **Directions:** From Malahide Village through arch into Marina.

Malahide   Danieli Restaurant

RESTAURANT   The Green Malahide Co Dublin **Tel: 01 806 188**

Danieli has brought a continental air to the foreshore here, with its alfresco dining area and a smart canvas awning - which improves the rather plain office-like brick building considerably. Inside, the restaurant is broken into several areas, allowing some tables a view, and menus are adventurous and varied - with an understandable emphasis on seafood. In the Guide's experience, the cooking is very good: quality ingredients are handled with expertise, producing handsome dishes which taste as good as they look colourful, fresh-tasting starters might include a warm salad of Parma ham (with asparagus, rocket and a softly poached egg), for example, and main course such as an elegant panache of shellfish, or a fine rack of lamb. Main course are very individual and quite substantial, so a good coffee will probably be all that is required to round off a satisfying meal. Prices (of both food and wine are on the high side, so bills can mount rather quickly, but a visit here shoul be an enjoyable experience. Mon-Sat, D from 5.30; Sun, L&D, open from 1pm A la carte. House wine around €20. **Directions:** On the front in Malahide looking towards the marina.

Malahide   Grand Hotel

Ⓑ HOTEL   Malahide Co Dublin **Tel: 01 845 0000** Fax: 01 845 098
                Email: info@thegrand.ie Web: www.thegrand.i

Just 8 miles from Dublin airport in one of Ireland's most attractive coasta towns, The Grand Hotel is well-situated for business and pleasure; set in si acres of gardens, the original building at the heart of this large hotel date back to 1835, which gives it a certain gravitas. Recent additions hav included an excellent leisure centre and extensive conference and banquetin facilities. Many of the bedrooms have sea views, the beach (a tidal estuary) just across the road, there are several golf courses nearby - also numerou other activities, including equestrian, fishing, tennis and watersports - an there is much of interest within walking distance in the town. Although th the hotel **restaurant** is rather lacking in atmosphere, dining here shoul otherwise be a pleasant outing as, in the Guides's recent experience, menu are interesting and the cooking is very good. Conference/banquetin (450/380). Business centre. Leisure centre (21 metre swimming pool, jacuzz gym). Own parking. Wheelchair accessible. Children welcome (under 12 free i parents' room; cots available, baby sitting arranged). No pets. **Rooms 150 (** suites, 7 junior suites, 39 executive, 15 shower only, 60 no-smoking, 1 f disabled). Lift. B&B about €175 pps. ss about €85. Special breaks offered. Closed 25-27 Dec. Amex, Diners, MasterCard, Visa, Laser. **Directions:** Centre of Malahide; near Dublin Airport and about 30 mins from Dublin city centre.

Malahide | **Jaipur**
RESTAURANT | St James Terrace Malahide Co Dublin
Tel: 01 845 5455 Fax: 01 845 5456
Email: malahide@jaipur.ie Web: www.jaipur.ie

féile bia This chic new-wave Indian restaurant is the third Jaipur - the others are in Dublin 2 and Dalkey; it's in the basement of a fine Georgian terrace and, although Malahide is particularly well-served with interesting eating places, it has earned a following. Cooking is crisp and modern - a contemporary take on traditional Indian food; head chef Sunil Ghai trained in the five-star Oberoi hotel in New Dehli and it shows in colourful, well-flavoured dishes that have a lot of eye appeal. Vegetarian choices are particularly appealing, old favourites like tandoori prawns take well to the contemporary treatment and even desserts - usually a total no-no in ethnic restaurants - are worth leaving room for. Meals: D daily, 5-11. Early D, €20 (5-7pm). Set menus €35-45 (incl 4-course Tasting Menu). House wine €18.Closed 25-26 Dec. Amex, MasterCard, Visa, Laser. **Directions:** In Georgian terrace facing the tennis club in Malahide.

Malahide | **Siam Thai Restaurant**
RESTAURANT | Gas Lane Malahide Co Dublin
Tel: 01 845 4698 Fax: 01 816 9460
Email: siam@eircom.net Web: www.siamthai.ie

Handily located in a laneway close to the marina, this was one of Dublin's earlier Thai restaurants and still regularly fills its tightly-packed tables. Sutchan Sutchudthad, who has been with the restaurant since 1994, presents menus that offer many of the Thai classics on an extensive à la carte as well as the set menus and, although perhaps blanded down a bit for local tastes, there's a willingness to vary the spiciness according to personal preference. No monosodium glutamate is used. A typically warm Thai welcome gets guests into the mood, and you may be shown to a small bar (where a pianist plays a grand piano on some nights) or taken to your ornately gold-framed chair at a white linen clad table in a large dimly-lit restaurant decorated with Thai paintings. Menus are very extensive - the indecisive might begin with Siam Combination appetisers (including chicken satay, spring rolls, special coated prawns, marinated pork ribs, prawns wrapped in ham and bags of golden wonton with plum sauce), followed perhaps by main courses like Ghung Phad Phong Garee Tiger prawns with scallions, mushrooms and basil leaves and a spicy sauce) and Ped Makham (boneless crisp-skinned duck with crispy noodles and plum sauce). Outstandingly warm and friendly staff are knowledgeable and efficient. Children welcome. Air conditioning. Live music (piano or live Thai band) most nights. **Seats 105.** D daily 5-11.30 (Sun to 10.30). Early D €20 (5-7.30); Set €33; à la carte also available. House wine €19.96. SC10%. Closed 25-26 Dec. Amex, Diners, MasterCard, Visa, Laser. **Directions:** In Malahide village, near marina; turn left at Church to end of road.

Malahide | **Silks**
RESTAURANT | 5 The Mall Malahide Co Dublin **Tel: 01 845 3331**

This smart Chinese restaurant is spacious, modern and airy, with cheerful decor and staff who are friendly and helpful, to match. Although the long menu is fairly predictable, the food is well above average and can show imagination and flair. Sizzlers and sweet & sours are there, but they are expertly done using quality ingredients, especially the seafood. Excellent crispy Peking duck with pancakes or a light, delicately spiced chicken and mushroom broth make good starters followed, perhaps, by fresh-flavoured main courses of crunchy salt & chilli squid and prawns with ginger and spring onions. Cantonese-style chicken is a speciality - tender slices of chicken in a light, fruit-based sauce with just a hint of spiciness - and desserts are unsurprising: banana fritters with an above average vanilla ice cream, perhaps, or a simple bowl of lychees. Reservations are essential as this restaurant has a loyal following and is busy every night of the week. **Seats 90** (private room 20). Air conditioning. D daily: Mon-Sat 6-12.30. Sun 5-11. A la carte. **Directions:** Opposite Garda Station.

Malahide Area
✓COUNTRY HOUSE

Belcamp Hutchinson

Carrs Lane Malahide Road Balgriffin Dublin 17
Tel: 01 846 0843 Fax: 01 848 5703
Email: belcamhutchinson@eircom.net
Web: www.belcamphutchinson.com

Dating back to 1786, this impressive house just outside Malahide takes its name from its original owner, Francis Hely-Hutchinson, 3rd Earl of Donoughmore. It is set in large grounds, with interesting gardens, giving it a very away-from-it-all country atmosphere - yet Belcamp Hutchinson is only about half an hour from Dublin city centre (off peak) and 15 minutes to the airport. The present owners, Doreen Gleeson and Karl Waldburg, have renovated the house sensitively: high ceilinged, graciously proportioned rooms have retained many of their original features and are furnished and decorated in keeping with their age. Bedrooms are very comfortable, with thoughtfully appointed bathrooms and views over the gardens and countryside. Although its convenient location makes this an ideal place to stay on arrival or when leaving Ireland, a one-night stay won't do justice to this lovely and hospitable place. Walled garden; maze. Golf, equestrian, walking, garden visits, tennis, sailing nearby. Not suitable for children under 10. Pets welcome. **Rooms 8** (all with full bath & overbath shower). B&B €70 pps, no ss. Closed 20 Dec-1 Feb. MasterCard, Visa. **Directions:** From city centre, take Malahide Road; pas Campions pub, 1st lane on left (sign on right pointing up lane).

Portmarnock
✓ Ⓑ HOTEL/RESTAURANT

Portmarnock Hotel & Golf Links

Strand Road Portmarnock Co Dublin
Tel: 01 846 0611 Fax: 01 846 2442
Email: sales@portmarnock.com Web: www.portmarnock.com

Originally owned by the Jameson family, Portmarnock Hotel and Golf Links enjoys a wonderful beachside position overlooking the islands of Lambay and Ireland's Eye. Very close to the airport, and only eleven miles from Dublin city centre, the hotel seems to offer the best of every world - the peace and convenience of the location and a magnificent 18 hole Bernhard Langer designed links course. Public areas, including an impressive foyer, are bright and spacious, with elegant modern decor and a relaxed atmosphere. The Jameson Bar, in the old house, has character and there's also an informal Links Bar and Restaurant next to the golf shop (open 12-9.30 daily). Accommodation is imaginatively designed so that all rooms have sea or golf course views, and all - including some in the original house which are furnished with antiques, two with four-posters and executive rooms with balconies or bay windows - are furnished to a high standard of comfort, with excellent bathrooms. Conference/banqueting (350/220) Business centre; secretarial services. Golf (18). Oceana, health & beauty, offers: gym, sauna, steam rooms & a wide range of treatments. Children welcome (under 3 free in parents' room, cots available without charge, baby sitting arranged). No pets. Garden. **Rooms 100** (17 executive, 16 no-smoking, 4 for disabled). Lift. 24 hour room service. B&B about€155 pps, ss €75. Open all year.

The Osborne Restaurant: Named after the artist Walter Osborne, who painted many of his most famous pictures in the area including the view from the Jameson house, the restaurant has been a major addition to the north Dublin dining scene since the hotel opened in 1996. The room is very formal, with beautifully appointed tables and fresh flowers, and head chef Mark Doe's menus are constructed with the international traveller in mind, using the best quality ingredients available - especially seafood from the nearby fishing port of Howth including, typically, a fillet of turbot with scallop ravioli and tarragon butter sauce. Tempting desserts may include a signature dish of grilled white peaches with mascarpone cheese & pistachio biscotti. The dining experience is generally pleasant, with nice details like good breads and petits fours; presentation is notable for its formality, making this very much a 'special occasion' restaurant. A good wine list matches the style of the menu and surroundings. Air conditioning. **Seats 80** (private room, 22). D only Tue-Sat, 7-10. Set D from €45, Tasting Menu from €70. A la carte available; house wine from €18.95; SC discretionary. Closed Sun, Mon. Amex, Diners, MasterCard, Visa, Laser. **Directions:** On the coast in Portmarnock.

SKERRIES

So far remarkably unspoilt, the fishing port of **Skerries** is not completely undeveloped but its essential atmosphere has remained unchanged for decades (perhaps because it does not yet have marina and all its attendant development) and it makes a refreshing break from the hurly-burly of Dublin city. The harbour is renowned for its fishing, notably Dublin Bay prawns, and the surrounding area is famous for market gardening, so it has always been a good place for a very subtstantial bite to eat - and there are several pubs of character to enjoy a pint before your meal - or the **Coast Inn**, just across the road from the **Red Bank** (see below), does a great line in cocktails. On Strand street, **Russell's** (01 849 2450) is a friendly neighbourhood restaurant, and while in the area, allow time to visit **Skerries Mills** (working windmills; Tel: 01 849 5208) and the beautifully located **Ardgillan Castle and Victorian Gardens** (Tel: 01 849 2212) nearby, where there are tea rooms. Near Skerries, at **Lusk**, the **Fingal Food Fayre** market is held at the Arts Centre, on the last Sunday of every month (12-5).

Skerries   **Red Bank House & Restaurant**

/ **Ⓑ** ♣ RESTAURANT/GUESTHOUSE   5-7 Church Street Skerries Co Dublin
                 Tel: 01 849 1005   Fax: 01 849 1598
                 Email: redbank@eircom.net   Web: www.redbank.ie

féile bia There's a double-entendre to the name of Terry and Margaret McCoy's restaurant - not only is there a sandbank of the same name nearby, but it's also in a converted banking premises, which makes a restaurant of character and practicality - even the old vault has its uses: as a wine cellar. Aperitifs and crudités, served in a comfortable bar/reception area, get arriving guests off to a good start, and it's a pleasant place to consider Terry's high individual menus before heading through to the traditional restaurant. One of the great characters of contemporary Irish cooking, Terry is an avid supporter of local produce and suppliers and fresh seafood from Skerries harbour (including local razor fish) provides the backbone of his menus, but without limiting the vision - this is a man who goes out at dawn with a bucket to gather young nettles for soup. Dishes conceived and cooked with generosity have names of local relevance - thus, for example, grilled goat's cheese St. Patrick is a reminder that the saint once lived on Church Island off Skerries. The dessert trolley is legendary - a large space should be left if pudding is to be part of your meal. Should the sauces and accompaniments prove too much, plainly cooked food is provided on request and dishes suitable for vegetarians are marked on the menu. A good wine list is informative and fairly priced; it includes a wide selection of house wines, and a good choice of half bottles. **Seats 55** (private room,10). D Mon-Sat, 6.30-10; L Sun only, 12.30-4.30. Early D €30 (Mon-Fri, 6.30-7.30); Set D €45, Set Sun L €26. A la carte also available. Interesting selection of about two dozen house wines €20-28; sc discretionary. Children welcome. Closed D Sun. Restaurant only closed 24-27 Dec.

Accommodation: As well as fine, comfortably furnished bedrooms with all the amenities normally expected of an hotel, there are facilities for private parties (50). Gourmet golf breaks are a speciality - up to 40 golf courses within 20 minutes drive. Children under 4 free in parents' room (cots available free of charge). Pets permitted by arrangement. **Rooms 18** (all superior & no-smoking). B&B €70 pps, ss €10 (DB&B rate is good value at €90 pps). Accommodation open all year. Amex, Diners, MasterCard, Visa, Laser. **Directions:** Opposite AIB Bank in Skerries.

Skerries   **Stoop Your Head**
RESTAURANT/BAR   Harbour Road Skerries Co Dublin
                                          Tel: 01 849 1144

After a quiet off season drink a few doors along at Joe May's, there can be no greater pleasure in north Dublin than to slip into 'Stoops' for some of Andy Davies' mainly seafood cooking. If it's busy you may have to wait at the little bar - where you can opt to eat if you like, or have a look at the menu while waiting for a table (they seem to turn over fairly fast). The surroundings are simple - chunky wooden tables, closely packed - and the menu is not elaborate but there is plenty to choose from, and there are blackboard specials every day too; what could be more delightful than starters of dressed crab, or moules marinière - or perhaps a classic fresh prawn Marie Rose? Prawns are landed in Skerries and a speciality - and like crab claws, are offered as starters or main courses, in irresistible garlic butter . You don't have to eat seafood here - there are other choices like Asian chicken salad, or pasta dishes or even fillet steak medallions - but it would be a pity to miss it. Super fresh and delicously simple, it's a treat. **Seats 30** (outdoor seating, 20). No reservations. Children welcome. L & D daily: L 12-3, D 5.30-10 (Sun D 4-8). House wine €16. Closed 25 Dec & Good Fri. Visa. **Directions:** On the harbour front in Skerries.

SWORDS

Bypassing this busy town near the airport may prove to be the making of it although still busy, it's a much more pedestrian-friendly place recently, and easier on the nerves all round. Points of interest in and around the town include a 75' round tower, **Swords Castle** (built around 1200) and, close by, the exciting contemporary premises of **Fingal County Council** (built around 2000) **Newbridge House & Traditional Farm** (01 843 6534), which is on the coast at Donabate, about halfway between Skerries and Malahide, is an interesting place to visit with pleasant walks in extensive grounds - and tea rooms.

Swords

RESTAURANT

Old Schoolhouse Restaurant

Church Road Swords Co Dublin

Tel: 01 840 2846 Fax: 01 840 5060

Email: sincater@gofree.indigo.ie Web: www.oldschoolhouse.ie

féile bia In a quiet riverside site close to the Northern Cross motorway, and only a short drive from the airport, the Sinclair family's restored 18th century stone school building has been an attractive and highly regarded country-style restaurant since 1982. However, although still operating as a restaurant at the time of going to press, major changes are planned which will greatly extend the premises - and it will become a large bar offering imaginative informal food (and possibly retention of a smaller dining area something like the old restaurant.) Children welcome. **Seats 70** (private room, 12) Air conditioning. L Tue-Fri, 12.30-2.30, D Tue-Sat 6.30-10.30. Set L €19.50. Early D €25 (Mon-Fri, 6.30-7.30); Set D €25; à la carte also available; house wine €18; SC discretionary. Closed Sun, Mon, Christmas/New Year, bank hols. Amex, Diners, MasterCard, Visa, Laser. **Directions:** Coming from Dublin, turn left after Lord Mayor's Pub.

SOUTH COUNTY DUBLIN

BLACKROCK

From a gastronomic viewpoint, this well-heeled suburb just a 15 minute DART ride from the city centre has blossomed in recent years and has some good restaurants and a sprinkling of interesting shops. **Cakes & Co**, on Rock Hill, specialise in celebration cakes - even "just looking" is very worthwhile for these inventive creations - although roaming foodlovers should perhaps make a visit to Eileen Bergin's well-established shop, **The Butler's Pantry** on Mount Merrion Avenue (also in Donnybrook and Dun Laoghaire) the first port of call, especially if there's a picnic in the offing, or you want a proper home-cooked meal to come home to without cooking it yourself. Should something be needed to wash it down, **McCabes Wine Merchants** next door will have the solution - in spades. Lovers of Thai food might head up to the shopping centre on Newtown Park Avenue, where **The Blue Orchid** (01 283 17677) is in the premises previously occupied by the famous AyumiYa Japanese Restaurant. And, if gardens are your thing, make a point of visiting the Italianate garden and herb garden at "**Deepwell**"on Rock Hill if the dates suit. (Call 01 288 7407 for information on opening times of both house and garden). Further out, at Sandyford, **Fernhill Gardens** are also a great destination for garden lovers (01 295 6000).

Blackrock   **Dali's Restaurant**

RESTAURANT   63-65 Main Street Blackrock Co Dublin
Tel: 01 278 0660 Fax: 01 278 0661

These premises have been home to several of Dublin's most successful restaurateurs and there's a chic little bar just inside the door, leading to a rather tightly packed dining area, at a slightly higher level, beyond - all attractively set up in a style that is contemporary but without hard-edged minimalism. Menus are appealingly light and colourful, including zesty first courses salmon fishcakes with a chive beurre blanc, which are a speciality followed by main courses that could include some unusual variations on old favourites - Dali's Irish Stew. Booking is essential, especially at weekends. Set lunch menus offer a choice of four or five dishes on each course and are good value. Children welcome. Air conditioning. **Seats 65**. L Tue-Sun, 12-3; D Tue Sat 6-10.30. Set L from about €15. A la carte L&D available; house wine about €20, sc discretionary except 10% on parties of 6+. Closed D Sun, all Mon, 25 27 Dec. **Directions:** Opposite Blackrock Library.

Blackrock   **Tonic**

BAR   5 Temple Road Blackrock Village Co Dublin **Tel: 01 288 7671**
Email: mail@tonic.ie Web: www.tonic.ie

This smart designer bar is a younger sister of IN in Dalkey (see entry) and has brought some welcome style to Blackrock village with its cool walnut woodwork cube chairs, cream leather banquettes and artwork for sale on exhibition - all of which, plus a big screen upstairs, have made it the in place for the trendy young crowd. Informal menus are offered through the day - brunch, daytime and evening bistro - and there's a patio area for al fresco dining in fine weather however, in the Guide's experience, the food may be a little disappointing, so perhaps it's more a place to drop into for a drink in stylish surroundings. Open 11am-11.30 pm (later at weekends). Bar food served 12-11 (L12-3.30, D 4-11) Café, **Seats 53**: 7.30-11. Toilets wheelchair accessible. **Directions:** Centre of Blackrock village.

DALKEY

Dalkey is a charming old-world place with a distinctly villagey atmosphere, a delightful little harbour and lots of characterful pubs and good restaurants to choose from. On St Patrick's Road there's also an innovative shop, **On the Grapevine** which, predictably enough, specialises in wine; this is does very well, but they can do better - not only do they stock some very delicious specialist foods as well, but their website has an on-line purchase facility, tasting notes and Food & Wine information. If you can't get to the shop, perhaps a virtual visit to www.onthegrapevine.ie would do instead!

Dalkey	**Daniel Finnegan**
✓ ATMOSPHERIC PUB	2 Sorrento Road Dalkey Co Dublin
	Tel: 01 285 8505

An immaculately maintained pub of great character, much-loved by locals and visitors alike. It's bright, comfortable and cosy, with wood panelling and traditional Irish seating in 'snugs', has now 'blended in' the large extension built a couple of years ago. Food is served at lunchtime only - a full hot bar lunch, including starters such as baked Dalkey crab, brie fritters with apple coulis and main courses like roast stuffed pork steak, honey roast half duck and grilled cod steak, followed by traditional desserts like apple pie and lemon cheesecake. The fresh fish (from the harbour nearby) is excellent, the vegetables predictable but tasty and value good. No reservations - get there early to avoid a long wait. Carpark nearby. Bar food 12.30-3pm Mon-Sat. Closed 25 Dec, Good Fri & & New Year. **Directions:** Near Dalkey DART station.

Dalkey	**IN**
BAR/CAFÉ	115-117 Coliemore Road Dalkey Co Dublin
	Tel: 01 275 0007 Fax: 02 275 0009
	Email: info@indalkey.ie Web: www.indalkey.ie

This stylish contemporary café-bar in the centre of Dalkey has found a niche, offering something rather different from pubs and restaurants in the area. The atmosphere is relaxed and what you get here is informal dining in comfortable, pleasant surroundings: menus offer a choice ranging from the ubiquitous steak, and bistro dishes like lamb shank (deliciously tender) or crisp confit of duck to seafood dishes - including a range of platters available for groups of four to eight (€20-40), which is an interesting idea. Judging by the Guide's recent experience cooking may be uneven, but this is an attractive bar and useful to know about. Wheelchair accessible. Open 11 am-11.30pm (Fri & Sat to 1.30). Bar meals daily: 12-10 (Fri & Sat to 11). L Mon-Fri 12-4, D 5.30-10. Sun brunch (2.30-4.30). **Directions:** At the end of Dalkey's main street.

Dalkey	**Jaipur Restaurant**
RESTAURANT	23 Castle Street Dalkey Co Dublin
	Tel: 01 285 0552

féile bia This stylish south County Dublin branch of the small chain of well-regarded progressive Indian restaurants has become established as a favourite in the area. (See entries under Dublin 2 and Malahide). D daily, 5.30-1. Set D from €20, also à la carte. House wine €18. Closed 25-26 Dec. **Directions:** On Dalkey's main street.

Nosh

Dalkey
RESTAURANT

111 Coliemore Road Dalkey Co Dublin
Tel: 01 284 0666 Email: comments@nosh.ie Web: www.nosh.ie

féile bia Samantha and Sacha Farrell's bright, contemporary restaurant is next to the famous Club Bar and, with its clean lines and lightwood furniture, no-nonsense menus and quality ingredients, its place in the Dalkey dining scene seems assured. Head chef Julie Sheils' contemporary seasonal menus have a slight bias towards fish and vegetarian food, and change throughout the day: their great weekend brunch menu has become very popular, and offers hot dishes (anything from the traditional Irish 'Nosh brunch', or potato pancakes with scrambled eggs and smoked salmon, to omelettes, buttermilk pancakes with grilled bananas and maple syrup, to smoked haddock & chips or fish pie with Nosh mash) and a wide range of coffees and other hot and cold drinks, including home-made lemonade). For lunch there's some overlap from the Brunch menu and a dozen or so other choices, ranging up to the "Posh Nosh" special of the day. In the evening, you might begin with prawn pil-pils in sizzling garlic & chilli oil (an enduring favourite) and proceed to fish & chips with home-made chips & tartare sauce (another speciality) or an appealing vegetarian dish such as pea & asparagus risotto. Desserts are home-made and there's a limited but well-chosen wine list, with a few half bottles, offered throughout the day. Not suitable for children after 8pm. Wheelchair accessible. Air conditioning. **Seats 45**. L Tue-Fri, 12-4 (Sat & Sun, Brunch 12-4); D Tue-Sun 6-10. A la carte. House wine €17.50. Closed Mon, bank hols. **Directions:** End of Dalkey town, take left.

The Queen's Bar & Restaurant

Dalkey
PUB/RESTAURANT

12 Castle Street Dalkey Co Dublin **Tel: 01 285 4569**
Fax: 01 285 8345 Email: queens@clubi.ie

The oldest pub in Dalkey, and also one of the oldest in Ireland, The Queen's was originally licensed to 'dispense liquor' as far back as 1745, and renovations and improvements in recent years have been done with due respect for the age and character of the premises. As well as a busy, characterful bar, there is a restaurant (previously La Romana) offering popular international food - pizzas, pastas, steak, a little (well cooked) fish - in an informal atmosphere. Very good bar food: chowders, salads, pies, steak sandwiches etc also available every afternoon and and evening, and can be served to patio areas at the back and front in fine weather. Wheelchair accessible. Restaurant Seat 70; D daily. Bar menu daily,12-5, light evening bar menu Mon-Fri. Closed 25 Dec & Good Fri **Directions:** Centre of town,beside Heritage Centre.

Ragazzi

Dalkey
RESTAURANT

109 Coliemore Road Dalkey Co Dublin
Tel: 01 284 7280

Possibly Dublin's buzziest little bistro, this is the pizza place where everyone goes to have their spirits lifted by theatrical Italian waiters and great value. Lovely pastas, luscious bruschettas - but best of all the pizzas, renowned for their thin, crisp bases and scrumptious toppings. But it's the atmosphere that counts - every town should have a place like this.

Thai House Restaurant

Dalkey
RESTAURANT

21 Railway Road Dalkey Co Dublin **Tel: 01 284 7304**
Email: info@thaihouseireland.com
Web: www.thaihouseireland.com

Established in 1997, well before the current vogue for Thai food, Tony Ecock' restaurant has earned a loyal following and head chef Wilai Khruekhcai ha maintained a reputation for including dishes that do not pander too much to bland western tastes. In typical oriental style, a number of set menus are offered for groups of various sizes and there is also an extensive à la carte which offers a wider choice. After an aperitif in the wine bar/reception area, begin, perhaps, with the Thai House Special Starter Pack, a sampling plate of six starters, well-balanced in flavour and texture and including some vegetarian options: Thai prawn toast, chicken satay with peanut sauce, deep-fried corn cakes with herbs & curry paste, crispy vegetarian spring rolls, deep-fried prawn cakes with sweet chilli sauce From a choice of soups that includes the famous Tom Yam Gung (spicy prawn soup with lemon grass and chilli) Tom Yam Rumit - a spicy soup with prawns, squid, crab and mussels is perhaps the most interesting. Main courses include a range of curries - a speciality is fresh monkfish dumplings in green curry sauce with wild ginger - and vegetarian dishes are listed separately. Groups of four can share a dessert platter (usually with coconut and/or banana). The wine list includes a page of house favourites (all under €25) and a Thai beer. Not suitable for children after 8pm. Air conditioning. **Seats 34**. D Tue-Sun. Closed Mon. **Directions:** 100 metres from Dalkey DART Station.

DUN LAOGHAIRE AREA

With its three traditional yacht clubs and a rather dashing new passenger terminal at the ferry port, Dun Laoghaire is putting on a smart contemporary face these days. Seafood is of course well-represented - notably at both **Brasserie na Mara**, and nearby at **Caviston's** very special shop and restaurant (see below), while **Passion**, on Patrick Street, supplies all sorts of other goodies. There's a branch of **Itsabagel** at the Pavilion Centre and, at the time of going to press, an ambitious new restaurant, **Purple Ocean** (01 284 5590; www.purpleocean.ie), had just opened its doors on St Michael's Pier, in the ferry port of Dun Laoghaire. With harbour views, a grand entrance staircase from the harbour plaza (or lift from the harbour carpark under the plaza) and outdoor dining options on the balcony, it promises to be an exciting development. The executive chef is Paul Lewis, formerly of The Old Schoolhouse Restaurant, Swords, Co Dublin. Simpler food is served at **Janet's Coffee House**, Upper George's Street (01 663 6871), where Roberto Morsiani and his wife Janet (previously of Da Roberto in Blackrock, among other popular Italian restaurants) now serve wholesome daytime fare, including authentic pasta dishes, at reasonable prices. And, nearby in Glasthule, another small restaurant that has its heart in the right place is **Reubens** (01 236 5971); situated on Glasthule Road, Sandycove, it is earning a reputation for interesting, carefully sourced food using artisan foods; how fortunate they are to have **O'Toole's**, who specialise in organic meats, close by at Glasthule Road (O'Toole's also have a shop in Terenure). Dun Laoghaire can also boast a brace of **Farmers' Markets** - at the People's Park on Saturdays, 11-4, and at the Harbour Plaza on Thursdays, 10.30-4.

Dun Laoghaire | **Bistro Vino**
RESTAURANT

56 Glasthule Road Dun Laoghaire Co Dublin
Tel: 01 280 6097 Fax: 01 280 6097

Dermot Baker's small first floor evening restaurant (up steep stairs) is near the seafront at Sandycove. It pre-dates surrounding establishments in this now fashionable area by a long chalk. But it's still a hit with the locals, who appreciate the moderate prices, unpretentious, good food and informal

atmosphere. A la carte except for an inexpensive early set menu. D daily, 5-
"late". **Directions:** Opposite Eagle House pub.

Dun Laoghaire	**Brasserie Na Mara**
✓ **B** RESTAURANT	1 Harbour Road Dun Laoghaire Co Dublin

Tel: 01 280 6767 Fax: 01 284 4649
Email: brasserienamara@irishrail.ie

féile bia The old Kingstown terminal building beside the Dun Laoghaire DART station makes a fine location for this harbourside restaurant. Part of Irish Rail's art collection graces the walls - a Nora McGuinness, a Lambe, a Leech - and the current contemporary decor is stylish, with high ceilings and tall windows complemented by linen-covered tables, glistening glasses and a single fresh flower on each table - and the bar faces in towards the reception area, so you look out over the harbour while enjoying your aperitif. Interesting menus are in a bright, modern style to suit the decor and, while there is always plenty of choice, there is a special emphasis on seafood as one would expect: starters like shrimp & cod chowder, pan seared scallops, or a speciality dish of grilled seabass, served with sauce vierge, French beans & herb mashed potatoes. Popular meat and poultry dishes include baked ham with champ potatoes and roast breast of duck served oriental style with vegetable spring roll, coconut rice and ginger & chilli syrup; vegetarian dishes are always included - goats cheese, asparagus & sun dried tomato ravioli is typical. Tempting desserts like chocolate cookie millefeuille with mascarpone ice cream & strawberry compôte are well executed. Service is friendly, if slightly disorganised, but pleasing surroundings, quality ingredients, accomplished cooking and good value ensure the popularity of this well-located restaurant. A well-priced wine list includes an unusually good choice of half bottles. **Seats** **64** (private room, 45). Reservations advised. L Mon-Fri 12.30-2.30; D Mon-Sat, 6.30-10. [Mon-Fri: Set L €25; Set 'Value' D €35.] D also à la carte; house wine €20.65. SC 12.5%. Closed L Sat & all Sun, 25-26 Dec & 1 Jan, bank hols. **Directions:** Coast road, beside DART, opposite the Pavilion.

Dun Laoghaire	**Café Mao**
CAFÉ	The Pavilion Dun Laoghaire Co Dublin **Tel: 01 214 8090**

Fax: 01 214 7064 Email: info@cafemao.com

féile bia This large, informal contemporary café-restaurant near the harbour is a younger sister establishment to the popular Café Mao in the city centre, which was one of Dublin's first - and enduringly successful - fusion cafés. It is run on the same lines, with the philosophy of providing simple, quick and healthy food, with youthful appeal, at a reasonable price - and there's always a good buzz. Dishes with nuts are highlighted on the menu, also chilli strength, low fat and vegetarian dishes. Daily specials are particularly good value, and there's a daily cake selection - e.g. cappuccino with walnut gateau, toffee & apple gateau, pecan pie & Mississippi mud pie - and an interesting drinks menu. It's a good place for brunch, with tables outside for fine weather. **Seats 120** (outdoor seating, 40). Toilets wheelchair accessible. Open every day, 12 noon -11pm (Sun to 10). Bookings accepted. Closed 25 Dec, Good Fri. **Directions:** Dun Laoghaire seafront, near station.

Dun Laoghaire	**Caviston's Seafood Restaurant**
✓ RESTAURANT	59 Glasthule Road Dun Laoghaire Co Dublin

Tel: 01 280 9120 Fax: 01 284 4054
Email: caviston@indigo.ie Web: cavistons.com

Caviston's of Sandycove has long been a mecca for lovers of good food and was the Guide's Happy Heart Eat Out award-winner for 2001. Here you will find everything that is wonderful, from organic vegetables to farmhouse cheeses, cooked meats to specialist oils and other exotic items. But it was always for fish and shellfish that Caviston's were especially renowned - even providing a collection of well-thumbed recipe books for on-the-spot reference. At their little restaurant next door, they serve an imaginative range of healthy seafood dishes influenced by various traditions and all washed down by a glass or two from a very tempting little wine list. Caviston's food is simple, colourful, perfectly cooked - it speaks volumes for how good seafood can be. Children welcome. **Seats 26.** L Tue-Sat: 12-1.30; 1.30-3; 3-5. A la carte. SC discretionary. Closed Sun, Mon & Christmas/New Year. **Directions:** Between Dun Laoghaire and Dalkey, 5 mins. walk from Glasthule DART station.

Dun Laoghaire **Eagle House**

ATMOSPHERIC PUB 18 Glasthule Road Dun Laoghaire Co Dublin
Tel: 01 280 4740

This fine traditional establishment is full of interest and a great local. The interior is dark, but has a fascinating collection of model boats, ships and other nautical bric-à-brac and is arranged in comfortably sized alcoves and 'snugs' on different levels. Bar meals, available at lunchtime and in the evening, can be very good. Closed 25 Dec & Good Fri. **Directions:** 5 mins walk from Glasthule DART station, opposite Caviston's.

Dun Laoghaire **The Forty Foot**

BAR/RESTAURANT Pavilion Centre Dun Laoghaire Co Dublin
Tel: 01 284 2982

Named after a well-known local swimming place, this ultra-modern two-storey bar and restaurant in the redeveloped Pavilion Centre is designed to make the most of views over the harbour and Dublin Bay - particularly from the first floor restaurant - and to impress. Bright, spacious and airy, with acres of wood and huge windows the restaurant, especially, is a lovely space and (except at very busy times when you may be directed down to the bar), you can settle into a comfortable sofa to read the menu before being shown to a table simply laid with good linen and cutlery and handsome, plain glasses. The choice is wide and the menu reads well: colourful, fresh-sounding starters are offered - typically mozzarella with roasted peppers & rocket salad, or tian of salmon & crab with crème fraîche; main courses in a similar vein: expect pleasant, attractively presented food and you will not be disappointed; well-informed, attentive staff will, together with the pleasing ambience, ensure you wish to return. If you hit it on a sunny day, the large terraces outside both the bar and restaurant might also be a draw. Closed 25 Dec, Good Fri. **Directions:** At Pavilion Centre.

Dun Laoghaire **Glandore House**

GUESTHOUSE Glandore Park Lr Mounttown Rd
Dun Laoghaire Co Dublin
Tel: 01 280 3143 Fax: 01 280 2675
Email: info@glandorehouse.com Web: www.glandorehouse.com

Conveniently near the ferry terminal in Dun Laoghaire, Grainne Jackman and Louis Walshe's unusual guesthouse is a lovely place to stay - in large grounds surrounded by high hedges - and offers all the conveniences required by the discerning traveller in an old building of character. It was designed in the Venetian Gothic style in 1858, by the renowned Victorian architects Dean and Woodward, featuring carved sandstone, high ceilings and ornate windows. All the bedrooms are a good size, modern and and en-suite, with phone, television, tea and coffee making facilities - and there's even a lift. Ample parking. **Rooms**

12 (all en-suite, all shower only except 1 family room with bath). Lift. B&B from about €50. Closed mid Dec - mid Jan. **Directions:** 5 minutes drive from Dun Laoghaire ferry teminal.

Dun Laoghaire   # Gresham Royal Marine Hotel

Ⓑ HOTEL   Marine Road Dun Laoghaire Co Dublin **Tel: 01 280 1911**
Fax: 01 280 1069 Email: info@greshamroyalmarinehotel.com
Web: www.gresham-hotels.com

féile bia Overlooking Dublin Bay and the ferry port, this grand old Victorian hotel has ample parking and extensive landscaped gardens, yet it's only a twenty minute DART ride to the centre of Dublin. On entering the marble floored foyer a few steps take you up and through arched columns into the Bay Lounge (popular for afternoon teas) and the Powerscourt Restaurant. Eight bay-windowed suites have four-poster beds and free-standing antique furniture - a reminder of the age and character of the original building - but most rooms have fitted furniture and standard facilities, including neat bathrooms. Reflecting its popularity as a venue for functions, conferences and meetings, rooms on the executive floor provide extras for business travellers. Conference/banqueting (450/250). Garden. No pets. **Rooms 103** (8 junior suites, 55 executive, 20 no smoking, 2 for disabled). Lift. B&B from about €70 pps, SC15%. *Weekend specials from about €150. Closed Nov-Dec. **Directions:** Town centre, 200 yards from ferry terminal.

Dun Laoghaire   # McCormack & Sons

PUB   67 Lr Mounttown Rd Dun Laoghaire Co Dublin
Tel: 01 280 5519 Fax: 01 280 0145 Email: cormak@iol.ie

This fine pub (and 'emporium') has been run by the McCormack family since 1960. It's one of the neatest pubs around, with a landscaped carpark creating a pleasant outlook for an imaginative conservatory extension at the back of the pub. The main part of the pub is full of traditional character and the whole place has a well-run hum about it. Good bar food cooked to order includes fresh fish available on the day as well as classics like home-made hamburger (with mixed leaf salad, fries & a choice of toppings), hot sandwiches and salads. Evening menus offer tasty light dishes: zucchini fritters, warm crispy bacon and croûton salad, and steak sandwiches alongside more substantial dishes including a fish special, a 10 oz sirloin steak (with mushroom and Irish whiskey sauce perhaps) or pasta dishes with fresh parmesan. No children after 9pm. Wheelchair accessible. Bar food daily, 12-10. Closed 25 Dec, Good Fri. **Directions:** Near Dun Laoghaire at Monkstown end.

Dun Laoghaire   # Provence

RESTAURANT   1 Martello Terrace Sandycove Co Dublin
Tel: 01 280 8788 Fax: 0404 45702

At this appealing restaurant on the Dun Laoghaire seafront, the head chef (who had been with the restaurant, previously Southbank, since 1981) has been very much involved in the gradual shift towards a more definitely French style - something which suits this classical kitchen well. Fresh produce, used with respect, has remained the ethos - and proficient, gimmick-free cooking, personal, friendly service and good value. Expect sound renditions of classics like moules marinières, chicken chasseur, plaice with lemon butter, and crème caramel and you should not be disappointed. A keenly priced midweek menu, offered without time restriction, offers particularly good value. Not suitable for children under 8. **Seats 45**. D Tue-Sat (and Sun in summer) 6.30-9.30. A la carte. House wine about €18. Closed Mon, also Sun in winter, bank hols.

Directions: From Dun Laoghaire, take coast road to Sandycove; restaurant is on the right.

Dun Laoghaire   **Rasam**

✓ RESTAURANT   18-19 Glasthule Road Dun Laoghaire Co Dublin

Tel: 01 230 0600 Fax: 01 230 1000

Email: info@rasam.ie Web: www.rasam.ie

The latest in a series of distinguished restaurants to have occupied these premises over The Eagle pub in Glasthule, Rasam is owned by Nisheeth Tak - well known from earlier days in two other fine Indian restaurants, Jaipur and Vermilion (see entries) - and his partner Rangan Arulchelvan. It has always been an appealing dining space, and is now impressively decorated in dark teak, with traditional Balinese furnishings and generous, well-spaced tables. Rasam offers something different from other Indian restaurants, as the cuisine is lighter and more varied - the menu is laid out like a wine list with the name of the dish and a brief (but clear) description underneath and the name of the region it comes from opposite, alongside the (surprisingly reasonable) price. Starters begin with a modestly priced Tamatar Shorba, a chilled Indian tomato soup, from Hyderabad, rising to Jhinga Ajwaini (Jumbo prawns with lemon juice and carom seeds, grilled in the tandoor, served with tomato coulis, from Calicut), while main courses might include a relatively simple Kori Gassi, from Coorg, chicken simmered in a spicy masala of brown onions and tomatoes, with a special blend of coorgi masala) and extend to a large selection dish of lamb, fish and chicken, Mansahari Thali, which is very good value. Head chef Sanjay Vishwakarma came to Ireland specifically to take up this position and uses many special ingredients, including rare herbs and spices unique to the restaurant, all ground freshly each day; everything is made on the premises, including the poppodums. For a great dining Indian experience, Rasam has quickly earned a place at the top of the league. The wine list is thoughtfully selected, to ensure compatibility with Indian food. Children welcome. **Seats 75.** Reservations required. D daily, 5-11 (Sun 4.30-10.30). Closed 25-26 Dec, Good Fri. **Directions:** Over The Eagle pub.

Dun Laoghaire   **Roly @ The Pavilion**

✓ Ⓑ RESTAURANT   8 The Pavilion Dun Laoghaire Co Dublin

Tel: 01 2360 286 Fax: 01 2360 288

féile bia Roly Saul's purpose-built restaurant just across from the Royal St George Yacht Club is full of light, with gleaming contemporary decor balanced by some traditional gilded mirrors and leather upholstery in white and a shade that started out as black but (appropriately enough) is now ageing to a deep burgundy; different levels and a mixture of banquettes and high-back chairs are used to break the area up and give it interest and semi-private areas. It's a favourite haunt of many from the area (and beyond) who appreciate both the hospitality and the work of a youthful kitchen team, who relish the international cuisine, produce starters like rare tuna with ginger risotto spring roll & shitake broth, tian of crabmeat with guacamole & chilled gazpacho and mains of organic salmon, mussels, leek and diced potato stew or roast rump of lamb with chilli polenta chips, ratatouille & thyme jus. True to his philosophy of offering an accessible wine list and real value, Roly has managed to keep the (French) house wines to about €12.70 and the list has many other good bottles at fair prices. A set lunch menu at €19.50 is especially good value. Outside eating area. Air conditioning. Not Suitable for children under 7 after 7 pm. **Seats 100.** L&D daily. Closed 25-27 Dec, Good Fri. **Directions:** Opposite Railway Station.

GLENCULLEN

Although not far from the edge of the city, this tiny village in the Dublin Mountains feels very remote once you are there - which is undoubtedly a major part of its charm.

Glencullen   **Johnnie Fox's Pub**
♣ATMOSPHERIC PUB   Glencullen Co Dublin
                                          Tel: 01 295 5647 Fax: 01 295 8911
                      Email: info@johnniefoxs.com Web: www.johnniefoxs.com

féile bia Nestling in an attractive wooded hamlet in the Dublin Mountains, south of Dublin city, this popular pub dates back to the eighteenth century and has numerous claims to fame, including the fact that Daniel O'Connell was once a regular, apparently (he lived in Glencullen at one time), and it's "undoubtedly" the highest pub in the land. Whatever about that, it's a warm, friendly and generally well run place just about equally famous for its food – the "Famous Seafood Kitchen" – and its music – "Famous Hooley Nights" (booking advisable). Unlike so many superficially similar pubs that have popped up all over the world recently, it's also real. Kitsch, perhaps, but real nonetheless – the rickety old furniture is real, the dust is real and you certainly won't find a gas fire here – there's a lovely turf or log fire at every turn. It's a pleasant place to drop into at quieter times too, if you're walking in the hills or just loafing around and Dubliners find it an amusing place to take visitors from abroad. Reservations recommended for food. Own parking. Children welcome (under supervision). Traditional Irish music and dancing. **Seats 352** (private room, 120). Open daily, food 12.30-9.30; all menus à la carte, house wine €19.50. No SC. Closed 24-25 Dec & Good Fri. **Directions:** In Dublin Mountains, 30 minutes drive from Dublin city centre.

KILLINEY

Very much the posh end of the southern suburbs, Killiney Bay has been likened to the Bay of Naples and has Sorrento Terrace, a magnificent row of mansions inhabited (or at least owned by) pop stars and movie people, to prove it.

Killiney   **Fitzpatrick Castle Hotel Dublin**
🅱 HOTEL   Killiney Co Dublin **Tel: 01 230 5400** Fax: 01 230 5430
                  Email: dublin@fitzpatricks.com Web: www.fitzpatrickshotels.com

Located in the fashionable suburb of Killiney, this imposing castellated mansion overlooking Dublin Bay dates back to 1741. It is surrounded by landscaped gardens and, despite its size and grand style, has a relaxed atmosphere. Spacious bedrooms combine old-world charm with modern facilities, and a fitness centre has a 22 metre pool, jacuzzi, spa and relaxation deck. Although perhaps best known as a leading conference and function venue, Fitzpatrick's also caters especially well for business guests and 'The Crown Club', on the 5th floor functions as a 'hotel within a hotel', offering pre-arranged private transfer from the airport and a wide range of facilities for business guests. Five championship golf courses, including Druid's Glen, are nearby. Garden. Lift. **Rooms 113**. Room rate about €130. Closed 24-26 Dec. **Directions:** From Dun Laoghaire; south to Dalkey - top of Killiney hill.

MONKSTOWN

A village between Blackrock and Dun Laoghaire, Monkstown is a settled residential area with plenty of character enhanced by the shops, pubs and restaurants along the upper road on what is known as The Crescent - a visit to **Searson's** wine merchants here could be the beginning of a long affair.

Monkstown   ## Caviston

RESTAURANT   17 Monkstown Crescent Monkstown Co Dublin
Tel: 01 284 6012 Fax: 01 284 6051
Email: info@cavistonmonkstown.ie Web: www.cavistonmonkstown.ie

A younger sister of the well-loved Caviston' of Glasthule, you'll either love or loath the decor of this restaurant, which is designed to look and feel like the lower regions of a fishing trawler - with little natural light the gunmetal grey is relieved by some rather good, if eccentric, modern art work. Service is friendly but can be chaotic when the restaurant is busy - and it almost always is, even at lunchtime; it's not a place for a quick bite, as food is cooked to order - so go only if you have time to linger, don't mind the rather steep prices for the level of comfort offered, and can take the noisy atmosphere caused by all those hard surfaces. This is firmly a fish restaurant and with a fairly short menu that sets an expectation that the fish will be spanking fresh and local. You won't be disappointed and it's refreshing to see humbler fish like mackerel given pride of place on the menu of an up-market restaurant - although, at lunchtime, there may be a surprising lack of shellfish on the menu. The cooking is good, and head chef Stephane McGlynn is confident enough in his ingredients to offer a style of cooking that is refreshingly uncomplicated-classic French combined with contemporary Irish and the occasional Asian accent. A rather limited selection of vegetables, but excellent and interesting bread from Caviston's own bakery and simple, comforting desserts complete the menu. L Tue-Sun, 12-5; D Tue-Sat, from 6pm. Closed D Sun, all Mon. **Directions:** In Monkstown village.

Monkstown   ## Empress Restaurant

RESTAURANT   Clifton Avenue Monkstown Co Dublin
Tel: 01 284 3200 Fax: 01 284 3188

Over more than a decade, owner-chef Burt Tsang has earned a strong local following for this pleasant first-floor restaurant just off Monkstown Crescent. A warm welcome and charming, efficient service complement regional Chinese dishes - Sichuan, Shandong and Beijing - plus Thai and Vietnamese cuisine, offered in set dinners for varying numbers in addition to an à la carte. Specialities include Beijing duck, carved at the table and served with fresh vegetables and hoi sin sauce on pancakes, which requires 24 hours notice. Thai dishes may may seem to have been blanded down for local tastes but cooking overall is consistently good, presentation attractive and prices reasonable; a good choice of vegetarian options is always available, typically Thai vegetable curries. D 6-12 Mon-Sat; Sun open from 3pm. **Directions:** Just off the Crescent.

Monkstown   ## The Purty Kitchen

✓ ATMOSPHERIC PUB/CAFÉ   Old Dunleary Road Monkstown Co Dublin
Tel: 01 284 3576 Fax: 01 284 3576
Email: info@ourtykitchen.com Web: www.purtykitchen.com

Established in 1728 - making it the second oldest pub in Dublin (after The Brazen Head) and the oldest in Dun Laoghaire - this attractive old place has seen some changes recently, but its essential character remains, with dark wooden floors, good lighting, large mirrors and a good buzz. It's well set up for enjoyment of the bar food for which it has earned a fine reputation, with shiny dark wooden tables (a candle on each) and inviting menus which still have old favourites like the famous Purty Seafood Chowder and Purty Seafood Platter, but head chef Sheenagh Toal also offers creative cooking in dishes like crisp, fresh-tasting calamari with a sweet chilli sauce and pretty garnish, fish & chips (perfect goujons of fresh cod elegantly presented with perfectly cooked chips and a good tartar sauce) or moist panfried fillet of hake, topped with a tomato & cheese sauce. Lovely fresh food with a home cooked flavour, presented attractively on different shaped plates, make this an unusually enjoyable bar food experience. A list of House Favourites also includes some dishes that have stood the test of (considerable) time, such as a traditional breakfast, home-made beef burgers and seafood quiche, all at reasonable prices. A new garden terrace (previously a small garden centre) is a great addition to the premises, and there is a new Food & Wine Emporium specialising in artisan Irish foods. Live music on Saturday nights. Bar food 12 noon-10pm daily. **Directions:** On left approaching Dun Laoghaire from Dublin by the coast road.

STILLORGAN

Although it's a fair distance from the city centre, Stillorgan makes a good base, especially for business visitors who value the relative spaciousness of accommodation in the area - and ease of parking.

Stillorgan

RESTAURANT

Beaufield Mews Restaurant & Gardens

Woodlands Avenue Stillorgan Co Dublin
Tel: 01 288 0375 Fax: 01 288 6945
Email: beaumews@iol.ie Web: www.beaufieldmews.com

Dublin's oldest restaurant is located in a characterful 18th century coachhouse and stables - and, as the name implies, it is surrounded by beautiful mature gardens where guests can have an aperitif on the lawn before dinner, or take coffee afterwards, as the gardens are lit up by night. The effect in a built-up area is quite startling, as you are just a few hundred yards off one of Dublin's busiest roads and yet, with its mature trees, spacious surroundings and old-fashioned feeling in both the buildings and gardens, you could be forgiven for thinking you have been mysteriously transported to the country - there's even an antique shop where guests are encouraged to have a browse before dining (Open 3-9pm). This impression has been reinforced by recent changes - including the installation of a new 'Hayloft' bar and a new 'garden' look for the restaurant: atmosphere really is the trump card at this legendary restaurant and the cooking style and courteous service are in tune with the old-fashioned surroundings. A lovely outdoor patio area overlooking the gardens has recently been added too. Good wine list. Not suitable for children after 6.30pm. **Seats 200** (private room, 60; outdoor seating, 20). D Tue-Sat, 6.30-10; L Sun only, 12.30-2.30. Early D €20 (6.30-7.30); Set D €30.95; also à la carte. Closed Mon, bank hols, Good Fri. **Directions:** 4 miles from city centre, off Stillorgan dual carriageway.

China-Sichuan Restaurant

Stillorgan
✓ RESTAURANT

4 Lower Kilmacud Road Stillorgan Co Dublin
Tel: 01 288 4817 Fax: 01 288 0882

David & Julie Hui's unique restaurant runs in co-operation with the cultural exchange programme of the State-run China Sichuan Catering Service Company, which supplies chefs and special spices direct from Sichuan province. Since 1986 their refusal to 'bland-down' the style to suit local tastes has earned the restaurant widespread recognition for authenticity and it was the Guide's Ethnic Restaurant of the Year for 2005. Strong flavours are a characteristic of Sichuan cuisine, and spicy and chilli-hot dishes are identified here on menus - 'Bon Bon Chicken' for example, is a dish of cold chicken shreds in a hot and spicy sauce - but spicing can be varied to suit individual tastes. A speciality worth seeking out is smoked duckling in Sichuan style (€23): seasoned duck is smoked over bay leaves, camphor wood and black Chinese tea leaves, then served hot with plum sauce as a dip; count your blessings when enjoying this dish at it is not widely available, even in London - which may seem the most cosmopolitan of cities yet it has no Sichuan restaurant. While set menus are relatively limited (especially at lunch time), the à la carte offers plenty to tempt the most jaded palate including a wide range of seafood dishes and a particularly strong vegetarian section. Children welcome. **Seats 60.** Reservations required. Air conditioning. Toilets wheelchair accessible. L Mon-Fri 12.30-2, L Sun 1-2.30. D daily 6-10.30. Set L about €16 (Sun €17), Set D about €36; à la carte available; house wine about €15; SC10%. Toilets wheelchair accessible. Closed L Sat, 25-27 Dec & Good Fri. **Directions:** 5 miles south from city, through Stillorgan main road, turn right from Lower Kilmacud Road.

Stillorgan Park Hotel

Stillorgan
Ⓑ HOTEL/RESTAURANT

Stillorgan Road Stillorgan Co Dublin
Tel: 01 288 1621 Fax: 01 283 1610
Email: sales@stillorganpark.com Web: www.stillorganpark.com

féile bia This fine hotel on the Stillorgan dual carriageway is a sister establishment to the famous Talbot Hotel in Wexford; great improvements have been made in recent years and it is furnished in a dashing modern style throughout. Public areas include the stylish reception and lounge areas, and bedrooms - some with views of Dublin Bay - are spacious, attractively decorated in a bright contemporary tone, with well-finished bathrooms. Ample free parking is an attraction and good facilities for business guests include work space and fax/modem lines in rooms. Conference/banqueting (500/400); business centre, secretarial services. Children welcome (under 4 free in parents' room, cots available without charge, baby sitting arranged). Pets permitted by arrangement. **Rooms 125** (4 suites, 125 executive rooms, 50 no-smoking, 4 for disabled) Lift. B&B €80 pps, ss €70. No SC.

The Purple Sage Restaurant: An attractive, informal restaurant with seating in several areas, and welcoming staff. Menus are appealing in a fairly contemporary style - potato, blue cheese, pear & rocket salad with pesto dressing, for example, or a speciality of stir-fried prawns & monkfish with peppers and pak choi, and Thai jasmine rice. Imaginative vegetarian cooking has always been a feature and the hotel regularly runs special themed dining weeks, including one when 'healthy options' are highlighted on the menu. Children welcome. **Seats 110.** Reservations unnecessary. Air conditioning. Toilets wheelchair accessible. L & D daily, 12-2.30 & 5.45-9.30. Set L €23, Set Sun L €26.50; à la carte D available; house wine €22; no SC. Closed 25 Dec. **Directions:** Situated on main N11 dual carriageway.

WEST COUNTY DUBLIN

The area just west of Dublin city is changing very rapidly at the moment, as business parks and new residential developments radiate out from the M50. The 130 bedroom **Clarion Liffey Valley Hotel** (01 623 6421; www.hotelchoice.com) is due to open at the junction of N4 Lucan Road and Fonthill Road shortly aster we go to press. Lucan and Leixlip have both benefitted from by-passing, which has allowed them to regain something of their real character. Leixlip is in an unusual position, as the section east of the bridge is in County Dublin and the western part (which is most of the town) is in County Kildare. (Information on establishments beyond the limit of County Dublin can be found in our companion guide to the whole country, "Georgina Campbell's Ireland - The Best Places To Eat, Drink & Stay".)

LEIXLIP

Leixlip
ⓑ HOTEL

Becketts Country House Hotel

Cooldrinagh House Leixlip Co Dublin
Tel: 01 624 7040 Fax: 01 624 7072

A handsome house on the County Dublin side of the river that divides Leixlip, this house was once the home of Samuel Beckett's mother and it is now an unusual hotel, offering a personalised service for business guests: from the moment you arrive a butler looks after all your needs, whether it be dining, laundry, limousine facilities or tailored requirements for meetings or conferences. Imaginatively converted to its present use, luxurious accommodation includes four boardroom suites and six executive suites, all furnished to a high standard in a lively contemporary style. All have a workstation equipped for computers, including modem/Internet connection and audio visual equipment, private fax machines etc. are also available on request. Public areas, including a bar and a stylish modern restaurant, have a far less business-like atmosphere. Cooldrinagh House overlooks the Eddie Hackett-designed Leixlip golf course, for which golf tee off times may be booked in advance. Conference/banqueting (350/250) Business centre/secretarial services. Golf. Wheelchair accessible. No pets. **Rooms 10** (4 suites, 6 executive rooms) B&B about €75. Open all year except Christmas. **Directions:** Take N4, turn off at Spa Hotel, next left after Springfield Hotel.

LUCAN

Lucan
ⓑ HOTEL

Finnstown Country House Hotel

Newcastle Road Lucan Co Dublin
Tel: 01 601 0700 Fax: 01 621 4059
Email: manager@finnstown-hotel.ie Web: www.finnstown-hotel.ie

Approached by a long tree-lined driveway, this fine old manor house is set in 45 acres of woodland and (despite a large, blocky extension), is full of charm. It may not be immediately obvious where the hotel reception is, but an open fire in the foyer sets a welcoming tone and all of the large, well-proportioned reception rooms - drawing room, restaurant, bar - are elegantly furnished in a traditional style well-suited to the house. Although quite grand, there is a comfortable lived-in feeling throughout. Bedrooms vary and include some studio suites, with a small fridge and toaster in addition to the standard tea/coffee making facilities; although most rooms have good facilities including full bathrooms (with bath and shower), some are a little dated, and the view can be disappointing if you are looking over the extension. Residential golf breaks are a speciality. Conference/banqueting (300/200). Business centre; secretarial services. Leisure centre. Swimming pool. Tennis. Snooker; pool. Shop. Children welcome (Under 12 free in parents' room; cots available without charge, baby sitting arranged). Pets permitted. Parking (200). Wheelchair accessible. **Rooms 53** (28 executive, 10 no-smoking, 1 for disabled). B&B €95, ss €20. Open all year.

The Dining Room: As in the rest of the house, the decor of this comfortable room, is pleasantly quirky - and, with good lighting and ventilation and lovely piano playing, the atmosphere is relaxing. Tables are a little cluttered, perhaps, but nicely set up with fresh flowers, and menus are not over-ambitious, offering about five choices on each course; many are familiar enough although there are some surprises (a starter ragout of venison in a red wine and juniper jus in a puff pastry case, for example), and what arrives on the plate is far from the average hotel meal: sound, down to earth cooking with an emphasis on flavour is based on good quality ingredients and attractively presented without ostentation, all making for an enjoyable meal that is also good value for money. **Seats 90** (private room, 25). L daily 12.30-2.10 (Sun 1-5); D daily 7.30-9.30/ Set L €20, Set Sun L €28.95. set 2/4 course D, €38 /44. L&D also à la carte. House wine €18.95. **Directions:** Off main Dublin-Galway Road (N4): take exit for Newcastle off dual carriageway.

SAGGART

Saggart

Citywest Hotel Conference Leisure & Golf Resort

ⓑ HOTEL   Saggart Co Dublin **Tel: 01 4010 500** Fax: 01 4588 756
Email: info@citywesthotel.com Web: www.citywesthotel.com

féile bia Only about 25 minutes from the city centre and Dublin airport (traffic permitting), this large hotel was planned with the needs of the rapidly expanding western edge of the capital in mind. It is set in its own estate, which includes two 18-hole golf courses and a comprehensive leisure centre with a large deck level swimming pool and a wide range of health and beauty facilities. The other big attraction is the hotel's banqueting, conference and meeting facilities, which include a convention centre catering for 6,500 delegates, making Citywest one of the largest venues in the country. All round, a valuable amenity for West Dublin. Conference/banqueting (6,500/2,200); secretarial services, video-conferencing. Leisure centre, swimming pool. Hairdressing/beauty salon. Children welcome (under 6 free in parents' room, cots available free of charge). Restaurant: L Mon-Fri, D daily. **Rooms 333**. Lift. B&B about €75 pps. Open all year. **Directions:** Off Naas Road - N7 (from Dublin, take left after Independent printers & follow road for about a mile.

DUBLIN RESTAURANTS BY CUISINE & SPECIALITY

American

Elephant & Castle, D2
Franks, D2
Gotham Cafe, D2
Mermaid Café, D2
Town Bar & Grill (New
    York/Italian), D2
Shanahans, D2
TriBeCa, D6
Independent Pizza Co, D9

Asian Fusion

Café Mao, D2
Wagamama, D2
Diep Noodle Bar, D6
Kelly & Ping, D7
Cafe Mao, Dun Laoghaire

Chinese

Good World D2
Imperial Chinese D2
Furama, D4
Kites, D4
Wongs, D15
Silks, Malahide
Empress, Monkstown
China-Sichuan, Stillorgan

French

Halo, D1
Dax Wine Bar, D2
L'Gueleton, Bistro, D2
La Mère Zou,
    French/Belgian, D2
Les Frères Jacques, D2
The Old Mill,
    French/Moroccan, D2
Maison des Gourmets, D2
Pearl Brasserie, D2
R. Patrick Guilbaud, D2
Thornton's, French/ Classic
    European, D2
The French Paradox, D4
Bijou Bistro, D6
Locks, French/Country, D8
Provence, Dun Laoghaire

Indian/Pakistani

Jaipur (Various Branches)
Montys of Kathmandu, D2
Rajdoot Tandoori, D2
Saagar, D2
Shalimar, D2
Tulsi, D2
Kinara, D3
Poppadom, D6
Vermilion, D6
Indian Brasserie, D14

Italian

Condotti, D1
Enoteca delle Langhe, D1
Panem, D1
Ar Vicoletto Osteria
    Romana D2
Da Pino D2
Dunne & Crescenzi, D2, D4
    & D8
La Corte, D2
Il Primo, D2
Milano, D2
Pasta Fresca, D2
Steps of Rome, D2
Town Bar & Grill, D2
Unicorn, D2
Ristorante Da Enzo, D3
Ciao Café, D4
Talavera, Radisson SAS, D4
Antica Venezia, D6
Bar Italia, D8
Ragazzi, Dalkey

Japanese

Aya Deli @ IFSC, D1
Aya @ Brown Thomas, D2
Wagamama, D2
Yamamori Noodles, D2

Spanish/Mexican

Acapulco, D2
Salamanca, D2
Havana Tapas Bar, D8

Thai

Bangkok Café, D1
Chili Club, D2
Diep le Shaker, D2
Pad Thai, D2
Papaya, D2
Baan Thai, D4
Diep Noodles, D6
Thai House, Dalkey
Siam Thai, Malahide

Ethnic, Miscellaneous

Allilang, Korean, D1
Acapulco , Mexican, D2
Ho Sen,Vietnamese, D2
Silk Road Café, Med/mid
    East, D2
Bahay Kubo, Filipino, D4
Bella Cuba Cuban, D4
Langkawi, D4

Seafood

Les Frères Jacques, D2
Ouzo, D2 & D6
Lord Edward, The, D8
Brasserie Na Mara,
    Dun Laoghaire
Caviston's, Dun Laoghaire
Johnnie Fox's, Glencullen
King Sitric, Howth
Caviston, Monkstown
Purty Kitchen, Monkstown
Red Bank, Skerries
Stoops, Skerries

Vegetarian

Cornucopia, D2
Nude, D2

European Classic

Shelbourne/No 27, D2
Ernies, D4
Lobster Pot, D4
Bon Appetit, Malahide

European Classic/ Retro

Trocadero, D2
Beaufield Mews, Stillorgan

Contemporary / International

Expresso Bar Café IFSC, D1
Chatham Brasserie, D2
Darwin's, D2
Pearl Brasserie, D2
The Exchange/Westin, D2
Glass Onion, D6
Nosh, Dalkey
Roly @ The Pavilion,
   Dun Laoghaire
Ella, Howth
Cruzzo, Malahide
Danieli, Malahide
Osborne, Portmarnock

Irish/Contemporary

Chapter One, D1
Avoca Café, D2
Bang Café, D2
Bleu Bistro Moderne, D2
Cafe Bar Deli, D2
Cellar Restaurant,
   Merrion Hotel, D2
Cookes, D2
Eden, D2
Fado D2
Fitzers, D2
La Stampa, D2
Jacobs Ladder, D2
L'Ecrivain, D2
One Pico, D2
Tea Room, D2
O'Connells, D4
Roly's Bistro, D4
Elysium, D6
Mint, D6
Bistro One, D18
Aqua, Howth

Irish Traditional/ Informal

Ely, D2
Fitzers D2
Kilkenny, D2
Canal Bank Café, D4
The Still Room OJD, D7
Washerwomans Hill
   Restaurant, D9
Kingswood Country House,
   D 22
Daniel Finnegan, Dalkey
The Wheelhouse, Howth

Café-Bars/Tea Rooms

The Vaults, D1
Ba Mizu / Mimo, D2
Café en Seine, D2
Clarendon, D2
Odessa, D2
Queen of Tarts, D2
Expresso Bar Café, D4
Ocean, D4
Forty Foot The,
   Dun Laoghaire

Wine Bars/Cafés

Dobbins, D2
Ely, D2
La Cave, D2
Peploe's, D2
Romanza, D2
French Paradox, D4
Dax Wine Bar, D6
Andersons Food Hall, D9

Daytime/Coffee

Insomnia, D1
Soupdragon, D1
Avoca, D2
Dome, D2
Kilkenny, D2
Relax Café @ Habitat, D2
Queen of Tarts, D2
Berman & Wallace, D4
Panem, D7
Stillroom, OJD, D7

Chorus Café, D8
Gallic Kitchen, D8
Guinness Storehouse, D8
Grass Roots Café, D8

Contemporary Bars

Odessa Lounge & Grill, D2
Inn on the Green D2
12th Lock, D15
Tonic, Blackrock
IN, Dalkey

Pub Food

Davy Byrnes, D2
Porterhouse, D2
Market Bar, 'Tapas', D2
The Old Stand, D2
O'Neill's, D2
Merrion Inn, D4
Hole in the Wall, D7
Nancy Hands, D8
Brazen Head, D8
Addison Lodge, D9
Daniel Finnegan, Dalkey
Eagle House,
   Dun Laoghaire
McCormack & Sons,
   Dun Laoghaire
Johnnie Fox's, Glencullen
Abbey Tavern, Howth
Purty Kitchen, Monkstown

Traditional Pubs

International Bar, D2
John Mulligan, D2
Kehoe's, D2
McDaids, D2
Neary's, D2
O'Donoghue's, D2
Palace Bar, D2
Stag's Head, D2
The Long Hall, D2
Toners, D2
Ryans Parkgate Street, D8
John Kavanagh/
   Grave Digger, D9
Yellow House, D14

— Weekends Away —

A 'Baker's Dozen' of suggested places for short breaks within an hour or two of Dublin city. For more places to visit, in every style and price range, consult our main guide, **Georgina Campbell's Ireland - The Guide** (www.ireland-guide.com), which gives independent recommendations throughout Ireland.

- *Belfast:* **TENsq** (028 9024 1001; www.ten-sq.com)
  10 Donegall Square South, Belfast.
  Luxurious city centre boutique hotel, with two fine restaurants

- *Co Carlow:* **Lorum Old Rectory**, Bagenalstown (059 977 5282; www.lorum.com)
  Charming old-world country comfort, with a Euro-Toques chef doing the cooking

- *Co Carlow:* **The Step House**, Borris (059 977 3209; www.thestephouse.com)
  House of character & luxury in a delightfully unspoilt village

- *Co Kildare:* **Barberstown Castle**, Straffan (01 628 8157; www.barberstowncastle.ie)
  A real 13th century castle lies at the heart of this lovely hotel next door to the K Club (Ryder Cup 2006)

- *Co Kilkenny:* **Lacken House**, Kilkenny (056 776 1085; www.lackenhouse.ie)
  Féile Bia Award-winning restaurant and newly refurbished rooms in the medieval city

- *Co Kilkenny:* **Mount Juliet Hotel**, Thomastown,
  (056 77 73000; www.mountjuliet.com)
  A gracious mansion near Kilkenny, with glorious grounds, and golf

- *Co Laois:* **Castle Durrow**, Durrow (0502 36555; www.castledurrow.com)
  Recently refurbished 18th century country house midway between Dublin & Cork

- *Co Louth:* **Ghan House**, Carlingford (042 937 3682; www.ghanhouse.com)
  Country house & cookery school with views of Mourne Mountains

- *Co Meath:* **Neptune Beach Hotel**, Bettystown
  (041 982 7107; www.neptunebeach.ie)
  Modern hotel with on-site golf and miles of sandy beach to walk

- *Co Offaly:* **Kinnitty Castle** (0509 37318; www.kinnittycastle.com)
  Theatrical castle in 650 acres of parkland, complete with armour and dungeon bar

- *Co Westmeath:* **Wineport Lodge**, Glasson, Athlone
  (090 643 9010; www.wineport.ie)
  Waterside restaurant and sumptuous rooms in stunning away-from-it-all location

- *Co Wicklow:* **Rathsallagh**, Dunlavin, (045 403 112; www.rathsallagh.com)
  Rambling country house with romantic accommodation, great dinners, memorable breakfasts and golf

- *Co Wicklow:* **BrookLodge Hotel**, Macreddin (0402 36444; www.brooklodge.com)
  Luxurious new hotel with organic food, farmers markets, and a lovely rural location.

— A Great Day Out —

Some interesting places in and around Dublin that make a great day out *(full details from Tourist Information offices)*.

DUBLIN CITY & COUNTY

▸ **Croke Park** GAA Stadium and Museum, Dublin 3 (01 855 8176)
▸ **Farmleigh House,** Phoenix Park, Dublin 8 (01 815 5900)
▸ **War Memorial Gardens,** Islandbridge, Dublin 8, Sir Edwin Lutyens (01 677 0236)
▸ **Botanic Gardens,** Glasnevin, Dublin 9 (01 837 4388)
▸ **Drimnagh Castle,** Moat, formal 17th century gardens (01 450 2530)

▸ *Balbriggan/Skerries:* **Ardgillan Castle,** (01 849 2212)
▸ *Donabate:* **Newbridge House,** park and traditional farm (01 843 6534)
▸ *Malahide:* **Malahide Castle & Demesne,** (01 846 2184)
▸ *Rathfarnham:* **Marlay Demesne,** Gardens and craft courtyard (01 493 7372)
▸ *Sandyford:* **Fernhill Gardens,** Himalayan species (01 295 6000)
▸ *Skerries:* **Skerries Mills,** Working windmills and visitor centre (01 849 5208)

CO WICKLOW

▸ *Ashford:* **Mount Usher Gardens** (0404 32484)
▸ *Blessington:* **Russborough House & Gardens** - Beit art collection (045 865239)
▸ *Enniskerry:* **Powerscourt House & Gardens** - boutique shopping (01 204 6000)
▸ *Glendalough:* Monastic site, (Visitor Centre 0404 45325 / TIO 0404 45688; farmers market (2nd Sundays: 0404 43885); walking

CO MEATH

▸ *Newgrange:* prehistoric sites, including Dowth & Knowth (041 988 0300)
▸ *Oldcastle:* **Loughcrew Passage Tombs**, 3000 BC (049 854 2009)
▸ *Donore:* **Bru na Boinne Visitor Centre** (041 9880300)
▸ *Hill of Tara:* interpretive centre; walking; tea rooms (046 25903)
▸ *Kells Grove:* House & Tropical Bird Sanctuary (046 923 4267)

CO KILDARE

▸ *Celbridge:* **Castletown House,** Ireland's premier Palladian mansion (01 628 8252)
▸ *The Curragh:* **Curragh Racecourse** (01 441205)
▸ *Kilcock:* **Larchill Arcadian Gardens,** follies (01 01 628 7354)
▸ *Tully:* **Japanese Gardens** (045 521251)
➤ *Straffan:* **Steam Museum** (01 627 3155)

INDEX